THE AMERICAN BAR ASSOCIATION

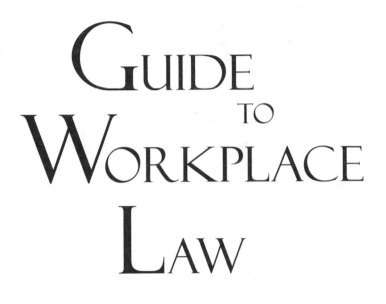

GUIDE TO WORKPLACE LAW

SECOND EDITION

Other Titles by the American Bar Association

The American Bar Association Guide to Credit and Bankruptcy

The American Bar Association Legal Guide to Home Renovation

The American Bar Association Guide to Marriage,
Divorce, and Families, Second Edition

The American Bar Association Legal Guide for Women

The American Bar Association Family Legal Guide, Third Edition

The American Bar Association Guide to Wills and Estates,
Second Edition

The American Bar Association Complete and Easy Guide
to Health Care Law

The American Bar Association Legal Guide for Small Business

The American Bar Association Legal Guide for Older Americans

THE AMERICAN BAR ASSOCIATION

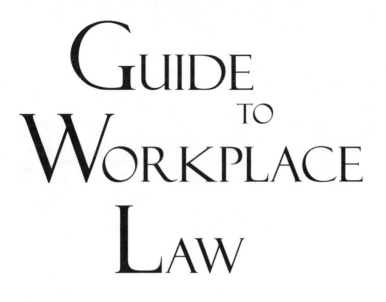

GUIDE
TO
WORKPLACE
LAW

SECOND EDITION

RANDOM HOUSE REFERENCE
NEW YORK   TORONTO   LONDON   SYDNEY   AUCKLAND

Please address inquiries about electronic licensing of reference products for use on a network, in software, or on CD-ROM to the Subsidiary Rights Department, Random House Reference, fax 212–572–6003.

This book is available for special discounts for bulk purchases for sales promotions or premiums. Special editions, including personalized covers, excerpts of existing books, and corporate imprints, can be created in large quantities for special needs. For more information, write to Random House, Inc., Special Markets/Premium Sales, 1745 Broadway, MD 6–2, New York, NY, 10019 or e-mail specialmarkets@randomhouse.com.

Visit the Random House Reference Web site: www.randomwords.com.

Library of Congress Cataloging-in-Publication Data

Fick, Barbara J.
The American Bar Association guide to workplace law. — 2nd ed.
p.   cm
"Principal author, Barbara J. Fick"—CIP galley.
Includes bibliographical references and index.
ISBN 0-375-72140-1 (alk. paper)
1. Labor laws and legislation—United States—Popular works. I. American Bar Association. II. Title. III. Title: Guide to workplace law. IV. Title: Workplace law.

KF3319.6.F53 2006
344.7301—dc22   2006045186

Second Edition
Printed in the United States of America

10 9 8 7 6 5 4 3 2 1

ISBN-13: 978-0-375-72140-3
ISBN-10: 0-375-72140-1

American Bar Association

Bert Z. Tigerman
The Wartnick Law Firm
San Francisco, California

Mary T. Torres
Modrall Sperling
Roehl Harris et al
Albuquerque, New Mexico

W. Scott Welch
Baker Donelson
Jackson, Mississippi

David Williams
Vanderbilt University
Law School
Nashville, Tennessee

CONTENTS

FOREWORD

Robert A. Stein, *Executive Director,*
American Bar Association

When American families are asked to describe their legal needs, the topics that come up repeatedly are housing, personal finance, wills and estates, family and domestic concerns, and employment-related issues. The books in the *American Bar Association Legal Guide* series are designed to address these key legal areas, and provide information about the law in plain, direct language.

The goal of this book is to give helpful information about legal issues that employees and employers encounter in the workplace every day, including the law relating to hiring, firing, and the issues that arise in the course of employment. The book is designed to help you make informed decisions on how best to handle your own particular questions—whether you're an employer or an employee—by providing information on the range of options that can be used in solving everyday legal problems. We hope this book will be able to help you negotiate the legal issues in the workplace; we also hope that it will help you feel more comfortable with the law generally, and will remove much of the mystery from the legal system.

As the largest voluntary professional association in the world and the nation's premier source of legal information, the American Bar Association is in a unique position to provide authoritative guidance on legal issues. The ABA also provides support for lawyer referral programs and pro bono services (where lawyers donate their time), so that finding the right lawyer and receiving quality legal help within your budget is an attainable goal.

This book was written with the aid of ABA members—including lawyers, judges, and academics—from across the country. Their contribution is invaluable because they have experience in dealing with employment law issues every day; their perspectives and expertise make this a better book.

The ABA's Standing Committee on Public Education provided oversight for this project. The programs, publications, and resources of the ABA Division for Public Education are designed to educate the public about the rule of law, and ensure that people understand and participate in our legal system. Public education and public service are two of the most important goals of the American Bar Association. Through publications, outreach, and our website (www.abanet.org), the ABA strives to provide accurate, unbiased legal information to our members, to the media, and to the general public.

Robert A. Stein is the Executive Director of the American Bar Association. He was formerly dean of the University of Minnesota Law School.

INTRODUCTION

Alan S. Kopit, *Chair*
ABA Standing Committee on Public Education

At any given time, almost half of all Americans—over 143 million of us—are working for wages. In addition, millions of retirees are affected by workplace laws governing pension rights, and the spouses and dependents of workers can be directly affected by laws covering health benefits. In fact, laws regulating the workplace potentially affect almost everyone.

There are many federal and state laws that regulate employment. How people are affected by these laws depends on several factors, including the size of the employer, the state the employer is in, and the type of job. Both employers and employees are at a big disadvantage if they're not familiar with the law of the workplace. A basic understanding of what the law requires can help both employers and employees develop realistic expectations, anticipate problems, and avoid trouble.

This book can help you understand more about the law of the workplace, whether you're paying wages or working for them. It describes federal and state labor and employment laws, and details the rights and protections available to employees, the limitations placed on employers, and the ways that employment laws are enforced. It also provides an overview of the legal rights and duties that affect both workers and bosses in the workplace. This book will help employees determine if the law can help them resolve problems they encounter at work, and it will help employers determine if their policies are consistent with the law.

NEW AND IMPROVED EDITION

This book is a complete revision and update of an earlier book in the *American Bar Association Legal Guide* series. We've expanded on some important material from the first edition, and broken the book into shorter chapters. We've also taken into account all the changes in the law, and added a new chapter on monitoring and surveillance.

Our principal author is Barbara Fick, an associate professor of law at Notre Dame Law School who has written widely on labor and employment law. Her manuscript was intensively edited and reviewed by lawyers who are experts in the field. The entire project was completed under the guidance of the ABA's Standing Committee on Public Education. Together, we've worked to provide you with easy-to-read information that will help you understand the law that affects employment. Our goal is to help you spot problems before they become major—when they're easiest to handle.

SPECIAL ACKNOWLEDGMENT

We would like to acknowledge the substantial effort and assistance of the Labor and Employment Law Section of the ABA for its expertise in editing and revising the manuscript.

WRITTEN WITH YOU IN MIND

We've made a special effort to make this book practical, by using situations and problems you are likely to encounter. You won't find legal jargon or technicalities here—just concise, straightforward discussions of your options under the law. Each chapter opens with a description of a real-life problem that shows the practical ramifications of the subject. Within chapters, you'll find sidebars with the following icons:

- ▶, which share practical tips that could be of benefit to you;
- ⓘ, which signal key additional information;
- ⚠, which warn you about potential pitfalls that you can navigate with the right information and help;

- 📄 , which give clear, plain English definitions to legal terms;
- ( ) , which highlight experts' responses to practical questions, giving legal information that may help you as you grapple with similar issues within your own family.

You'll find two additional features at the end of each chapter:

- "The World at Your Fingertips," which contains tips on where to go for more information if you'd like to explore a topic further.
- "Remember This," which highlights the most important points that the chapter has covered.

One word of caution: when reading this book, and other books in the series, keep in mind that these books cannot and do not pretend to provide legal advice. Only a lawyer who understands the facts of your particular case can do that. Although every effort has been made to present material that is as up-to-date as possible, laws can and do change. Laws can also vary widely from one jurisdiction to the next. If you are thinking about pursuing legal action, you should consult first with a lawyer; to find one, contact a bar association or lawyer referral service.

With that in mind, this book can help you to make informed decisions about a wide range of problems and options. Armed with the knowledge and insights this book provides, you can be confident that the decisions you make will be in your best interest.

Alan S. Kopit is a legal-affairs commentator who has appeared on national television for more than fifteen years. He is chair of the ABA's Standing Committee on Public Education and is an attorney in private practice with the firm of Hahn Loeser & Parks, LLP, in Cleveland, Ohio.

CHAPTER 1

How Law Affects the Workplace

From Government Regulation to Private Agreements

John is a retail clerk who works for a large department store. Jennifer works as a secretary for a lawyer who runs his own law office. Peter works in the parks department for the city government. Betty picks grapes for a winery. Does the law address each of their workplace situations in the same way?

Though people often think of workplace law as a single, unified body of law, there's no one set of laws that governs every workplace; metaphorically speaking, workplace law is more of a patchwork quilt than a single piece of fabric. There are many federal and state laws that cover different aspects of working in different settings, but they don't necessarily affect every business and every employee. For example, while federal laws apply to work sites all over the country, they typically exempt businesses that employ fewer than a certain number of employees—and that number varies from law to law. One federal law may not apply to a business unless it employs at least twenty employees; another might apply only to businesses that employ more than fifty employees. The result is that an employee of a small business may be covered by some laws, but not others. Coverage may depend on the type of business, or on certain characteristics of the business in which the employer is engaged. The law may apply to government employers but not to non-government employers; or may exclude agricultural employers from coverage, to name just a few examples.

In addition to the federal government, state governments may also enact laws that apply to the workplace. Maybe your state has stepped in to fill a gap in federal law by passing laws that apply to workers of smaller businesses. Or perhaps your state has simply duplicated the federal provisions, or expanded these provisions for workers in your state to give employees more protections. In addition, your city or county may have passed ordinances that cover some aspects of the workplace environment.

Even when federal law applies to an employer, it does not regulate *every* aspect of the employment relationship. For example, federal law prohibits employers from firing employees based on race, but it does not require employers to have a "good reason" for firing someone. As far as federal law goes (as well as most state law), most of us are what the law calls **employees at will**. This means that we can be refused employment, disciplined, or fired for any reason (or no reason at all), as long as it is not for a reason prohibited by law.

Before workplace laws can apply, there's the issue of whether you are an employee in the first place. The focus of this book is on the laws that regulate the relationship between employers and employees. We don't discuss laws dealing with **independent contractors**, who are not considered to be employees and thus aren't affected by many of the laws that affect employees. (See the sidebar on page 4 titled "The Trend toward Contingent Workers" for more information about why companies are turning to independent contractors.)

The following is a list of factors courts consider when deciding whether an individual is an employee or an independent contractor:

- the extent to which the employer exercises control over the details of the work;
- whether the individual is engaged in a distinct occupation or business;
- whether the work is usually done under the direction of an employer or by a specialist without supervision;
- the skill required in the particular occupation;
- whether the employer or the individual supplies the tools for doing the work;
- the length of time for which the person is employed;

(i) EMPLOYEES VS INDEPENDENT CONTRACTORS

For purposes of applying workplace law, what is the difference between an employee and an independent contractor? Although there is no one determining factor, there are several criteria that bear upon the answer to this question. For example, an employee usually is paid a salary or wage while an independent contractor is usually paid per project. In addition, employees are usually furnished the equipment used to perform their work, while independent contractors usually supply their own equipment. A third indicator is the individual's relationship with the employer. If an employer controls, directs, and supervises the individual in the performance of his or her work, then that individual would probably be considered an employee. On the other hand, if a company merely specifies the result to be achieved, and the individual uses personal judgment to achieve that result, then it's more likely that the individual is an independent contractor.

• whether payment is calculated based on the time worked or on completion of a specified job; and

• whether the work is part of the regular business of the employer.

Here's an example in which someone acts as an independent contractor and not an employee: ABC Company retains Jill to put up a fence for $1,000. ABC does not supervise Jill's work or give her tools or pay her a salary; it only wants to get its fence built. Jill only wants profits, not wages and benefits. Her relationship with ABC ends after the job is done. Jill is an independent contractor, and workplace law will not apply to her relationship with ABC.

Workplace law consists of more than just laws enacted by Congress, state legislatures, and local governments. There is also **case law**, which consists of decisions in which state and federal courts interpret the law and create precedent for other courts. **Civil service rules** are another very important aspect

THE TREND TOWARD CONTINGENT WORKERS

What business wouldn't want to reduce its expenses for injuries, workers' compensation insurance, and unemployment claims? How about lowering other employee-related expenses and lessening the impact of workplace laws?

Enter **contingent workers**: temps, part-timers, and independent contractors. In the past decade, availability of jobs for these types of workers has increased faster than availability of traditional full-time jobs, and contingent workers now make up more than 25 percent of the workforce. The trend is not surprising; after all, experts estimate that contingent workers cost from 20 to 40 percent less than full-time workers.

Part of the reason for the increase in the number of contingent workers is that such workers aren't always covered by the same workplace laws as full-time employees. Some observers believe that one purpose of corporate downsizing and outsourcing is to limit the effect of government regulation on companies by reducing the number of full-time employees and using more contingent workers, who come with fewer legal entanglements.

For example, if they work less than a certain number of hours, part-time employees are not covered by some laws, such as the Family and Medical Leave Act. In addition, using temporary workers or independent contractors instead of employees may keep businesses small enough to be exempt from certain workplace laws.

Whether a worker is classified as a temporary worker or an independent contractor depends on the factual context of the relationship between the worker and the employer, and not on the title used by the employer to describe the worker. The contractual arrangement between a temporary labor agency and a client firm may give the temp agency the authority to hire, train, pay, discipline, and discharge workers. In such a situation, the temp agency—and not the client firm—is the employer of the workers. The client firm may, however, become a **joint employer** of a worker by exercising control over the worker, such as by assigning and supervising work, determining the hours of work, deciding which workers to "accept" or "reject" in referrals from the agency, and having a significant say in the discipline or discharge of the worker.

Some observers speculate that increased efforts to guarantee workers' rights have, ironically, contributed to the trend toward increased use of contingent workers. By adding to employers' labor costs, workplace laws may encourage employers to pursue alternative forms of labor.

The downside for companies of using contingent workers is the considerable risk of lower morale on the job, reduced quality and productivity, and the need to seek and train workers constantly. When figuring in these factors, companies may conclude that the cost savings are illusory, and that they're better off with experienced, full-time employees.

of the law affecting government employees. The law of the workplace may also be affected by **employment contracts** between an individual worker and employer; an example would be a contract between a professional athlete and a team. More common are **collective-bargaining agreements,** which are contracts between an employer and a union. Collective-bargaining agreements cover everything from rate of pay to working conditions and protections against arbitrary dismissal. (Contracts like these often give you more protections than if you're an at-will employee.) **Company personnel handbooks** may also affect the employment relationship, as might employer practices.

At first glance, all this might appear confusing, but don't despair. There's help, too. This book will explain the basic principles of employment law and will help you understand how the law might affect you, whether as an employer or employee. Appendix I defines key terms found in federal laws. As a ready reference, Appendix II lists the major federal employment laws, grouped into categories, and tells you where you can find detailed information about them.

⚠ NOTICE POSTING

Almost all federal labor and employment laws (as well as many state laws) require employers to post notices informing employees of their rights under the law. These notices must be posted conspicuously and in enough places so employees can see them as they enter and exit the workplace.

To ensure that they will remain prominently posted as required, and not get frayed, defaced, or lost, it is a good idea for employers to post these notices in glass or clear-plastic cases. To make sure they are accessible to employees, employers should place them near time clocks and at the various entrances to the workplace.

FEDERAL LAWS

Federal laws will be discussed extensively throughout this book, and are summarized in Appendix II. Below is a list of some of the most important ones. The description following each law gives some indication of its content, but is not meant to provide a detailed analysis. For that, turn to the appropriate chapter of this book—or consult a lawyer or employment law expert.

Antidiscrimination Legislation

• **Title VII** of the **Civil Rights Act of 1964**, as amended, prohibits discrimination in employment based on race, sex, pregnancy, religion, national origin, or color.

• The **Age Discrimination in Employment Act (ADEA)** prohibits discrimination in employment based on age against persons who are forty years of age or older.

• **The Rehabilitation Act** and **Title I** of the **Americans with Disabilities Act (ADA)** prohibit discrimination in employment against persons with disabilities.

Wages and Hours of Work

• The **Fair Labor Standards Act (FLSA)** requires employers to pay employees a minimum wage rate per hour and to pay $1\frac{1}{2}$ times an employee's regular rate of pay for each hour over forty worked during any given workweek; it also imposes restrictions on the employment of children under the age of eighteen.

• The **Equal Pay Act (EPA)** requires employers to pay equal wages to male and female employees who are performing jobs that require equal skill, effort, and responsibility under similar working conditions, unless the differential is based on a factor other than sex.

Workplace Safety

• The **Occupational Safety and Health Act (OSH Act)** requires employers to furnish a workplace free from hazards likely to cause death or serious injury, and to comply with safety and health standards under the statute.

Pensions

• The **Employee Retirement Income Security Act (ERISA)** establishes eligibility and vesting rights for employees in employer pension plans, as well as administrative, fiduciary, funding, and termination requirements for pension plans.

Immigrant Workers

• The **Immigration Reform and Control Act (IRCA)** prohibits employers from hiring aliens who are not authorized to work in the United States; requires employers to verify the work eligibility status of applicants; and prohibits discrimination in employment based on citizenship status against lawfully admitted aliens.

Union-Management Relations

• The **National Labor Relations Act (NLRA)**, as amended, requires employers to engage in collective bargaining with unions designated as the representative of their employees, and prohibits discrimination in employment based on union activities or participation in other protected concerted activity.

Other Terms of Employment

• The **Uniformed Services Employment and Reemployment Rights Act** of 1994 (**USERRA**) prohibits discrimination against employees for their service in the Armed Forces Reserve, the National Guard, or other uniformed services, and requires employers to provide job-protected leaves to certain employees during their service.

• The **Worker Adjustment and Retraining Notification Act (WARN Act)** requires covered employers to give sixty days' advance notice of plant closings or mass layoffs to employees or their union representatives and to state and local governments.

• The **Employee Polygraph Protection Act (EPPA)** prohibits employers from requiring employees or applicants to take lie detector tests except under very limited circumstances.

• The **Family and Medical Leave Act (FMLA)** requires covered employers to grant eligible employees up to twelve weeks of unpaid leave during a twelve-month period for the birth or adoption of a child, because the employee has a serious health condition, or because the employee has to care for a parent, spouse, or child with a serious health condition.

• The **Jury System Improvements Act** prohibits employers from disciplining or discharging employees because they are serving on a federal jury.

STATE LAWS

In addition to federal laws, many states have their own workplace regulations. States also play a major role in the enactment and extension of employment rights for employees. Thus, whether you're an employee or an employer, when you're confronted by a workplace problem, you shouldn't just look at federal law; try to find out whether your state has a law dealing with the issue. A lawyer will be able to give you detailed information on employment law in your state.

In the area of employment discrimination, for example, many state statutes offer protections mirroring those offered by Title VII, the Age Discrimination in Employment Act, and the Americans with Disabilities Act. Some of these state laws expand coverage to smaller employers that do not fall within the coverage of the federal laws, while others add categories of workers entitled to protection. Thus, federal laws protect employees on the basis of race, color, religion, national origin, sex, pregnancy, age, and disability, but some state laws also prohibit discrimination based on marital status, sexual orientation, or arrest record. The federal age discrimination law applies only to employees who are forty or older, but some states prohibit age discrimination regardless of age.

In the area of union-management relations, many states have enacted their own versions of the National Labor Relations Act (NLRA) that apply to smaller employers not covered by the federal law. In some states, for example, agricultural labor relations laws regulate the union-management relationships of farm workers who are excluded from the coverage of the NLRA. There is no federal law governing union-management relations for state and local government employees, but many states have passed laws granting government employees the right to be represented by unions and to bargain collectively. In some states, all categories of government employees have these rights; in others, only limited classes of employees, such as police and firefighters or schoolteachers, are given these rights.

In the field of wage-and-hour laws and workplace health and

safety, some states have laws that give employees a greater level of protection than they enjoy under federal law. For example, federal law requires employers to pay a minimum wage of $5.15 an hour; at least fifteen states, however, set a higher minimum wage ranging from $5.70 to $7.35 an hour. Similarly, some states' workplace safety regulations impose stricter safety and health standards than those required by federal law.

States have also passed legislation dealing with issues that federal law has simply left unregulated. For example, there are state laws:

• prohibiting employers from discriminating against employees who have engaged in legal off-duty behavior such as smoking;

• requiring employers to give employees time off to vote in elections; and

• requiring employers to allow employees to inspect their own personnel files.

Two very important sources of workers' rights—**workers' compensation laws** that pay employees for injuries incurred at work, and **unemployment insurance laws** that pay benefits to employees who have lost their jobs—are also administered by the states.

Throughout this book, as we discuss workplace issues, we will refer to the range of state laws that supplement federal statutes. While we cannot give details on the laws of each specific state, we do discuss state law generally, provide a few examples of laws in different states, and point out how such laws can affect the work relationship. Since it is rare for any two states to have identical laws, we cannot provide guidance on each state's different workplace laws; such a project is beyond the scope of this book.

THE RELATIONSHIP BETWEEN FEDERAL AND STATE LAW

Federal and state laws interact in three ways. First, in some circumstances federal law **preempts** any attempt by states to regulate the same conduct as the federal law. This means that a state or local government cannot pass *any* law that regulates conduct already covered under federal law. Second, in other circumstances the state is allowed to **supplement** federal law, as long as the state law does not undermine the federal law. Third, a state can **regulate** an area of law if there is no existing federal regulation on that topic, or if some employers are not subject to federal law because they do not meet the guidelines for coverage. In these circumstances, a state can decide whether it will regulate the conduct and the extent of that regulation.

Examples of Preemption

Both the NLRA and the Employee Retirement Income Security Act (ERISA) preempt any attempt by the states to regulate the activity covered by these federal laws. For example, the NLRA regulates how employees select unions to bargain collectively for them. So, a state cannot require a labor union to register with the state before it can represent employees—such a state law would not be enforceable, because it would be preempted by federal law. Similarly, ERISA provides the rules for the vesting of pension benefits. A state is preempted from passing a law that regulates the vesting of pensions.

Examples of State Law
Supplementing Federal Law

Except in those areas preempted by federal law, states may supplement the employee protections provided by federal law. The federal law represents a "floor"—that is, a minimum level of protections beneath which the state may not venture—but allows the states to raise that floor if they so desire. For example, the Family and Medical Leave Act (FMLA) requires covered employers to provide twelve weeks of unpaid leave to employees in certain circumstances. State law could supplement that protection by requiring those same employers to provide thirteen weeks of unpaid leave, or by requiring employers to provide paid instead of unpaid leave.

Extending Coverage

Even when the federal government does regulate an issue, employers that are not covered by the federal law can be subject to state laws that vary in content from the federal law. For example, the FMLA applies only to employers with fifty or more employees. A state, therefore, can pass family leave legislation covering employers with fewer than fifty employees. For example, while the FMLA requires employers covered under the statute to provide a minimum of twelve weeks of unpaid leave, a state could mandate that employers with fewer than fifty employees also provide a specified amount of unpaid leave.

Regulating Where There Is No Federal Law

When the federal government does not regulate an activity, the states are generally free to decide whether or not they wish to pass legislation covering that activity, and the extent of that regulation. For example, although there is a federal law that prohibits employers from discharging employees called to serve jury duty in federal court (the **Jury System Improvements Act**), the law does not cover employees who are called to serve jury duty in state courts. Therefore, some states have enacted legislation to address the issue of state court jury duty; other states have not.

State regulation may result not only from laws passed by state legislatures, but also from state court decisions interpreting the **common law**. The common law is a body of law that is based on precedents set by courts, rather than on legislative enactments. There is no federal law requiring employers to honor promises made in company manuals, for example, but some state courts have interpreted the common law of contracts to make such promises enforceable under certain circumstances.

( ) TALKING TO A LAWYER

Q. *I own two grocery stores. One is located in northern Indiana and the other is ten miles away, across the state line in Michigan. My business office is in Indiana and most of my employees also live here in Indiana, although a few live in Michigan. Employees often transfer between store locations. It would cause bad feelings if I had different rules for each store. Since my business is in more than one state, does only federal law apply? Or should I follow Indiana laws, since most of my connections are with Indiana?*

A. Each of your stores must comply with the laws of the state where it is located, as well as any applicable federal laws. To avoid bad feelings about unequal treatment, if Michigan state law is more favorable to employees than Indiana law (or vice versa)—for example, if it mandates a higher state minimum wage—you might voluntarily choose to apply the more favorable standard to employees in both locations.

—Answer by members of the ABA Section
of Labor and Employment Law

A. Federal law would apply to any union activity, and to any issues regarding wages and hours, safety and health, and many forms of discrimination. But depending on where the employees in question work, either Indiana or Michigan law would also apply to most of these areas (except for union-management regulation), and would be exclusive in certain areas, such as the areas of workers' compensation and *individual* employment contracts. To avoid the "different rules" problem, you would have to meet the minimum standards of *all* these jurisdictions.

—Answer by Theodore St. Antoine, Degan Professor
Emeritus of Law, University of Michigan Law School

THE WORLD AT YOUR FINGERTIPS

• The Workplace Fairness website, at *www.workplacefairness. org*, provides access to information on how the law affects all aspects of the employment relationship. You can also find general information on the laws of specific states and the state agencies responsible for overseeing enforcement by clicking on "Resource Guide," then "Government," then "Agency-State Guide," and then selecting your state.

• The U.S. Department of Labor website also links to the websites of state labor departments. These state agencies are responsible for enforcing many state labor laws, and their websites often contain information on the content of state workplace laws. Go to *www.dol.gov*, click on "Services by Location," and then pick your state.

• *Employment Law in a Nutshell* by Robert Covington and Kurt Decker (2nd ed. 2002) provides an overview of the various sources of law, both federal and state-based, that affect the employment relationship.

• Findlaw provides links to information on all aspects of employment rights at *www.employment.findlaw.com*.

REMEMBER THIS

• One size does not fit all. Which law applies to a workplace depends on many factors.

• The law consists of many sources: federal statutes, state statutes, regulations, common law, and city and county ordinances.

• Don't forget to check state and local law. Each state, and sometimes each city and county, has different laws, and these laws may provide protections or impose regulations beyond the requirements of federal law.

• Different types of employees enjoy different levels of protection under the law.

CHAPTER 2

The Antidiscrimination Principle

Don't Let Discrimination Affect You at Work

*"No Irish Need Apply." "Help Wanted: Young, Pretty Reception-
ist." "I'm sorry, but we don't hire black people." "What a joke!
That girl just asked me to hire her as a truck driver."*

*Thanks to federal, state, and local antidiscrimination laws,
one rarely runs across these kinds of statements in today's workplace. But that doesn't mean that antidiscrimination laws have
outlived their usefulness. Unfortunately, illegal discrimination
still sometimes occurs in the workplace.*

*For example, a 2003 study by the Discrimination Research
Center concluded that temporary employment agencies in Los
Angeles preferred white applicants four to one over African-
Americans. This same group conducted another study a year
later and found that job applicants with Arab- or South Asian-
sounding names received significantly fewer responses from
temporary staffing agencies in California than other applicants.*

The antidiscrimination principles codified in federal, state,
and local legislation affect many aspects of the employment
relationship. This chapter provides a basic introduction to these
principles. Their specific application to particular employment
situations will be discussed in subsequent chapters.

FEDERAL ANTIDISCRIMINATION LAWS

Title VII of the Civil Rights Act of 1964 (Title VII) prohibits
employment discrimination against any individual based on
race, color, religion, sex, pregnancy, or national origin. The **Age
Discrimination in Employment Act (ADEA)** prohibits employment discrimination against individuals forty years of age

or older. Title I of the **Americans with Disabilities Act (ADA)** prohibits employment discrimination against qualified individuals with a disability, and requires employers to make reasonable accommodations to such individuals. The sidebar below provides further information about which employers, unions, employment agencies, and training programs are subject to these laws.

Two other federal laws that address employment discrimination are the **Uniformed Services Employment and Reemployment Rights Act (USERRA)** and the **National Labor Relations Act (NLRA)**. USERRA, which applies to all private- and public-sector employers regardless of size, prohibits discrimination against current and former members of the military. The NLRA, which applies to most private-sector employers, prohibits employment discrimination against employees because of union activity or because of other protected, concerted activity. (See chapter 13 for a discussion of the coverage requirements and protections afforded under the NLRA.)

HOW TO TELL IF THE LAW APPLIES TO YOU

Each of the antidiscrimination laws mentioned above establishes standards for determining which employers, unions, employment agencies, and training programs it covers.

TITLE VII COVERS:

- all employers, both public- and private-sector, that employ at least fifteen employees for each working day in at least twenty calendar weeks during the calendar year;

- all employment agencies that regularly procure employees for a covered employer;

- any labor union that operates a hiring hall, or has at least fifteen members and is recognized as the collective-bargaining representative of a covered employer, or is certified as a representative under the National Labor Relations Act (NLRA) or the Railway Labor Act (RLA), or is affiliated with any union that is so recognized or certified; and

- all joint labor-management committees controlling training programs.

THE ADEA COVERS:

- all employers, both public- and private-sector, that employ at least twenty employees for each working day in at least twenty calendar weeks during the calendar year;

- all employment agencies that regularly procure employees for a covered employer; and

- any labor union that operates a hiring hall, or has at least twenty-five members and is recognized as the collective-bargaining representative of a covered employer, or is certified as a representative under the NLRA or the RLA, or is affiliated with any union that is so recognized or certified.

The coverage requirements for the ADA are the same as those for Title VII, except that the ADA does not apply to the federal government. There is a separate statute, the **Rehabilitation Act**, that prohibits discrimination on the basis of disability by the federal government, federal contractors, and those employers who receive federal grants or other financial assistance.

Title VII, the ADEA, and the ADA all base employer coverage on the number of employees employed during a calendar week. For purposes of these laws, individuals who are on vacation or sick leave are counted as employees, as are part-time employees.

PROHIBITED DISCRIMINATION

Not every decision made by an employer that affects an employee in the workplace is subject to scrutiny under antidiscrimination laws. In order to be subject to such scrutiny, the law requires that a decision have a significant adverse effect on an employee's employment or employment opportunities, or cause a significant adverse change in benefits or compensation.

Not every action that displeases an employee rises to the level of an adverse employment action under the law. For example, a lateral transfer that does not affect compensation or job prospects generally does not constitute an adverse employment action for purposes of antidiscrimination law. However, many employer decisions regarding hiring, firing, wages, promotions, discipline, and benefits are clearly decisions that can have significant effects on employment, and thus may be subject to scrutiny under these laws.

Federal antidiscrimination laws prohibit employers from making employment decisions based on an individual's membership in a protected class. An employment decision motivated by an employee's protected status is an example of **intentional discrimination** (also called **disparate treatment**). An employment decision that is neutral on its face but has a disproportionate negative impact on a protected class is an example of **adverse-impact discrimination** (also called **disparate impact**).

 ## DEFINING THE PROTECTED CLASS

The protections afforded by antidiscrimination laws are limited to individuals who are members of a protected class, as defined by the applicable statute. See Appendix I for a complete definition and explanation of the protected classes for each statute.

Intentional Discrimination

In a case alleging intentional discrimination, the issue is whether the employer is treating individuals differently because of their membership in a protected class. In such cases, courts look for evidence of the employer's motive at the time it made the employment decision in question. Was the employer motivated by race, or was the employer's motive legitimate and nondiscriminatory? In trying to discern an employer's motive, courts may look to either **direct** or **indirect evidence** of intent.

Direct evidence consists of statements, made by people who have the authority to make employment decisions, that indicate what those people were thinking at or near the time they made the decision in question. For example, in one prominent case, comments made by managers about a woman up for promotion were found by the court to constitute direct evidence of sex discrimination. The comments included statements that the female candidate "overcompensated for being a woman"; that she should "take a course at charm school"; and that she should "walk more femininely, talk more femininely, dress more femininely, wear make-up, have her hair styled, and wear jewelry."

Indirect evidence of discrimination requires examining the context in which the decision was made to see if impermissible motives can be discerned from the circumstances. For example, suppose an employer asserts that it fired a Hispanic employee because he came to work late. The evidence shows, however, that several white employees were also late and were given warnings but not fired. This evidence might lead to the conclusion that the employer fired the worker not because he was late (since the employer had not fired other tardy workers), but rather because he was Hispanic. As with this example, most discrimination cases rely on indirect evidence for proof.

Adverse Impact

Even if an employer does not intentionally treat employees differently based on their membership in a protected class, an em-

ployer's actions may still have an adverse effect on employees.
For example, suppose an employer uses a written test to decide
who should get a promotion. On its face, this policy does not discriminate against workers in any protected category. However,
if disproportionately more women fail the test than men, then
the policy would have a discriminatory effect—also called an
adverse impact (or **disparate impact**)—regardless of the employer's actual intent.

Adverse-impact discrimination is prohibited under Title VII
unless an employer can prove that the policy in question is required by business necessity and is significantly related to the requirements of the job. Under the ADEA, an employer can avoid
liability for adverse-impact discrimination if it shows that its actions were based on a reasonable factor other than age.

Refusal to Accommodate

A third way in which an employer's decision may cause unlawful
discrimination is if it constitutes a **refusal to accommodate**.
Title VII requires an employer to accommodate the religious
practices of an employee, unless the accommodation would impose an undue hardship on the employer's business. Similarly,
the ADA requires an employer to provide reasonable accommodation to individuals with disabilities where such accommodation is necessary for the disabled employees to perform essential
functions of the job, unless the accommodation would impose
an undue hardship on the employer's business.

For example, suppose an employee who is a Seventh-day Ad-
ventist asks her employer if she may have Saturdays off, because
Saturday is her Sabbath. But the employer requires all employees to work on Saturdays, because its business is open on Saturdays. In this example, there is no intentional discrimination
against the worker; she is being treated the same as all other employees. And while the Saturday requirement has an adverse effect on individuals whose religion requires Saturday Sabbath
observance, the employer can prove that its policy is a business

(i) UNDUE HARDSHIP UNDER TITLE VII AND THE ADA

Although both Title VII and the ADA use the same phrase, "undue hardship," to define the statutory limit of the employer's duty to accommodate employees in protected classes, the precise meaning of the phrase is different under the two statutes. For purposes of Title VII, accommodating a religious practice is considered an undue hardship if such accommodation involves more than a **de minimis** (minimal) cost. The ADA, however, envisions that an employer may have to expend additional resources in order to achieve an accommodation. Whether that expenditure amounts to undue hardship under the ADA depends on the financial resources available to the employer. For a Fortune 500 corporation, purchasing a braille keyboard or a TDD (telephone device for the deaf) for a disabled employee would be unlikely to constitute an undue hardship; for a smaller, less-wealthy company, such an accommodation might be deemed more burdensome.

necessity (because the business is open on Saturday) and is required by the job (because employees are needed to work when the business is open). So there is no case of adverse-impact discrimination under Title VII. Nonetheless, Title VII still requires that the employer try to accommodate this employee's religious practice unless it will cause an undue hardship. Can the employer find an employee who will agree to substitute for the worker? Can the employee make up her work by working on a different day?

The ADA also requires the employer to take affirmative steps to accommodate employees with disabilities. For example, suppose an applicant for a position as a typist is blind, but is able to type if provided with a braille keyboard. In this example, the employer would be required to provide a braille keyboard unless doing so would pose an undue hardship.

STATE AND LOCAL LAWS

State and local legislation also address discrimination in employment. Many state and local laws mandate protections that mirror those of Title VII, the ADEA, or the ADA. However, there are also significant differences between many state laws and their federal counterparts.

First, many state laws regulate employers that are not covered by the federal laws. For example, Massachusetts antidiscrimination law covers employers with six or more employees; New York's statute covers employers with four or more employees; and in South Dakota all employers are covered regardless of how many employees they have.

Second, the list of protected classes may be more extensive under state law than under federal law. For example, some states prohibit employment discrimination based on:

- marital status;
- arrest or conviction records;
- sexual orientation;

ⓘ EMPLOYEES WORKING OVERSEAS

Most legislation applies only to conduct that occurs within the territorial jurisdiction of the United States. However, most federal antidiscrimination laws also apply to the overseas operations of companies controlled by U.S. corporations, even if those companies are incorporated overseas. Title VII, the ADEA, and the ADA protect *U.S. citizens* employed overseas by companies controlled by U.S. corporations, and USERRA protects *both* U.S. citizens and permanent resident aliens employed overseas. All of these statutes exempt the employer from compliance with U.S. law if such compliance would violate the law of the foreign country where the workplace is located.

- political affiliation;
- height and weight; or
- genetic disorders.

Lastly, the monetary remedies available for violations of state law may be more (or less) extensive than the remedies provided under federal law, and the statutes of limitations may be different.

One should also be aware of city and county ordinances. These local laws may also be more extensive than federal laws and, in some cases, may even offer more protections than state laws. For example, the city of Seattle prohibits discrimination based on political ideology and sexual orientation, even though Washington state includes no such prohibitions in its state antidiscrimination laws.

Sovereign Immunity

The principle of **sovereign immunity**, set forth in the U.S. Constitution, provides that a state cannot be sued in federal court by one of its own citizens. The implication of this principle is that, while state employers are prohibited from engaging in acts of discrimination under both the ADEA and the ADA, the principle of **sovereign immunity** prevents individuals from filing lawsuits in federal court against states in order to enforce their rights under those two statutes. However, the Equal Employment Opportunity Commission (EEOC) can file a lawsuit against a state government on an employee's behalf to enforce his or her individual rights under the ADEA or the ADA. Moreover, if a state has waived its right to rely on sovereign immunity, then it can be sued by individuals. Although most states have not agreed to waive this right, a few states, such as Minnesota, have done so. The sovereign-immunity defense does not apply to Title VII discrimination lawsuits.

The principle of sovereign immunity does not protect *local* governments from individual lawsuits, so individual workers who have been discriminated against by city or county government employers can vindicate their rights in federal court.

( ) TALKING TO A LAWYER

Q. I work in a large factory in a city that has an ordinance prohibiting discrimination based on national origin. Our state law also prohibits
national-origin discrimination, as does Title VII. I think I was passed
over for a promotion because I'm from Pakistan. Which law should I
use to address my problem? Can I make a claim under all of them?

A. Because you work in a large factory, it is likely that your employer is
covered by federal, state, and local antidiscrimination laws. You may
file a charge with the federal Equal Employment Opportunity Commission and request that the charge be cross-filed with your state's
Fair Employment Practices agency, or vice versa. Additionally, you
should consult with an attorney regarding whether local laws require
that you file a charge with a local agency. You and your attorney
should consider whether the possible forms of relief available under
the various laws differ. In some cities and states, you may be able to
recover greater damages under city or state law than under federal
law. Conversely, your state or city may afford you less relief than Title
VII. You may also not have the same right to a jury trial under city or
state law that you do under Title VII. Although you may be able to file
claims under all of the various laws, sometimes the suits will be consolidated, and you will not be allowed to recover cumulative damages
for the same discriminatory action.

—Answer by members of the ABA Section
of Labor and Employment Law

THE WORLD AT YOUR FINGERTIPS

• For more information about federal antidiscrimination laws,
visit the website of the U.S. Equal Employment Opportunity
Commission at *www.eeoc.gov*.

- For an overview of the federal antidiscrimination laws, consult Mack Player's *Federal Law of Employment Discrimination in a Nutshell* (5th ed. 2005).
- The website of the Legal Information Institute at Cornell University provides a summary of federal employment discrimination laws, with links to the text of the laws and recent court cases, at *straylight.law.cornell.edu* (click on "Law About," and select "Employment").
- The Workplace Fairness website answers the most commonly asked questions about employment discrimination. Visit *www.workplacefairness.org*, click on "Know the Law," and then click on "Discrimination."
- Findlaw provides links to information on all aspects of employment discrimination. Visit *www.employment.findlaw.com*, and click on "Discrimination & Harassment."

REMEMBER THIS

- Federal law prohibits employment discrimination based on race, color, religion, national origin, sex, pregnancy, age, disability, military status, union activity, and other concerted activity.
- State and local laws may prohibit employment discrimination based on additional categories not included in federal law, such as sexual orientation, height, weight, marital status, political affiliation, or genetic disorders.
- Disparate-treatment discrimination occurs when employers base employment decisions on individuals' membership in protected classes.
- Adverse-impact discrimination occurs when neutral employment policies adversely affect the employment opportunities of persons in protected classes, unless employers prove that the policies in question are related to the job and required by business necessity. In the case of the ADEA, discrimination occurs when neutral employment policies that are not based

on a rational factor other than age have an adverse effect on the employment opportunities of those aged forty or over.

• Discrimination also occurs when an employer fails to reasonably accommodate an employee's religious practice or disability, unless doing so would cause an undue hardship on the business.

CHAPTER 3

Beginning the Hiring Process

Qualifications and Job Ads

Ben works in human resources for Acme Manufacturing. It is important to Ben that Acme hire the best-possible people. He is currently writing a help-wanted ad to place in the local newspaper. It reads:

HELP WANTED: PRODUCTION WORKERS
Acme is now hiring for positions on its widget assembly line. Must have a high-school diploma, excellent job references, two years' experience, no attendance problems, and be physically agile and in good health. Shift hours are Monday to Friday, 8 A.M. to 6 P.M. Apply in person at Acme Mfg.

The director of human resources is reviewing Ben's ad. What should he consider in determining whether to modify the wording or to place the ad as written?

For an employer, hiring employees usually involves several steps. First, an employer determines the qualifications needed to perform the job in question. Next, the employer circulates a job description and solicits applications for the position. The employer then interviews all qualified applicants. Finally, the employer hires someone from among the applicants. A variety of laws—including child labor laws, immigration laws, and antidiscrimination laws—affect each of these stages in the hiring process.

CHILD LABOR LAWS

The federal **Fair Labor Standards Act (FLSA)**, which dates back to the New Deal, regulates the employment of **child labor**, and limits when and under what conditions employers can hire individuals under the age of eighteen. In order to comply with the FLSA (and similar state laws), employers are required to set minimum age requirements for certain jobs.

As a general rule, employers cannot employ children under the age of fourteen. There are three exceptions to this rule: minors working for a parent who is the sole proprietor of a business; minors working as actors; and minors working as news carriers.

Minors who are fourteen or fifteen years old are prohibited from working in certain hazardous occupations. The aim of this restriction is to keep children away from activities in which they could be severely injured. Minors who are fourteen or fifteen can be employed in some retail and service industry jobs, but even these industries place limitations on minors' performance: they cannot be employed at hazardous jobs, they cannot work in a warehouse unless performing clerical work, and they cannot work on ladders or unload trucks.

If an employer employs minors who are fourteen or fifteen, the law limits the number of hours that minors can work. For example, minors cannot work any hours during which they are expected to be attending school. They may work a maximum of three hours on a school day, up to eighteen hours per week. On nonschool days, minors can work for a maximum of eight hours a day, up to forty hours per week. In any event, minors cannot work before 7:00 A.M. or after 7:00 P.M. (9:00 P.M. in the summer).

The FLSA does not restrict the number of hours worked by sixteen- or seventeen-year-old minors, but it does prohibit employing them in certain types of hazardous jobs.

Some states have passed stricter limitations on child labor than those found in the FLSA. For example, some states have a more extensive list of hazardous jobs and activities, and also limit the number of work hours for all minors under eighteen— not just for those under sixteen. Lastly, some states require that employers obtain age certificates to verify the age of employed minors, or require minors to get work permits from school authorities.

(i) DANGER! MINOR WORKING

Some jobs that are generally considered hazardous for fourteen- and fifteen-year-olds are:

- transportation jobs;
- construction jobs;
- mining jobs;
- operating power-driven machinery;
- maintaining and repairing equipment; and
- working in or around a boiler room.

Some examples of jobs considered hazardous for sixteen- and seventeen-year-olds are:

- logging jobs;
- operating elevators;
- operating power-driven, meat-processing, bakery, or paper-product machinery;
- operating circular saws or band saws;
- driving a motor vehicle;
- performing wrecking and demolition work;
- roofing; and
- excavation work.

For a complete list of work restrictions for employees under eighteen, visit *www.dol.gov/dol/allcfr/ Title_29/Part_570/toc.htm.*

( ) **TALKING TO A LAWYER**

Q. *I operate a fast-food franchise and most of my employees are high-school kids. I know I have to check their ages to make sure they're at least fourteen, but are there any other obligations of which I need to be aware?*

A. Be aware that: (1) minors cannot work any hours during which they are required to attend school; (2) minors may work a maximum of three hours on school days, eight hours on nonschool days, and a maximum total of forty hours per week; and (3) minors may not perform hazardous work.

—Answer by Theodore St. Antoine, Degan Professor Emeritus of Law, University of Michigan Law School

UNAUTHORIZED ALIENS

The federal **Immigration Reform and Control Act (IRCA)** prohibits employers from hiring individuals who are not authorized to work in the United States. As part of the hiring process, employers must complete an eligibility form (**Form I-9**) for each new employee. The purpose of this form is to ensure that the employer has verified the legal eligibility of the applicant to be employed in the United States. The law requires that the form be completed for *all* employees hired. The employer must retain the eligibility form for three years after hiring, or for one year after the employee is terminated, *whichever is later.*

◖◗ TALKING TO A LAWYER

Q. *I know that before I hire someone I'm supposed to verify work autho-rization, but what happens if somebody uses a fake ID?*

A. Remember that just checking a potential employee's driver's li-cense—the typical form of identification used as a fake ID—is not enough. To ensure that a potential employee is authorized to work, you must also check his or her Social Security card or birth certificate.

—Answer by members of the ABA Section
of Labor and Employment Law

The following are some of the documents that can be used to verify an individual's authorization to work:

- Social Security card plus driver's license with photograph;
- U.S. passport;
- unexpired foreign passport with temporary I-551 stamp;
- alien registration receipt card;
- permanent resident card (green card); or
- U.S. birth certificate plus driver's license with photograph.

While it is illegal to hire someone who is not eligible to work in the United States, it is also illegal for employers to discrimi-nate, on the basis of national origin or citizenship status, against U.S. citizens and people intending to become citizens. (See the sidebar below, "Employment Protection for Unauthorized Aliens," for further information.) The antidiscrimination provi-sions of the IRCA are designed to protect U.S. citizens and so-called intending citizens from overly cautious employers who might otherwise simply refuse to hire persons who look or sound foreign.

▤ INTENDING CITIZENS

An **intending citizen** is an alien who is actively pursuing naturalization and has been:

1. lawfully admitted to the U.S. for permanent residence (a green-card holder),

2. granted temporary residence in the U.S. under IRCA's legalization program,

3. granted asylum in the U.S. under the **Immigration and Nationality Act**, or

4. admitted to the U.S. as a refugee under the Immigration and Nationality Act.

Executive Order 12989 prohibits federal government contractors from knowingly hiring aliens not authorized to work in the United States. Any government contractor found to have knowingly hired illegal aliens can lose its government contracts and be barred from any future government contracts for a year.

ⓘ EMPLOYMENT PROTECTION FOR UNAUTHORIZED ALIENS

Whether they are legally authorized to work or not, all individuals employed by an employer are protected under federal and state workplace laws. Therefore, for example, an employer who fires an unauthorized alien because that person has joined a union, or who pays that person less than minimum wage, has violated the law. Though there are some limitations on the types of remedies available for such employees, the employer remains liable and is subject to legal sanctions in the event of a violation.

ⓘ LICENSING REQUIREMENTS

Some state laws require special **licenses** for certain categories of jobs. For example, an employer hiring a lawyer, teacher, cosmetologist, or nurse often must require the applicant to have a specialized license. In such cases, the employer cannot legally hire applicants who have not acquired the appropriate license.

Some states also require employers to complete criminal-background checks before hiring individuals for certain jobs, such as health-care jobs, child-care jobs, or teaching jobs.

DRUG TESTING LAWS

The U.S. Department of Transportation requires preemployment drug testing for truck drivers, and the Federal Aviation Administration has similar regulations covering airline flight personnel. If applicants fail the required tests, they may not be hired.

The **Drug-Free Workplace Act** does not require federal contractors to give drug tests to their applicants or employees. This law merely requires contractors to establish drug-free awareness policies and communicate those policies to their employees. More information about preemployment drug tests is provided on page 59.

ANTIDISCRIMINATION LAWS

The federal government and most states have antidiscrimination laws in place protecting applicants and employees from hiring and employment decisions based on race, color, religion, national origin, sex, pregnancy, age, disability, union affiliation, or veteran status. (Some states also prohibit discrimination based on other categories, including sexual orientation, marital status, and arrest record.)

Thus, if an employer decides not to hire an applicant because he is African-American, the employer has violated the law. But if the employer chooses a white applicant over an African-American applicant because the white candidate has better job skills and more work experience, the employer has not violated the law. The question is whether the reason for the employer's action is based on the applicant's **protected status** (in this example, the question is whether the decision to not hire the applicant was based on the applicant's status as an African-American).

Setting Nondiscriminatory Requirements

Except by limiting child labor or requiring licenses for certain occupations, the law generally does not dictate what qualifications an employer should establish for a job. Rather, the law allows employers to establish basic job requirements and work standards—as long as those requirements and standards do not result in discrimination based on protected classifications under federal and state employment discrimination laws.

A requirement that a job applicant be of a specific gender, national origin, religion, or age will almost always violate both federal and state antidiscrimination laws. These laws require employers to consider applicants based on their individual abilities, not on stereotypical assumptions. As an example, suppose a factory job entails regular lifting of items weighing forty pounds or more. An employer cannot require that applicants be young men based on the assumption that young men are strong and older people and women are weak. However, subject to its obligation to reasonably accommodate employees with disabilities, the employer can require that all employees—regardless of age or gender—be able to regularly lift items weighing forty pounds or more.

"Neutral" Job Requirements

Even job requirements that appear to be neutral on their faces can create problems for employers under antidiscrimination

(i) THE BFOQ EXCEPTION

In a few rare situations, it is an objective fact (not a stereotypical assumption) that members of a protected class are not qualified for a particular job. For example, only men are qualified to play male roles in movies. In this example, sex is a **bona fide occupational qualification (BFOQ)** for the job in question, so filmmakers may require that candidates for such jobs be male.

Both Title VII and the Age Discrimination in Employment Act (ADEA) allow an employer to exclude applicants from consideration for a job based on sex, religion, national origin, or age if the employer can prove that a BFOQ warrants such exclusion. In order for a particular trait to qualify as a BFOQ, the employer must prove that there is an objective factual basis for believing that all applicants from the excluded group would be unable to safely and efficiently perform the duties of the job. The employer must also prove that the duties involved are so important to the business that the business would be undermined if members of the excluded group were hired.

The BFOQ is a very limited exception to the otherwise general rule that an employer can never specify a particular religion, gender, national origin, or age as a requirement for a job. What if customers prefer members of a particular protected category? Such a preference is not enough for the trait in question to qualify as a BFOQ, nor are stereotypical assumptions about the abilities of members of a protected group, or costs associated with hiring members of a particular group. Moreover, race, color, and disability can never qualify as BFOQs.

laws. For example, requiring applicants to pass a written test or hold a college degree may result in disproportionate exclusion of members of protected classes. More men than women may be able to pass a mechanical-aptitude test, or—in a particular geographic area—many more white than African-American applicants may hold college degrees. Such criteria could thus have an adverse impact, excluding disproportionately more individuals

ⓘ DO THE MATH

How does an employer determine whether a neutral requirement creates an adverse impact? Employers should compare the protected group's rate of success in satisfying the requirement with the success rate of the majority group. The touchstone is whether the difference in success rates is statistically significant—as a general guideline, whether the success rate for the protected group is at least 80 percent of the success rate for the majority group.

For example, suppose ten men and ten women take a mechanical-aptitude test; eight men and four women pass the test. The success rate for men is thus 80 percent, and the success rate for women is 40 percent. Comparison of these success rates reveals that only 50 percent as many women as men passed the test. Since this figure is less than 80 percent, the employer could reasonably conclude that the test in question has an adverse impact on women.

who are members of a certain protected class—in this example, women and African-Americans.

Does an adverse impact automatically mean that an employer has violated antidiscrimination laws? No. When neutral job criteria have an adverse impact, they are considered to violate employment discrimination laws *unless* the employer can show that the criteria are related to successful performance of the job in question. Therefore, an employer could justify using a mechanical-aptitude test as a means of screening candidates for a job as a mechanic, but may not be able to justify using it to screen applicants for a clerical position. Similarly, the employer could justify requiring a college degree for a job as a high-school teacher, but not necessarily for a job as an assembly line worker.

⚠ CRITERIA THAT CAN GET THE EMPLOYER IN TROUBLE

Examples of neutral criteria that have been found to have adverse impacts on protected classes include:

- height and weight standards (which may adversely impact women and members of certain ethnic groups);
- fluency in the English language (which may adversely impact members of certain national-origin groups);
- standards relating to arrest and conviction records (which may adversely impact members of certain racial and ethnic groups); and
- standards relating to history of garnishment (which may adversely impact members of certain racial and ethnic groups).

Remember, though, that even if neutral criteria create an adverse impact, an employer can still make use of such criteria if it can show that the qualifications measured are necessary for successful performance of the job.

Scheduling Requirements

Besides the qualifications needed to perform the work in question, most jobs also have other kinds of requirements. Most jobs require employees to be at work during scheduled workdays and working hours. But such requirements may exclude people with certain religious beliefs. Title VII of the Civil Rights Act of 1964 requires employers to **reasonably accommodate** an applicant's sincerely held religious beliefs, unless the accommodation would cause undue hardship to the employer's business. This does not mean that an employer cannot establish work schedules and make all applicants and employees abide by such schedules. But it does mean that, if an individual cannot comply with a work schedule *because of that individual's sincerely held religious beliefs*, the employer must work with the employee to

(i) "I WANT SUNDAYS OFF, TOO!"

Though Title VII requires employers to reasonably accommodate an employee's sincerely held religious beliefs, employers are *not* required to accommodate every employee's whim relating to hours worked. For example, an applicant who requests time off on Sundays to attend church services may be entitled to reasonable accommodation, but an applicant who wants Sundays off to play golf is not entitled to the same accommodation.

reach a reasonable compromise that will both meet the employer's business needs and allow the employee to honor his or her religious beliefs.

An employer is only required to accommodate an employee's religious beliefs, however, if such accommodation does not cause **undue hardship** to the employer's business. For example, if changing the work schedule would prove extremely costly or would unduly disrupt the employer's business, the accommodation would be deemed an undue hardship. If an accommodation imposes more than de minimis (minimal) costs on the employer, it will be deemed an undue hardship. This is an extremely low standard. For example, in one case, $150 was considered more than a de minimis cost. Many work schedule problems, however, can be resolved without any hardship to the employer. For example, where an employee requests time off for religious observance, another employee might volunteer to swap work schedules, or the employee seeking accommodation could work longer hours on another day to finish his or her work.

Job Requirements and Disabilities

Some job requirements may also have the effect of screening out individuals based on disability. The **Americans with Disabilities Act (ADA)** obligates employers to justify any requirements that exclude individuals because of disability. Under the ADA, in order to show that a criterion is related to successful performance of the job in question, an employer must show that the criterion is related to an *essential* function of job performance and not merely an incidental aspect of the job. For example, if a job description for a receptionist position states that an essential function is typing, then for purposes of Title VII, so long as the receptionist performs some typing while on the job, that crite-

ⓘ WHAT CONSTITUTES "ESSENTIAL"?

Equal Employment Opportunity Commission (EEOC) regulations list several factors to consider in determining the essential functions of a job under the ADA:

1. Does the position exist to perform the function in question? For example, a secretarial position exists to facilitate typing of letters and documents, whereas a receptionist position may exist to facilitate greeting and directing of visitors and answering the telephone.

2. Are there a limited number of employees available to perform the function? Even though a receptionist's primary function is not to type, if there is only one secretarial employee at a company and the receptionist must perform his or her duties when the secretary is sick or on vacation, then typing may be an essential skill for the receptionist.

3. What is the amount of time spent performing the function? The larger the amount of time devoted to the function, the more likely it is to be deemed essential.

4. What is the effect of not requiring the person to perform the job function in question? For example, a firefighter may be called upon to carry a heavy person from a burning building only rarely (thus spending only a small portion of time performing this duty), yet failure to perform this function could cost a life; the skill may thus be considered essential.

5. What have been the job responsibilities of employees who have previously performed this job?

rion would be considered job related. However, if the receptionist spends only a small amount of his or her time typing—say, 5
percent—it is possible that this skill would not be considered essential to the job under the ADA. When evaluating applicants for
a job, employers should explain the essential functions of the job
to all applicants and ask every candidate if he or she can perform
these functions.

THE BOTTOM LINE

In formulating hiring criteria, employers should remember the
Supreme Court's mandate that job qualifications should "measure the person for the job and not the person in the abstract."
Employers should carefully consider which functions constitute
the essential functions of the job in question, and what types of
skills are necessary to perform those functions. When the required skills are shown to be directly related to the performance
of the job, the hiring criteria in question are lawful.

Quite apart from legal concerns, employers will benefit from
thinking hard about what goals a job is intended to accomplish,
what skills are necessary to get the job done, and what schedule
is necessary for performance of the job. Having determined the
skills and qualifications necessary to perform the job, the employer will be in a better position to write up and circulate a job
description that will not only meet the requirements of state and
federal laws, but will also be precisely targeted to fill the job in
question—and more likely to result in finding someone to do
it well.

GETTING THE WORD OUT

In order to attract the most qualified applicants or employees,
ads and job descriptions should avoid words that suggest the employer prefers applicants of a particular race, sex, religion, national origin, age, or other protected trait under the relevant

▶ **AVOIDING TROUBLE**

Employers can avoid problems by disseminating news of job openings as widely as possible. Placing ads in newspapers and magazines with wide circulation bases and using employment agencies or state job service divisions can help employers to reach a wide variety of qualified applicants.

state or local law. For example, an ad that employs the phrase "recent college graduate" instead of "college degree required" could imply a preference for young people and discourage older applicants from applying. Likewise, using the term "salesman" instead of "salesperson" could suggest that only men should apply.

Employers should also use care when deciding how to disseminate information about available jobs. The method an employer uses to get out the word about job openings can create problems if that method has the effect of foreclosing applicants from a protected class. For example, if the employer's current workforce is predominantly white, and the employer depends on employee word of mouth to circulate news of upcoming job openings, the news may only spread to the employees' acquaintances, who might also be predominantly white. As a result, members of ethnic and racial minority groups may never hear about the job. Or, to take another example, help-wanted ads placed in college newspapers and not in other newspapers may only target younger people, to the exclusion of older applicants.

APPLICATION FORMS

Many employers require candidates to fill out job application forms. These forms usually ask for an applicant's personal information and information about his or her educational background and previous work experience. While such applications

( ) TALKING TO A LAWYER

Q. Are employers required to use written application forms, or can they hire people based on telephone inquiries, letters, or e-mail?

A. Employers are not required to use written applications; however, having a written record of an employee's or applicant's qualifications is a good employment practice.

—Answer by members of the ABA Section
of Labor and Employment Law

are generally permissible, federal and state laws do regulate the type of information that can be requested from applicants.

The ADA prohibits an employer from asking any questions relating to the applicant's physical or mental health. Questions that seek such information either directly (such as "Do you have a disability?" or "Do you have any health problems?") or indi-

▶ BE CAREFUL WHAT YOU ASK

Neither Title VII nor the ADEA specifically prohibits employers from asking certain questions. However, the EEOC warns that either direct or indirect requests for such information (i.e., information relating to race, color, religion, national origin, sex, or age), unless otherwise explained, may constitute evidence of discrimination prohibited by Title VII. The reason for this warning is that the law prohibits employers from using information about race, color, religion, national origin, sex, or age as the basis for making hiring decisions. And if the information cannot legally be used, why would an employer need to ask about it? Only in those rare instances where religion, national origin, sex, or age qualifies as a BFOQ should an employer ask questions pertaining to these subjects.

Some state laws may also explicitly restrict allowable questions on application forms. West Virginia, for example, expressly prohibits preemployment questions on race, religion, color, national origin, sex, and age. Wisconsin prohibits questions about an applicant's arrest record. Michigan prohibits questions on race, color, religion, national origin, age, sex, height, weight, marital status, or arrest record. These are just a few examples of the wide variations found in state law.

Employers should review their application forms in light of their states' specific laws. State constitutions, as well as the U.S. Constitution, also may limit the types of questions that government employers may ask applicants. These restrictions are discussed in chapter 14, which deals with public-sector employment issues.

rectly (such as "Have you ever filed a claim for workers' compensation?" or "Do you take any prescription medications?") are forbidden. Rather, as discussed previously, employers should ask all applicants if they can perform the essential functions of the job. For example, if the job requires sitting down for eight hours a day, the application should ask whether the applicant is physically able to meet that requirement.

The National Labor Relations Act (NLRA) prohibits any questions about union membership or activities. For example, questions such as "Do you belong to a labor organization?" or "Have you ever participated in a strike?" are against the law.

THE WORLD AT YOUR FINGERTIPS

• You can find more information on all aspects of the hiring process at the Findlaw website. Visit *www.employment.findlaw. com* and click on "The Hiring Process."

• The Department of Labor enforces child labor laws; its website, at *www.dol.gov/dol/topic/youthlabor/index.htm*, provides links to a wide range of resources dealing with child labor issues.

• The Office of Special Counsel enforces the provisions of the IRCA dealing with immigration-related unfair employment practices. Its website, at *www.justice.gov/crt/osc*, features links to the applicable law and regulations.

• See the resources listed at the end of chapter 2 for additional information on how antidiscrimination laws affect the hiring process.

REMEMBER THIS

• With few exceptions, individuals under the age of fourteen cannot work.

• Teenagers aged fourteen and fifteen can work only limited hours and cannot work in dangerous jobs.

• Teenagers aged sixteen and seventeen cannot work in hazardous jobs.

• Employers must verify the work authorization of all employees.

• Job requirements cannot violate antidiscrimination laws, and should be related to performance of the job.

• Employers may need to make accommodation for applicants based on their disabilities or sincerely held religious beliefs.

CHAPTER 4

Selecting the Right Employee

Interviews, Tests, and More

Fran is a recent college graduate looking for her first profes-sional job. She just finished a day-long interview process at Jones & Sons, an investment banking firm. It was a very gruel-ing day. First she spoke with a psychologist who asked her many personal questions. Then a nurse took a blood sample to test for drugs. After that she took a two-hour written test on economics, mathematics, and business finance. Finally she had a series of personal interviews with several of the firm's partners.

As she reflects on the day's events, she wonders whether all job interviews are like this. Can employers really make you jump through all these hoops?

After reviewing applications and eliminating candidates who are not qualified for the job, an employer's next step is to hire the most-qualified candidate.

In choosing from among many qualified applicants, employ-ers must try to determine who will best perform the job. In mak-ing their decisions, they usually rely on personal interviews, references and other background checks, and test results. Some-times an employer's decision may also be influenced by affirmative-action considerations. Each of these selection meth-ods is regulated by state and federal law.

PERSONAL INTERVIEWS

By their very nature, job interviews are subjective. During an in-terview, an employer cannot help but form impressions about an applicant's ambition, motivation, creativity, dependability, and

responsibility. Even so, given the inherently subjective nature of
the interviewing process, employers should strive to make interviews as objective (i.e., fact-based) as possible. Concentrating on
objective information helps avoid decisions (or the appearance
of decisions) based upon an applicant's status as a member of
one or more protected classes. It focuses the selection process
where it should be focused—on an individual's qualifications
and employment experience. Interviews that focus on job-
related issues and relate to legitimate business interests usually
will not violate the law.

Employers should also attempt to make job interviews as
uniform as possible. To this end, the same set of questions
should be addressed to all applicants for the same position. This
type of uniformity provides a better basis for comparing candidates, and helps avoid any appearance of discrimination. For example, suppose that an employer asks female applicants whether
they plan to marry, but does not ask the same question of male
applicants. This difference may imply that the employer rejects
women who plan to marry, but does not reject men for the same
reason. In any event, employers should not ask this type of question because it is not relevant to any job requirement.

Obviously, employers should never ask questions in an interview that they are prohibited from asking on a job application

---

▶ **TAKE NOTE OF THIS**

In the interest of creating a written record of the information used to
make hiring decisions, employers should take careful notes during interviews. Besides being helpful in defending hiring decisions if they're chal-
lenged in the future, keeping accurate, job-related interview notes
improves the quality of the selection process itself. However, employers
should avoid writing on resumes, and should only write notes that per-
tain to an applicant's ability to perform the functions of a job.

ⓘ HANDLING BIASED QUESTIONS

As an applicant, what should you do if an interviewer asks a question that seems out of bounds?

You can either swallow hard and answer the question (and hope the job is worth it), or indicate that the question seems inappropriate—and risk antagonizing the interviewer and losing any chance at the job. If you're willing to take that risk, you may later wish to complain to the employer's human resources director about the inappropriate question. Even if you don't get the job, your complaint could at least prompt the employer to counsel the interviewer about which questions are legal and which are inappropriate.

A tactful middle course might be to answer the question by providing the information the interviewer is actually trying to elicit. For example, you could respond by saying "If you're wondering whether I'll be able to work long hours, I can assure you that I will. My current boss can attest to it!"

In any event, you would be well advised to make note of offending questions as soon as possible after an interview, in case you later decide to seek legal advice.

form. (See chapter 3 for further discussion of this topic.) Interview questions should relate only to the job's requirements and the applicant's qualifications, work experience, and history. Even when seeking information related to the job, interviewers should be careful to phrase questions to avoid any inference of discrimination. For example, an employer may have a legitimate interest in determining a potential employee's commitment to the company and the job. But the best way to get this information is to ask for it outright—not to ask whether the applicant has a family, is married, or is planning to have children. (Familial status, marital status, and pregnancy are all protected categories under some state laws.) A more neutral way of obtaining this information is to ask *all* applicants such questions as: "What are your career objectives?" or "Where do you see yourself in five years?" If an applicant provides information related to a protected category—for example, that she is pregnant—the interviewer's response should politely emphasize the employer's neutrality in the hiring process (e.g., "We don't take that information into consideration when making hiring decisions, but please accept our congratulations!").

CANDIDATES WITH DISABILITIES

Under the Americans with Disabilities Act (ADA), employers cannot discriminate against a "qualified individual with a disability who, with or without reasonable accommodation, can perform the essential functions of the employment position." Therefore, in interviewing and making hiring decisions about an individual with a disability, employers must be careful to base their decisions on the individual's ability to do the job, and not on the disability. Even if a disability is obvious, employers may not question an applicant about the nature or severity of the disability, whether it will interfere with his or her ability to perform the job, or whether he or she will need treatment or leave time because of the disability. Employers may ask applicants how they

 BUT IT COSTS MORE MONEY!

If a reasonable accommodation would allow an applicant with a disability to perform the essential functions of a job, the ADA prohibits an employer from refusing to hire that person because it would have to provide the accommodation. In other words, if the employer is choosing between two candidates, one of whom has a disability requiring an accommodation, the employer is forbidden from choosing the nondisabled candidate because it would be cheaper. The employer can, however, select the nondisabled candidate if he or she is better qualified for the job.

would perform the job, but should ask this question of all applicants—not just those who appear to have a disability or medical impairment.

If an applicant cannot perform a job's essential functions, the first question is whether the inability is due to lack of qualifications or to the disability. For example, suppose an employer is hiring for a secretarial position in which the essential function is typing. If an applicant happens to be blind, and also cannot type, then the employer could refuse to hire that candidate—because that individual is not qualified for the job. However, if an applicant is blind but has typing skills, then the question becomes whether he or she—with or without reasonable accommodation—could perform the job in question. The ADA requires employers to provide reasonable accommodation for individuals with disabilities unless to do so would cause an undue hardship for the business. The blind applicant may be unable to use the employer's existing computer keyboard, but could perhaps perform the job by using a braille keyboard. In that case, providing the braille keyboard may be an accommodation that could allow the applicant to perform the essential functions of the job. Whether the employer would be required by law to provide the keyboard would depend on whether the accommodation would cause an undue hardship to the operation of the business.

What is a Reasonable Accommodation?

Common examples of reasonable accommodations include:
- making existing facilities readily accessible;
- job restructuring to facilitate part-time or modified work schedules;
- modifying equipment; and
- providing readers or interpreters.

Some specific examples of accommodations include providing a deaf employee who answers phones with a TDD, and modifying an employee's work hours to accommodate regularly scheduled appointments for medical treatment. Employers are not required to provide equipment or devices primarily for an in-

( ) TALKING TO A LAWYER

Q. Some of the employees at my company handle toxic chemicals. Despite all our precautions, spills sometimes occur and we need to evacuate the plant immediately. If an individual is unable to hear the warning siren or is not mobile enough to quickly leave the premises in the event of an emergency, I won't hire that person. Am I violating some law?

A. You may be violating the ADA. For a hearing-impaired employee, could you use flashing lights in addition to the warning siren? If an employee has impaired mobility and moves slowly, could he or she be assigned to a workstation near the emergency exit? These may be reasonable accommodations that you would be required to make, unless they would cause an undue hardship.

> —Answer by members of the ABA Section
> of Labor and Employment Law

dividual's personal use—such as corrective glasses, hearing aids, or wheelchairs—but may be required to build access ramps so that individuals in wheelchairs can enter the workplace. Under the ADA, employers and employees must engage in interactive dialogue to determine whether reasonable accommodation is necessary—and, if so, what that accommodation might be.

Is There an Undue Hardship?

The ADA defines an **undue hardship** as "an action requiring significant difficulty or expense, when considered in light of the [following] factors":

    1. the nature and cost of the accommodation needed;

    2. the overall financial resources of the employer's facility, the number of persons employed at that facility, the effect on expenses and resources at the facility, and the impact on the operation of the facility;

▶ **LET'S TALK ABOUT IT**

Frequently, when a qualified individual with a disability requests a reasonable accommodation, the appropriate accommodation is obvious. The individual may suggest a reasonable accommodation based on his or her own experience. However, when the appropriate accommodation is not readily apparent, employers should make a reasonable effort to identify one. The best way to do this is to consult informally with the applicant about potential accommodations. If this consultation does not identify an appropriate accommodation, the employer or applicant can often obtain suggestions for appropriate accommodations from the EEOC, state or local vocational-rehabilitation agencies, or state or local organizations representing or providing services to individuals with disabilities.

3. the financial resources of the employer as a whole, and the overall size of the business; and

4. the type of business that the employer operates, including the composition, structure, and function of the workforce and the relationship of the facility to the employer as a whole.

Whether or not an accommodation causes an undue hardship is determined on a case-by-case basis. For example, purchasing a TDD may constitute an undue hardship for a small family-owned grocery store, but not for a Fortune 500 company.

It is generally the applicant's responsibility to inform employers of the need for an accommodation. Also, an employer may require an applicant to prove a qualifying disability and the need for an accommodation, if the disability is not obvious.

PROTECTING PRIVACY

Employers should also be careful not to ask questions that constitute unwarranted intrusion into an individual's personal life.

The law in some states protects individuals from intentional intrusions into their private affairs in a manner that a reasonable person would find offensive.

Many states have also passed laws that prohibit an employer from discrimination based on an employee's off-duty lifestyle. For example, at least twenty-eight states—including Indiana, South Carolina, and Wyoming—prohibit employment discrimination based on an employee's off-duty use of tobacco. Other states, such as Wisconsin and Illinois, prohibit employment discrimination based on an employee's off-duty use of *any* lawful product (such as alcohol). However, if an employee's off-duty use of tobacco or alcohol negatively affects his or her performance in the workplace—for example, if the employee comes to work intoxicated—then an employer can take disciplinary action.

Lastly, a few states such as Colorado and New York prohibit employment discrimination based on *any* lawful off-duty conduct by employees. Constitutional protections available to government workers are discussed in chapter 14.

( ) TALKING TO A LAWYER

Q. *I'm two months pregnant and I've been turned down for several jobs. Some of the interviewers told me that they can't hire me because I'll soon need time off, and they need someone on a full-time basis. Is this legal?*

A. No. The Pregnancy Discrimination Act and many state laws specifically prohibit discrimination in employment, including hiring decisions against female applicants who are pregnant but otherwise qualified for the position sought.

—Answer by members of the ABA Section
of Labor and Employment Law

REFERENCES AND BACKGROUND CHECKS

Both federal and state laws regulate the ability of employers to request references and other information. The federal Fair Credit Reporting Act (FCRA) regulates what type of background information employers can obtain and how they can use it. Reference checks that unnecessarily request private information or use unreasonable methods to gather data may subject an employer to liability for invasion of privacy, though such liability is admittedly rare. As a rule, when conducting reference checks, employers should inquire only about issues relating to an individual's past work performance.

Some employers run credit checks or criminal-history checks for job applicants and/or employees. These procedures raise questions under both Title VII and the FCRA. Courts interpreting Title VII have held that requiring good credit as a condition of employment can result in adverse-impact discrimination, since disproportionately more nonwhites than whites live below the poverty line. Basing decisions on arrest and conviction records may also have an adverse impact on certain minority groups, and is prohibited by some state antidiscrimination laws.

⚠ REFERENCES CAN BACKFIRE

Background checks can also pose dangers for former employers, who can face defamation suits for providing false or misleading references about former employees. To protect themselves from possible liability for defamation, many employers will only verify that an employee worked for them for a particular period, and will not provide an assessment of that employee's performance. (See the discussion above for further information about references.)

The FCRA also regulates the use of consumer information. An employer using a third-party consumer reporting agency to get information on a prospective employee is subject to the FCRA. An employer can get two types of information from a reporting agency: a consumer report and an investigative consumer report. Under the FCRA, before an employer can request a consumer report or an investigative consumer report on an applicant or employee, it must give notice to the applicant or employee and obtain his or her authorization. This notice must be on a form separate from the employment application. Some states impose specific requirements for a notice to be effective.

If an employer decides not to hire someone based in whole or in part on any information contained in a consumer report, the FCRA requires the employer to so advise the applicant and provide a copy of the report and the name and address of the consumer reporting agency that provided the report, and to advise the individual of his or her rights under the FCRA. Employers intending to obtain investigative consumer reports on applicants must notify them in writing within three days of requesting such reports, and inform them of their right to request a complete and accurate disclosure of the nature and scope of the investigation. Some states impose additional restrictions on the use of consumer credit reports.

 ## TWO DIFFERENT TYPES OF REPORTS

A **consumer report** contains information about an individual's creditworthiness, credit standing, character, and general reputation, none of which is obtained from personal interviews. An **investigative consumer report** contains more detailed and subjective information on a person's character, reputation, and mode of living, and is obtained through personal interviews of friends and associates of the consumer.

TESTS

Employers may use any of several types of tests during the employee selection process. Such tests include written-ability tests, polygraph tests, honesty tests, medical tests, personality tests, drug tests, and AIDS/HIV tests. Each of these tests is regulated in some way by federal or state law, and some are permissible only in certain situations.

However, before we address specific types of tests, let's discuss some considerations that apply to all tests. Any test given by employers that has the effect of disproportionately excluding members of a protected class creates potential problems under Title VII, the Age Discrimination in Employment Act (ADEA), and the ADA (see chapter 2 for a detailed discussion of antidiscrimination law under these statutes). If a test with an adverse impact on candidates in protected classes is not related to successful performance of the job in question, it likely violates federal law. Of course, many types of tests have been shown not to have an adverse impact, and their use is not forbidden under employment antidiscrimination laws.

A second general concern about tests arises with respect to the ADA. When giving tests to applicants with disabilities, employers must ensure that test results reflect the skills that the tests are meant to measure, and that the results are not affected by an applicant's disability. For example, suppose an employer administers a timed, written test to measure mathematical aptitude. An applicant who is paraplegic and uses a mechanical device for writing might fail the test because he does not have sufficient time to complete it. In that instance, the applicant's disability would affect the test result. If an applicant has a disability impairing his ability to take the test, the employer must determine whether it needs to modify the test to accommodate that disability.

But if the purpose of a test is to measure a skill that is itself impaired by an applicant's disability, the employer is not required to accommodate the applicant in question. For example, an applicant who is a paraplegic might fail a speed-typing test because his disability prevents him from typing quickly. However, since the test is designed to measure speed—the very skill impaired by the applicant's disability—the employer generally would not be required to modify the test to accommodate that applicant.

As discussed previously, the burden is on applicants taking tests to inform employers of their need for accommodation.

Besides the above concerns that apply to all employment tests, both federal and state laws regulate specific types of tests, as detailed below.

Polygraph Tests

The Employee Polygraph Protection Act (EPPA) prohibits almost all private-sector employers from requiring job applicants to take lie detector tests. Under the terms of the EPPA, employers cannot:

- request or suggest that applicants undergo lie detector tests;
- administer lie detector tests to applicants; or
- refuse to hire an individual because he or she has refused to take a lie detector test.

Included in the statute's definition of **lie detector test** are polygraphs, deceptographs, voice stress analyzers, psychological-stress evaluators, and any similar mechanical or electrical devices that provide a diagnostic opinion about an individual's honesty.

⚠ BE CAREFUL OF STATE LAW

Some states—including Alaska, California, and Idaho—prohibit *all* private-sector employers from requiring polygraph tests.

(i) LEGAL STATUS OF LIE DETECTOR TESTS

The general rule in most states is that the results of lie detector tests are not admissible as evidence in court. However, the fact that their results are inadmissible as evidence does not keep lie detectors from being used by employers. Before the EPPA was passed, about 2 million tests were administered each year by private employers.

Two types of employers are exempted from the EPPA's requirements: employers manufacturing or distributing controlled substances, and employers whose primary business is to provide armored-car services, security systems, or security personnel. These employers can administer such tests to employees, but only to employees who either have access to controlled substances or themselves perform security services. Thus, most clerical and administrative employees who work for drug manufacturers or security companies are protected under the EPPA.

As set forth in the EPPA, federal law forbids only the administration of honesty tests that are mechanical or electrical; it does not apply to pen-and-paper honesty tests. However, even though such tests are not covered by the EPPA, a few states regulate them. For example, Maine and Rhode Island prohibit employers from administering written as well as mechanical honesty tests.

(An employer's use of polygraphs to investigate its current workforce is discussed in chapter 10.)

Medical Tests

The ADA strictly forbids employers from giving **medical tests** to *any* applicants. However, an employer may require such tests after an offer of employment has been made and before an applicant begins working, but only if:

1. all employees for the job in question are required to undergo a medical exam (i.e., particular candidates cannot be singled out for an exam);

2. any information obtained from the exam is maintained in a separate medical file (not the applicant's personnel file) and kept confidential; and

3. the information is not used to discriminate against the employee because of a disability.

A test to determine the presence of the AIDS/HIV virus is a medical test, and as such is subject to ADA restrictions. Moreover, AIDS/HIV is a disability within the meaning of the ADA, and basing an employment decision on the fact that an applicant has AIDS/HIV is prohibited. Many states have specific laws that place even further limitations on AIDS/HIV testing. A few states, such as Massachusetts and Florida, prohibit employers from requiring an AIDS/HIV test as a condition of employment. Many more states, like California, Delaware, and Michigan, prohibit AIDS/HIV testing without informed consent and place severe restrictions on disseminating test results.

Many states have also enacted laws regulating employer use of genetic testing. At least twenty-five states either prohibit the use of genetic testing for employment purposes (Connecticut, Iowa, and Oregon) or impose confidentiality requirements on the use of such information (Arizona and Illinois). Moreover, a genetic test is a medical test and is thus subject to the limitations on medical tests imposed by the ADA.

Personality Tests

As a general rule, the law does not regulate **personality tests** that employers use to determine innate intelligence, general personality, or psychological characteristics of applicants or employees. However, if use of such a test provides evidence of a mental disability, the test may be considered a medical test, and thus subject to the ADA's strict regulations on medical tests. Also, if such tests have the effect of disproportionately screening out individuals with mental disabilities, they could be deemed to have an adverse impact under the ADA. In that case, the tests would be unlawful unless the employer could prove that administering such tests was a job-related business necessity.

Drug Tests

The ADA specifically excludes **drug tests** from its definition of "medical examinations." Therefore, neither the ADA nor any other federal law prohibits employers from requiring applicants to undergo drug tests. However, constitutional guarantees limit the circumstances under which government employers may use drug tests. These limitations on government employers are discussed in chapter 14.

In addition, most states have adopted some form of legislation regulating drug testing in the employment setting. Many of these laws are limited to specific employment sectors, such as the government or transportation sectors. Typically, these laws do not restrict when an employer may administer drug testing, but instead regulate technical matters such as certification of laboratories and chain of custody of urine or blood samples. Some state laws encourage drug testing by mandating discounted workers' compensation premiums for employers that test applicants or employees.

Several states, however, have more stringent requirements with regard to drug testing. For example, Maine and Rhode Island allow drug testing only after an offer of employment has been extended (and only if the job is conditional on a clean test result). Rhode Island law also requires that test samples be collected in private, and that positive results be confirmed. In Minnesota, an employer may not require an applicant to undergo arbitrary or capricious drug testing, and can require a test only after a job offer has been made; moreover, any testing must conform to a written drug-testing policy and be conducted by an approved laboratory. Hawaii, North Carolina, and Utah allow drug testing so long as certain procedures are followed that provide for reliable testing results. Some states, such as California, provide for a constitutional right to privacy that limits drug testing by private as well as public employers.

Finally, if the method used by an employer in administering a drug test (such as direct observation of urination) is deemed "outrageous," that employer could be subject to tort liability for invasion of privacy or intentional infliction of emotional distress.

AFFIRMATIVE ACTION

Affirmative action affects some hiring decisions. Affirmative action is permissible under federal law, as long as it is practiced according to a valid **affirmative-action plan (AAP)**.

An AAP establishes guidelines for recruiting, hiring, and promoting women and minorities in order to eliminate the present effects of past employment discrimination. In crafting an AAP, an employer analyzes its current employment practices and the makeup of its workforce for any indications that women and minorities are excluded or disadvantaged. If the employer identifies problems, it devises new policies and practices aimed at solving the problems. The employer then develops goals for measuring progress in correcting the problems and ensuring that women and minorities have equal employment opportunities.

The Supreme Court has held that voluntary private sector AAPs are lawful if they remedy obvious racial or gender imbalances in traditionally segregated job categories. Voluntary AAPs must, however, maintain a balance, and ensure that minority employees are free from the effects of unlawful discrimination while respecting the employment interests of nonminority employees.

Neither Title VII nor the ADEA nor the ADA requires employers to create AAPs. Employers that have government con-

(i) WHAT MAKES AN AFFIRMATIVE ACTION PLAN VALID?

The courts look to several factors in determining the validity of a private-sector AAP:

1. The AAP should be designed to eliminate obvious racial- or gender-based imbalances in the workforce.

2. The plan cannot "unnecessarily trammel the interests" of nonminority workers. It should not automatically exclude nonminority employees from consideration for the job in question. The minority employee favored by the AAP should be qualified for the job; employers should avoid favoring unqualified workers.

3. The AAP should not adopt strict quotas. It should strive toward realistic goals, taking into account turnover, layoffs, lateral transfers, new job openings, and retirements. These goals should also take into account the number of qualified minorities in the area workforce. Moreover, goals should be temporary, designed to achieve—not maintain—racial and gender balance.

4. Courts are more likely to validate AAPs that focus on recruiting, hiring, and promotion practices, rather than plans that provide special treatment in the event of a layoff. However, the courts are more willing to protect a nonminority employee's interests in his current job (as in a layoff situation) than any speculative expectations an applicant might have about a job that he doesn't currently hold (as in the case of hiring and promotions).

tracts, however, are often required to develop AAPs. **Executive Order 11246** requires any federal contractor with a contract exceeding $50,000 and a workforce of at least fifty employees to develop an AAP. Many states, such as Iowa and Pennsylvania, require employers that have state contracts to implement AAPs.

ⓘ EMPLOYMENT AGENCIES

With the increase in the use of part-time and temporary employees, more employers are using employment agencies for recruitment. Employment agencies are chiefly regulated through antidiscrimination laws.

When referring applicants, employment agencies may not discriminate based on protected classifications. In this context, discrimination includes not only intentional discrimination, but also adverse-impact discrimination. For example, an employment agency could not refuse to refer a worker because he is African-American, even if the company asking for the referral specifically requested only white workers. Moreover, an employment agency using a test to determine which applicants to refer is required to justify the test as job-related if the test disproportionately excludes members of a protected class. Also, in administering any tests, an employment agency should ensure that its manner of administering the test does not discriminate based on an applicant's disability. (See the "Tests" section of this chapter for further discussion of the ADA's impact on employment tests.)

In addition, the Immigration Reform and Control Act prohibits an employment agency from recruiting or referring aliens unauthorized to work in the United States, as well as from discriminating in recruitment or referral based on national origin or citizenship status.

The ability of public-sector employers to utilize AAPs is more strictly limited than that of private-sector employers. Evidence of workforce imbalance is not a sufficient justification for a government employer to use an AAP. Rather, there must be a strong evidentiary basis for concluding that the specific government employer engaged in illegal discrimination in the past. Second, any AAP must be limited in duration, and flexible enough to respond to changes in circumstance. Lastly, there must be no other method that would be as effective in remedy-

( ) TALKING TO A LAWYER

Q. *I run a construction company. This guy applied for a job, but my fore-man told me he's a paid union organizer who only wants to work here so he can get my crew to join the union. Surely I don't have to hire him!*

A. You cannot discriminate against an applicant solely because he or she supports or is a member of a union. Even if you know the applicant intends to try to organize your workforce, you cannot use that knowledge as a basis for not hiring the applicant.

—Answer by members of the ABA Section
of Labor and Employment Law

ing the discrimination. A few states, such as California and Washington, prohibit the use of affirmative action by any governmental employer.

MAKING THE FINAL SELECTION

Having narrowed the field of qualified applicants through the use of interviews and tests, an employer must make its final decision: Who should be hired? Once again, the antidiscrimination principle comes into play; an employer cannot make its decision based on a protected characteristic of an applicant. For example, in making a choice between a Caucasian applicant and a Hispanic applicant, the employer cannot choose the Caucasian because he finds it difficult to understand the Hispanic worker's accent, unless communication skills are a job requirement. Nor may he choose a male candidate over a female candidate because the female is pregnant. Nor may he hire a Christian applicant over a Muslim because the latter wears a scarf covering her hair. In making any final employment decision, the employer must base its decision on criteria *not* related to the individual's membership in a protected class.

THE WORLD AT YOUR FINGERTIPS

- The Federal Trade Commission's website provides a link to the Fair Credit Reporting Act at *www.ftc.gov/bcp/conline/edcams/credit/index.html*.
- For more information on the Employee Polygraph Protection Act, visit *www.dol.gov/dol/compliance/comp-eppa.htm*. This site also provides information on rights and responsibilities relating to the use of lie detector tests.
- For information on affirmative-action programs, visit *www.dol.gov/dol/topic/hiring* and click on "Affirmative Action."
- Findlaw provides links to sources of information on state laws regulating drug testing. Visit *www.employment.findlaw.com/employment/employment-employee-hiring* and click on "Drug Tests."
- See the resources listed at the end of chapter 2 for information on how the antidiscrimination laws impact employee selection procedures.

REMEMBER THIS

- Make sure that applicant interview questions focus on the qualifications and skills needed for the job.
- Do not ask applicants questions about their medical histories or medical conditions.
- With few exceptions, applicants cannot be asked to take a polygraph exam.
- Many states regulate the procedures for administering drug tests to applicants and employees.
- Employers can be required to provide accommodations to applicants to enable them to take employment-related tests or to

enable them to perform the essential functions of the job in question.

• Employment tests that have an adverse impact on protected classes of applicants are permissible only if they are shown to be related to successful performance of the job.

• Be careful when running background checks on applicants; federal and state laws may regulate the methods used and the information sought.

CHAPTER 5

The Law on Wages, Hours, and Benefits

What the Law Requires

Jeremy started a new job on Monday. When he got to work, his supervisor filled him in on company procedures. Jeremy asked about benefits and was surprised to learn that his new job did not entitle him to health insurance coverage, paid vacation, or paid holidays. "You don't have to work on holidays, and you get one week of vacation per year," said his supervisor—then adding, "but you won't get paid for the days you don't work."

"This can't be right," thought Jeremy. "After all, every other job I've ever had has provided those benefits!"

Once employees are hired, their working lives are governed by their **terms and conditions of employment.** This phrase encompasses all aspects of the relationship between an employer and employee: pay, promotions, vacations, hours of work, training programs, leave time, working environment, discipline, and discharge.

Obviously employees care deeply about the terms and conditions of their employment, but often they have little or no say in how these terms or conditions are established. Terms and conditions are established in one of four ways: 1) through requirements imposed by federal or state law; 2) by employer decisions; 3) in a written contract between the employer and the employee; or 4) in a collective-bargaining agreement between a union and an employer. This chapter will examine the requirements imposed by law for setting wages, hours, and benefits; the next chapter will explore the ways in which employers set terms and conditions of employment. Chapter 13 will provide more information on collective-bargaining agreements.

THE LAW'S IMPACT

Before discussing specific laws, let's discuss an important general consideration relating to employment. Under antidiscrimination laws (discussed in chapter 2), members of a protected class cannot be discriminated against with respect to terms and conditions of employment. For example, suppose the law does not require an employer to provide a specific benefit—say, paid vacation. Nonetheless, if that employer decides to provide vacation benefits to *some* employees, those benefits must be made available to *all* employees—without regard to race, color, religion, national origin, sex, age, disability, or other protected status.

The implication of this general rule is that an employer may not give pay raises to men while refusing them to women. It may, however, give raises to assembly workers but not to office workers. Why the distinction? In the first instance, men and women are treated differently based on their membership in a protected class—i.e., sex. But in the second example, the reason for the differential treatment has to do with a difference in job duties—not with a difference in gender or other protected characteristic.

While the law leaves many aspects of the working relationship to the employer's discretion, it does establish a minimum level of benefits for certain terms and conditions of employment, as set forth below.

MINIMUM-WAGE LAWS

The **Fair Labor Standards Act (FLSA)** requires employers to pay employees a minimum of $5.15 per hour. A few employers are not covered by the FLSA, but most states have their own minimum-wage laws covering employers that do business there. Most states set their minimum wage at the same level as that established by the FLSA; about eight states have a lower minimum or no set minimum wage at all, and about fifteen states have a higher one. In states that have set a higher minimum wage than is required by federal law, the higher wage applies to *all* employers doing business in that state—even if those employers are also covered under the FLSA. For example, all employers doing business in Oregon must pay their workers a minimum of $7.25 an hour—even employers who are covered by the FLSA, which mandates a lower wage. However, in a state that requires a minimum wage lower than that set by the FLSA, only those employers who are covered under the FLSA are required to pay the higher FLSA rate; employers not covered by the FLSA may pay the lower, state-mandated wage.

In the last ten years, city and county governments have begun to pass "living wage" ordinances that set the minimum wage for businesses at a higher level than that of the federal minimum wage. Over one hundred cities or counties have passed such ordinances; the overwhelming majority of these ordinances apply only to those companies that have contracts with the local government or receive some type of tax abatement from the government. However, at least five cities have passed living wage ordinances that apply to all companies doing business within the geographic confines of the city.

Employers must pay the minimum wage for every hour employees work in any workweek; thus, an employee who works for twenty hours at the federal minimum wage must be paid a min-

---

ⓘ YOUTH SUB-MINIMUM WAGE UNDER THE FLSA

Under the FLSA, covered employees under twenty years of age may be paid a sub-minimum wage of $4.25 an hour during their first ninety consecutive calendar days of employment. After the first ninety days, however, employers must pay the regular minimum wage. Moreover, an employer is prohibited from discharging or reducing the hours of employees who are paid the regular minimum wage in order to hire youths at the sub-minimum rate. Be aware that state law may not have a similar allowance for sub-minimum rates.

imum of $103. For the purposes of minimum-wage laws, **hours worked** generally includes all the time spent by employees performing their job duties during the workday. When an employee's job requires travel during the workday, as in the case of a service technician who repairs furnaces at customers' homes, time spent traveling is considered hours worked for which the employee must receive compensation. Hours worked also may include certain preparatory time spent at the beginning of the workday. For example, workers at a meat processing plant must be compensated for time spent sharpening their knives, and workers at a chemical plant must be compensated for time spent changing into required protective clothing. Mandatory attendance at lectures, meetings, and training programs is also considered hours worked, as are rest periods and coffee breaks shorter than twenty minutes.

What is *not* considered hours worked for purposes of minimum-wage law? Examples include:
• time spent commuting to work;
• lunch or dinner breaks of at least thirty minutes;
• time spent changing clothes, if done for the benefit of the employee; and
• on-call time spent away from the employer's premises that the employee can use for his or her own purposes.

( ) TALKING TO A LAWYER

Q. I work at a call center. We have to begin work at 9 A.M. sharp. In order to be ready to work, I have to come in at least ten minutes early to log on to my computer and prepare my paperwork, but I don't get paid for that time. Should I?

A. Yes. An employer is required to pay its employees for preparatory time if tasks performed during such time are necessary to perform the job.

—Answer by members of the ABA Section of Labor and Employment Law

In determining whether workers should be paid for on-call time, courts look at how much control the employer has over the employee during that time, and whether the employee is free to use the time as he or she wishes. If an employee is prevented from performing only a limited number of tasks while on call (such as consuming alcohol), then the worker generally does not have to be paid.

In jobs where employees customarily receive more than $30 a month in tips (for example, waiter or beautician jobs), employers may credit the value of such tips against the required minimum wage. Of course, the employer may credit against minimum wage only the amount the employee actually receives in tips. Under the FLSA, an employer must pay a tipped employee at

▶ **THE COIN OF THE REALM**

The minimum wage must usually be paid in the form of money, but in some cases an employer may deduct the cost of providing certain noncash benefits to employees from the required minimum wage. For example, an employer can deduct from an employee's wages the reasonable cost of providing board, lodging, and other facilities—as in the case of lodging provided to a "house mother" who lives in a residential rehabilitation facility.

To receive credit for the cost of such noncash benefits, the employer must furnish the benefits for the employee's convenience and the employee must voluntarily accept them. Examples of noncash items that can be credited against the minimum wage are: meals furnished at a company cafeteria, housing furnished by a company for residential purposes, and fuel or electricity used by an employee for nonbusiness purposes.

For the purpose of minimum-wage laws, employers can't take a credit for discounts provided to employees, or for money employees are required to pay for breakage or cash shortages.

least $2.13 an hour. If the employee receives less than $3.02 an hour in tips (the amount that would allow the employee to make the federal minimum wage of $5.15 an hour), the employer is required to pay the additional amount necessary to ensure the employee receives the minimum wage. In other words, the employee must always receive *at least* the federal minimum wage when the values of wages and tips are combined.

Employers may not take the tip credit unless they inform their employees about it before the credit is taken. In addition, employers must be able to prove that the employee actually receives tips equal to the value of the credit taken.

As is the case with other employment laws, the rules relating to tip credits may be different under state law. For example, in those states where the minimum wage is higher than $5.15 an hour, the minimum wage for a tipped employee will be higher than $2.13 an hour. Moreover, even in states that set their minimum wage at $5.15, the amount allowed for the tip credit may

▶ **HOW THE TIP CREDIT WORKS**

Suppose a waitress works forty hours in a week and earns a total of $80 in tips, for a total of $2 in tips per hour. By federal law, her employer is allowed to take $2 per hour as credit against the $5.15 minimum wage. This means that the employer must pay the waitress a minimum wage of $3.15 per hour ($5.15 [federal minimum wage]–$2.00 [allowed tip credit] = $3.15). Since the waitress worked forty hours for the week, the employer must pay her at least $126 for that week's work ($3.15 [minimum wage adjusted for tip credit] x 40 [number of hours worked] = $126).

Now suppose that the same waitress works forty hours in a week and earns a total of $160 in tips, which is $4 in tips per hour. In that instance, her employer may only take credit for $3.02 in tips, and not the entire $4, because the law limits the total tip credit to no more than $3.02 per hour. Thus, the employer must pay the waitress $2.13 per hour (the requirement under federal law) for a total of $85.20 for the week.

not be as high as the amount set by federal law. For example, Idaho allows an employer to credit only $1.54 in tips toward the minimum wage, not the $3.02 allowed by federal law. Thus, all employers in Idaho must comply with the Idaho tip credit rules. Like Idaho, at least four other states have set their tip credit values lower than that of the FLSA.

OTHER WAGE LAWS

Employers performing work under certain types of contracts with the federal government are covered by a series of wage laws dealing with government contractors. A federal contractor manufacturing or furnishing to the government materials, supplies, articles, or equipment valued at more than $10,000 is covered by the **Walsh-Healy Act**. This law requires that all employees receive the prevailing minimum rate for similar work performed in a given locality. The prevailing minimum rate is determined by the Secretary of Labor.

The **Davis-Bacon Act** requires contractors on federal construction projects performing work valued in excess of $2,000 to pay their employees the prevailing wage and fringe-benefit rate for that area (as determined by the Secretary of Labor). The **Service Contract Act** requires that all employees performing service work under contract with the federal government (such as guards, janitors, and maintenance employees) be paid the minimum wage. If the value of the contract exceeds $2,500, then the employees must be paid the prevailing wage and fringe-benefit rate for that area (as determined by the Secretary of Labor).

OVERTIME

The FLSA and comparable state laws also regulate wage rates for overtime work. If employees work more than forty hours during any workweek, employers must pay them one and one-half times their regular rate of pay. The overtime rate applies to each hour, or fraction of an hour, worked over forty in any workweek.

Is an employee entitled to overtime for working a tough twelve-hour day? If he or she hasn't worked more than forty total hours for the week, then not necessarily. Under the FLSA and most state laws, overtime is calculated based on the number of hours worked per week, not the number of hours worked per day. Once again, however, there may be variations in state laws. California, for example, requires overtime for all hours worked in excess of eight hours in any workday, *or* in excess of forty hours in any workweek. A collective-bargaining agreement between an employer and a union may require overtime pay after eight hours in a day (or ten hours, or any number of hours to which the parties have agreed).

Overtime is based solely on time worked in excess of forty hours in a workweek, regardless of the days on which the hours are actually worked. Work on Saturday, Sunday, or a holiday does not automatically entitle an employee to overtime pay; it depends on whether the employee has already worked forty hours for that week. However, a collective-bargaining agreement may provide for overtime pay on weekends or holidays, regardless of whether an employee works forty hours that week.

The employer must use the employee's regular rate of pay—and not the minimum-wage rate—as the base rate for calculating overtime pay. When an employee is paid by the hour, the base rate used to calculate overtime pay is equal to the employee's hourly rate. When an employee is paid on salary or commission, the employee's pay must be converted to an hourly rate in order to properly compute overtime. The hourly rate is calculated by dividing the employee's pay for the week by the number of hours worked in that week.

Not all employers are covered by the FLSA. And even in the case of covered employers, the following categories of employees are exempt from the FLSA's provisions:

- outside salespeople;
- executive employees;
- professional employees;
- administrative employees; and
- computer systems analysts, computer programmers, and software engineers.

Whether these exemptions apply depends on the type of work performed by the employee in question, not the title of his or her job.

Retail commission salespeople must be paid at least the minimum wage, but are exempt from the overtime requirements if certain conditions are met. First, the salesperson's regular rate of pay must be more than one and one-half times the federal

▶ **DO THE MATH:**
CALCULATING OVERTIME

To calculate FLSA overtime for an hourly paid employee, consider the following example. An employee who is paid $6 an hour and works forty-three hours in one week is owed $27 in overtime pay. The calculation is as follows: $6/hour regular rate x $1\frac{1}{2}$ = $9/hour overtime rate; $9/hour x 3 (hours worked in excess of 40) = $27. The employee's salary for that week would be $267 ($6/hour x 40 hours = $240 regular salary + $27 in overtime pay).

To calculate overtime for a salaried employee, consider the following example. An employee is paid $250 a week as a standard salary for any week, including for a forty-hour workweek. One week the employee works forty-five hours. That makes the employee's regular hourly rate for that week $5.55 per hour ($250 divided by 45). The employer owes the employee an additional $41.60 for the five hours of overtime worked in that week. The calculation is as follows: $5.55/hour x $1\frac{1}{2}$ = $8.32 overtime rate; $8.32/hour x 5 (hours worked in excess of 40) = $41.60. The employee's salary for that week would be $291.60 ($250 regular salary + $41.60 overtime pay).

📋 PRIMARY DUTY

The term **primary duty** refers to the principal or most important duty that an employee performs. If performing exempt work takes up more than 50 percent of an employee's time, that work will generally be considered his or her primary duty. Factors to consider in determining whether exempt work constitutes an employee's primary duty include:

- the importance of the exempt work compared to other duties of the employee;
- the amount of time spent performing the exempt work;
- the relative freedom of the employee from direct supervision; and
- the relationship between the employee's salary and the wages paid to other employees performing the nonexempt work.

minimum wage (i.e., the regular rate of pay must be in excess of $7.73 per hour). Second, more than half of the salesperson's pay must come from commissions on goods or services.

Outside salespeople are exempt from both the minimum-wage and overtime requirements. An employee is considered an outside salesperson if:

- his or her primary duty is to make sales or to obtain orders or contracts for services; and

⚠ PAY ATTENTION TO STATE LAWS

Some state laws may have different requirements for exemption from the payment of overtime. As a result, an employee who meets the requirement for an executive exemption under federal law may not meet the exemption under state law, in which case the employee would be owed overtime under the terms of state wage law.

- he or she customarily and regularly spends time performing such sales work away from the employer's place of business.

Executive employees are exempt from overtime requirements if each of the following criteria is satisfied:

- The employee must be compensated on a salary basis at a rate of not less than $455 per week;
- The employee's primary duty must be managing the enterprise, or managing a customarily recognized department or subdivision within the enterprise;
- The employee must customarily and regularly direct the work of at least two or more full-time employees or their equivalent (e.g., four part-time employees who each work twenty hours per week); and
- The employee must have the authority to hire or fire other employees, or the employee's suggestions and recommendations

---

(i) WORK RELATED TO MANAGING THE BUSINESS

For purposes of overtime exemption, work that directly assists with the running or servicing of a business is related to the management of that business. Examples of such work include:

- accounting;
- budgeting;
- auditing;
- advertising;
- marketing;
- personnel management; and
- public relations.

But in performing this work, the employee must exercise independent judgment. For example, clerical workers in a company's accounting department would not qualify as exempt administrative employees.

as to hiring, firing, or change of status of other employees must be given particular weight.

Professional employees are exempt from overtime requirements if all of the following tests are met:

• The employee must be compensated on a salary basis at a rate of not less than $455 per week;

• The employee's primary duty must be the performance of work requiring **advanced knowledge**, defined as work that is predominantly intellectual in character and that requires the consistent exercise of discretion and judgment;

(i) SALARY DEDUCTIONS

The salary basis requirement for most of the overtime exemptions requires that the amount paid to the employee not be subject to reduction because of variations in the quality or quantity of work performed. To maintain this exemption, an exempt employee must receive the full salary for any week in which he performs any work, without regard to the number of days or hours worked. Deductions may, however, be made in the following circumstances:

• The employee is absent from work for one or more full days for personal reasons;

• The employee is absent for one or more full days because of sickness or disability, and there is a bona fide policy of providing compensation for loss of salary caused by sickness or disability;

• The employee receives a disciplinary suspension of one or more full days, imposed in good faith for infractions of written workplace conduct rules;

• The employee receives a penalty, imposed in good faith, for infractions of major safety rules; or

• The employee is on unpaid leave pursuant to the Family and Medical Leave Act.

• The advanced knowledge must be in a field of science or learning; and

• The advanced knowledge must be customarily acquired by a prolonged course of specialized intellectual instruction.

Administrative employees are exempt if all of the following tests are met:

• The employee must be compensated on a salary basis at a rate of not less than $455 per week;

• The employee's primary duty must be the performance of office or nonmanual work directly related to the management or general business operations of the employer or the employer's customers; and

• The employee's primary duty includes the exercise of discretion and independent judgment with respect to matters of significance.

Computer professionals who are paid on a salary basis at a rate of not less than $455 per week or who are compensated on an hourly basis at a rate not less than $27.63 an hour are exempt from overtime requirements if certain conditions are met. For purposes of overtime exemption, a computer professional is an employee who works as a computer systems analyst, computer programmer, software engineer, or other similarly skilled worker.

 MAKING A RECORD

The FLSA requires employers to maintain and preserve certain wage records to verify their compliance with the law. Employee payroll records must be retained for three years, and must contain such information as employee names, hours worked each workday and workweek, wages paid, deductions from wages, straight-time (non-overtime) wages, and overtime paid. The employer must also maintain for two years documentation in support of its payroll records, such as time cards, work schedules, and order and billing records.

Employees in this category are exempt if their primary work duties fall into one of the following categories:

• the application of systems analysis techniques and procedures, including consulting with users, to determine hardware, software, or system-functional specifications;

• the design, development, documentation, analysis, creation, testing, or modification of computer systems or programs;

• the design, documentation, testing, creation, or modification of computer programs related to machine operating systems; or

• a combination of the duties described in the preceding three categories, the performance of which requires the same level of skill.

SETTING WAGE RATES

Assuming the wage requirements of the FLSA and state law are met, an employer may use its discretion in setting wage rates for jobs, as long as it does not base pay differentials on membership in a protected class (i.e., race, gender, age, etc). Pay differentials based on a protected classification violate state and federal antidiscrimination laws. In addition, the **Equal Pay Act (EPA)** specifically prohibits employers from paying different wages to employees of the opposite sex for the same work. However, an employer may set different wage rates based on seniority, skill, merit, quality, or differences in job content.

EPA requirements apply to jobs that are **substantially equal**. For example, let's say a beauty salon hires a male barber and a female beautician. The beauty salon pays the barber $2.50 per hour more than it pays the beautician. These two employees are performing substantially equal jobs: the skill of cutting hair is the same, the effort used is the same, the responsibility the two employees have for cutting hair is the same, and they work under similar conditions in the same beauty salon. In this case, the employer has violated the EPA. However, if the barber has five years' experience cutting hair, and the beautician has only two years'

( ) TALKING TO A LAWYER

Q. *My employer requires me to wear a uniform at work, but I have to pay for it, launder it, and buy a new one when it wears out. Shouldn't my employer have to pay for this?*

A. In some states an employer may require employees to pay for the cost of uniforms, including laundry and replacement costs. However, an employee cannot be required to pay for the cost of such uniforms if doing so would reduce his or her wage below the level of minimum wage.

—Answer by members of the ABA Section
of Labor and Employment Law

experience, the employer could cite seniority as a justification for the difference in wage rate.

WAGE PAYMENTS AND GARNISHMENTS

While federal law does not specifically mandate when wages must be paid, virtually every state has a wage payment law that governs reasonable time frames for payment, deductions from wages, and garnishment. State law generally requires that employees be paid weekly, semimonthly or monthly.

Employers are *required* to deduct taxes and certain amounts that have been garnished from an employee's paycheck. They are *allowed* to deduct the value of certain items from an employee's paycheck if the employee has authorized the deduction. Examples of allowable deductions include: union dues, charitable contributions, and insurance premiums. These deductions are allowed even if the amount received by the employee after the deduction falls below the level of the minimum wage.

The value of other items cannot be deducted from paychecks if the deductions would cause the pay to fall below the minimum

⚠ STATE LAWS ON DEDUCTIONS

Most states prohibit certain deductions from pay regardless of the circumstances. For example, California prohibits deductions for the cost of a required preemployment physical exam; Connecticut prohibits any deductions without written authorization from the employee; and Hawaii prohibits any deductions for replacement costs for employee breakage.

wage. Examples of such deductions include: work uniforms (including cleaning work uniforms), employee breakage, and cash shortage debts.

Both the federal **Consumer Credit Protection Act** and state laws limit the amount that can be garnished from a worker's paycheck. A **garnishment** is a court order requiring that earnings be withheld from a worker's paycheck and paid to a person or business to whom the worker owes a debt. The federal law limits the maximum amount that can be garnished to 25 percent

▶ CALCULATING ALLOWABLE GARNISHMENT

Suppose an employee's take home pay is $400 a week. Currently, thirty times the federal minimum wage is $154.50; this worker's wage exceeds that amount by $245.50. But this excess amount is subject to garnishment only if it is less than 25 percent of the worker's wage. Since 25 percent of this worker's wage is $100, the maximum amount that can be garnished is $100.

On the other hand, if the employee's weekly take-home pay was $177, his wages would exceed thirty times the minimum wage by $22.50, and 25 percent of his wages would be $44.25. The maximum amount that could be garnished would be $22.50, which is the lesser of the two figures.

of an employee's disposable earnings (gross earnings less deductions required by law), or the part of disposable earnings that exceeds thirty times the federal minimum wage, whichever is less.

The law permits a larger amount to be deducted if the debt is owed for child support payments, Chapter 13 bankruptcy, or back taxes. Federal law also prohibits an employer from discharging an employee because his or her wages have been subjected to a single garnishment. However, there are no protections for employees whose wages are subject to two or more separate garnishments.

Most state garnishment laws feature the same limitations, but some states limit garnishment to a greater extent, in which case the employer must comply with state law. For example, Alaska limits the amount that can be garnished to the amount by which the employee's weekly net pay exceeds $350, and Delaware limits the amount to 15 percent of the employee's wages.

EMPLOYER BANKRUPTCY

Employers may file for bankruptcy to liquidate all of their assets (called **Chapter 7 bankruptcy**), or for the purpose of reorganizing the company and restructuring their debt (called **Chapter 11 bankruptcy**). In either situation, the payment of employee wages and benefits may be affected.

In a Chapter 7 bankruptcy, all the assets of a corporate entity are liquidated, the company goes out of business, and the money is used to pay off the company's debts. The law ranks the debtors to determine who gets paid off first. Unpaid wages due to employees and earned within ninety days of the bankruptcy filing receive third priority (after administrative fees of the bankruptcy proceeding and secured creditors), and are limited to $4,925 per person. Unpaid contributions to employee benefit funds receive fourth priority, and also have a limit based on a formula. In reality, there is often no money left after paying off the first- and second-priority debts, which often leaves employees with nothing. The plus side of the equation is that, thanks to most state wage payment laws, employers should never be more than a few weeks or a month in arrears in paying employee wages.

In a Chapter 11 bankruptcy, the employer tries to work out a debt repayment plan to pay off its creditors and restructure itself, so it can continue operations successfully in the future. Any unpaid wages and benefits owed to its employees up to the point when the employer files for bankruptcy are treated the same as under Chapter 7: they receive third and fourth priority respectively. The difference is that, in a Chapter 11 bankruptcy, the employer negotiates with all its creditors, including the employees, and tries to work out a repayment plan.

What about wages earned by employees after an employer files for bankruptcy, but while it is in Chapter 11 reorganization? Wages become the first priority, and any new money coming into the business will be used to pay ongoing salary expenses. However, the employer at this point will likely change its wage and salary schedules by decreasing the amount of wages it will pay. If there is no union representing its workers, the employer has the discretion to unilaterally change the wage rates. If a union represents the workers and there is a collective-bargaining agreement setting wages, the employer must first attempt to renegotiate the wage rate with the union. If the employer and union are unable to reach agreement on a modification to the wage rate, the employer may petition the bankruptcy judge for permission to reject the existing collective-bargaining agreement.

Under Chapter 11, if an employer is contractually bound to pay benefits to retired employees, it must negotiate with a union (if the benefits are part of a collectively bargained agreement) or with a representative of the retirees (if there is no collective-bargaining agreement) to attempt to reach an agreement to modify the benefits due. If the negotiations are unsuccessful, the employer may petition the judge for approval to modify the retiree benefits. If an insolvent employer modifies retiree benefits within 180 days before filing under Chapter 11, the court will reinstate the benefits unless the court finds that fairness favors the modification.

HOURS

Besides the FLSA, several federal laws affect the hours worked by certain employees. For example, federal laws regulate the hours worked by employees in interstate transportation. The **Hours of Service Act** limits the hours worked by railroad employees engaged in train operations. Train employees must be given eight consecutive hours off during a twenty-four-hour period, and cannot work more than twelve consecutive hours at any one time. A crew member who has worked the twelve-hour maximum must be given ten hours off before returning to work.

U.S. Department of Transportation regulations limit the hours worked by truck drivers working for employers regulated under the **Motor Carrier Act**, which generally covers interstate and commercial motor vehicle transportation companies. Limits on driving arise in two circumstances:

1. Drivers may not drive for more than eleven hours following ten consecutive off-duty hours;

2. Drivers cannot drive at all if they have been on duty (whether driving or not) for fourteen hours following ten consecutive off-duty hours.

Federal Aviation Administration regulations limit the hours worked by airline crew members. The limitations vary depending on the type of airline operation (overseas, domestic, non-passenger, etc). For example, flight crews that work on domestic and commuter passenger airlines cannot work more than one thousand hours per year, one hundred hours per month, or thirty hours in any seven consecutive days. Also, such crew members must be given scheduled rest periods of at least eleven consecutive hours for nine or more hours of scheduled flight time.

Outside the transportation industry, employers are generally free to set the work schedules of their employees. Some state laws and regulations, however, require employers to give employees certain rest and meal periods during the course of a workday. For example, Connecticut and Delaware require employers to give thirty-minute unpaid meal breaks to employees who work at least seven-and-a-half consecutive hours, while Maine requires employers to provide thirty consecutive minutes of rest time (which may be used for meals) to employees who work more than six consecutive hours. Minnesota requires employers to give reasonable bathroom break time every four hours, and Nevada requires a ten-minute rest break for every four hours worked.

COMPENSATION FOR JOB-RELATED INJURY AND ILLNESS

Workers' Compensation

Workers' compensation laws provide employees with the means to replace income lost as a result of employment injuries and illnesses, and provide for payment of medical expenses. In order to qualify for compensation under workers' compensation laws, employees are not required to prove that injuries were caused by an employer's negligence. These laws impose **strict liability** on employers for injuries suffered in the workplace. The rationale is that this arrangement places the burden of paying for injuries on the party most able to bear the cost. The trade-off for employers is that benefits under workers' compensation laws are limited—in other words, no pain-and-suffering or punitive damages are awarded—so employers are spared expensive surprises. The trade-off for employees is that they are assured of receiving some monetary compensation for workplace injuries, regardless of their own contributory negligence, though they are limited to the workers' compensation system as the exclusive means for receiving compensation. Generally speaking, employees cannot sue employers under state law to recover damages for workplace injuries.

Each state has its own law providing workers' compensation benefits. The general requirements of the laws are similar, although the dollar amounts recoverable and certain procedural and coverage details vary by state. There are separate federal workers' compensation laws covering federal government employees, employees of the railroad and maritime industries, and longshoremen and harbor workers.

The cost of providing workers' compensation is borne solely by the employer, usually by purchasing a workers' compensation insurance policy from an insurance company. The cost of providing this insurance cannot be deducted from an employee's wages. In some states, the state government provides the benefits for employees and uses taxes on employers (generally based on each employer's claims history) to fund those benefits.

Most employees injured at work are entitled to compensation under workers' compensation laws. Some state laws exempt certain categories of workers, such as casual employees, agricultural employees, domestic employees, and independent contractors. Moreover, a few states require coverage only if an employer employs a minimum number of employees. For example, Alabama imposes compulsory coverage only if an employer has at least three employees.

Injuries and illnesses that "arise out of and in the course of employment" are covered under workers' compensation laws. This means that, in order for an employee to obtain compensation for an injury under such laws, there must be some connection between an employment requirement and the cause of the injury. An automobile accident occurring during the commute to work is not covered, but a traveling salesperson who suffers an accident while on his or her way to a sales call could be compensated under the right circumstances.

Examples of **compensable injuries** include injuries caused at work by defective machinery, fires, explosions, repeated lifting of heavy equipment, or slipping on an oily floor surface. **Compensable illnesses** (or **occupational diseases**) are caused by working conditions that create a greater risk of contracting the illness on the job than in everyday life. Thus, a textile worker who contracts brown lung disease would likely be eligible for compensation.

The amount of money paid for an injury or illness varies by state and is based on the type of injury or illness. Workers receive a fixed weekly benefit, subject to a maximum amount, based on their regular salary. This wage payment is made for the period during which the employee is temporarily unable to work due to the injury.

Workers' compensation also pays for medical expenses associated with the injury or illness. Most state laws also provide some reimbursement for the costs associated with medical and vocational rehabilitation.

To collect workers' compensation benefits, an employee usually must notify the employer as soon as possible after sustaining an injury. In most states, the employee then files a claim with the employer or the employer's insurance agent. If the employer does not contest the claim, it proposes a settlement to the employee. If the employee accepts the settlement, payment begins.

What if the employer contests the claim or the employee rejects the settlement? Then the claim is usually filed with the state workers' compensation commission, which holds a hearing

---

(i) PERMANENT DISABILITY AND DEATH

If an employee suffers a permanent disability, whether partial or total, the employee may also be eligible for payment to compensate for the decrease in earnings attributable to the permanent nature of the disability. The amount may be determined by a **schedule** for specific disabilities, or as a percentage of the employee's weekly wage. States that pay a percentage of the employee's weekly wage may impose limits on the length of time for which the payments will be made.

If a workplace injury results in death, the benefit is generally provided to the surviving spouse and/or children. Death benefits generally consist of a burial allowance and a percentage of the employee's weekly wages. There may also be a maximum cap on benefits. Death benefits are provided to a spouse until remarriage, and to children until they reach the age of majority.

to determine whether the employee is entitled to benefits and, if so, the amount due. The commission's decision usually can be appealed to state court.

Social Security

The federal Social Security disability insurance system also provides compensation for injuries that prevent an employee from working. This system differs from workers' compensation in that the cause of the injury is irrelevant for purposes of Social Security. Under workers' compensation, an injury must arise out of employment; but for purposes of receiving benefits under Social Security, the injury need only prevent a person from being able to work (regardless of the cause of the injury). Thus, while an automobile accident suffered during the commute to work is not compensable under workers' compensation, a worker may be eligible for Social Security benefits if the injuries prevent him or her from earning a living.

An employee covered by Social Security is eligible to receive benefits for a disabling injury or illness if the employee has at least six quarters of coverage. A quarter of coverage is a calendar quarter in which an employee earns a minimum wage amount, as determined by the Secretary of Health and Human Services. Generally, Social Security covers every worker, except for certain federal employees such as postal workers, railroad employees, and certain state and local employees.

A **disabling medical condition** is one that is expected to last at least twelve months and prevent someone from gainfully working anywhere in the country. The **Social Security Administration (SSA)** has published a list of impairments that are considered disabling, such as severe epilepsy and loss of vision or hearing. A medical condition that does not appear on the list may still be considered disabling if the worker can show that the condition is the medical equivalent of a listed impairment, by showing that it is equal in severity and duration to a listed impairment. If an injury or illness cannot be shown to be the medical equivalent of a listed impairment, workers may still be eligible for benefits if they can prove by another means that they have a disabling medical condition. To do so, the individual would have to show that a condition or disease is so severe that it prevents the individual from performing his or her job, or other similar work. This is a difficult standard to meet.

To collect Social Security disability insurance benefits, an individual must file an application at the local Social Security office. The SSA decides whether employees are eligible for benefits. If the SSA decides in favor of the employees, they will receive a letter detailing the benefits to be received and the applicable entitlement dates. If the SSA denies benefits, the employee can request a reconsideration of the decision. If the reconsideration is still unfavorable, he or she can file an appeal and request a hearing before an administrative law judge. The decision of the administrative law judge is appealable to an appeals council, the decision of which can in turn be appealed to federal court.

◖◗ TALKING TO A LAWYER

Q. Before I began my job, my employer required me to attend a four-hour orientation session for which I didn't get paid. Does the employer owe me money?

A. If you had already been hired, then you are entitled to compensation for the mandatory training session. But if attending the orientation was required in order to apply for the job, then no compensation is owed.

—Answer by Theodore St. Antoine, Degan Professor Emeritus of Law, University of Michigan Law School

OTHER BENEFITS

Contrary to popular belief, there is no federal or state law requiring employers to provide any type of workplace benefit beyond those already discussed in this chapter. For example, there are no laws that require employers to provide paid vacations, holidays, health insurance, or pensions. Whether these or any other benefits are provided is determined either unilaterally by the employer, by negotiation between the employer and individual employees, or as a result of collective bargaining between a union and the company.

THE WORLD AT YOUR FINGERTIPS

• For more information on Social Security disability benefits, visit *www.ssa.gov*, and then browse the topic headings under "Disability and SSI."

• The Workplace Fairness website provides links to information on wage and hours laws at *www.workplacefairness.org*; click on "Know the Law," then "Pay & Hours." To find the workers' compensation agency for a particular state, scroll down to "Injuries/Illness."

• Findlaw provides information concerning the requirements imposed by federal and state wage laws; visit *www.employment. findlaw.com/employment/employment*, and click on "Wages & Benefits." Information about workers' compensation is available at *www.injury.findlaw.com/workers-compensation/*.

• The Department of Labor website provides a wealth of information on wages and benefits. You can find the minimum wage in your state by visiting *www.dol.gov/esa/minwage/america.htm*. An overview of the federal law on wage garnishment is available at *www.dol.gov/asp/programs/guide/garnish.htm*. And you can find more information about the Fair Labor Standards Act at *www. dol.gov/esa/whd*.

• *Workers' Compensation and Employee Protection Laws In a Nutshell* by Jack Hood, Benjamin Hardy, and Harold S. Lewis (1990) provides a comprehensive examination of the scope, coverage, and enforcement of workers' compensation law.

REMEMBER THIS

• All employees must be paid either the federal minimum wage or the state wage if it is higher.

• Unless employed in an exempt job, all employees must be paid overtime.

• Wage rates cannot be based on an employee's membership in a protected class.

• There are limits on how much money can be garnished from a worker's wages.

• Almost all employers must purchase workers' compensation insurance.

• Employees injured at work are entitled to workers' compensation benefits.

CHAPTER 6

Employer Policies on Wages, Hours, and Benefits

Information on Contracts, Handbooks, and Pensions

Bob is a production worker for Company A. Each year he enjoys a cost-of-living wage increase, company-provided health insurance, three weeks' paid vacation, and seven paid holidays.

Frank is a production worker for Company B. He does exactly the same kind of work as Bob. But Frank hasn't had a raise in two years, has no health insurance, and receives only one week of vacation and two paid holidays. Why is there such a big difference in their benefits?

Employers must provide the benefits required by law (as discussed in chapter 5), but benefits above and beyond those legally required are within each employer's discretion. Unless their employees are represented by a labor union, employers are not obligated to consult with the employees about what types of benefits to provide.

HANDBOOKS AND MANUALS

Many employers issue handbooks and policy manuals that list the benefits available to employees, as well as the employees' obligations. The contents of such manuals are determined by the company. Some state courts have held that promises employers make in manuals or handbooks may be binding as **implied contracts** (as opposed to explicit written contracts that were negotiated and signed by both parties). However, in order for such promises to be binding, certain requirements must be met.

⟨ ⟩ TALKING TO A LAWYER

Q. All the full-time employees at my workplace receive paid holidays, paid vacations, and paid health insurance. I work twenty-five hours a week and I don't get any of these benefits. Can my employer do that?

A. Probably. Employers aren't required to provide any particular group of employees with any particular group of benefits. Many employers provide lesser benefits to part-time employees, and there is generally nothing unlawful about this. However, if there is a contract in place that entitles you to these benefits (such as a collective-bargaining agreement or even, under certain circumstances, an employee handbook), your employer may be breaching that contract by not providing them.

—Answer by members of the ABA Section
of Labor and Employment Law

Even when manuals or handbooks create contracts, employers generally may revoke or revise them at any time. Once employers give notice to employees that policies have been changed, the old policies are no longer enforceable. For example, if an employer changed its policy from a specific promise of a 5 percent raise upon completion of a probationary period to a statement that a raise would merely be considered under the same circumstances, employees who completed their probationary period after the notice of change would not have the right to a raise. However, an employee who had already commenced or completed the probationary period before the change was made would likely have the right to a raise.

WRITTEN EMPLOYMENT CONTRACTS

Few employees have individual written employment contracts. Such contracts tend to be limited to high-level executives, teachers and professors, professional athletes, actors, and other highly

(i) WHEN A PROMISE BECOMES A CONTRACT

In order for courts to consider a manual or handbook a binding contract, the following conditions must generally be met:

- The manual must be circulated to employees. Manuals given only to managers or supervisors for use in dealing with employee problems do not create binding contracts.

- The language of the manual must contain clear and specific promises of benefits.

- The manual must not contain vague statements regarding fair treatment. For example, a policy stating that "any employee who successfully completes his probationary period will receive a 5 percent raise" may be specific enough to be enforceable. However, a policy stating simply that "employees who successfully complete their probationary period will be considered for a raise" may be too vague to create the binding promise of a raise.

- The manual must not contain an express disclaimer. Employers often seek to avoid creating a binding promise, even if the first two conditions listed above are met, by expressly stating that the policies contained in the manual or handbook are not meant to create a contract. Such an **express disclaimer** puts the employees on notice that they cannot rely on the policies as a statement of terms and conditions of employment. Some states give effect to such disclaimers if they are clear and unambiguous.

skilled professional workers. When such a contract exists, however, both the employer and employee are bound by it. Failure to live up to its terms is a breach of contract, and the breaching party is liable under state contract law.

One other group of employees has its employment conditions regulated by written contract: employees who are represented by a labor union that has negotiated a collective-bargaining agree-

(i) THERE'S ALWAYS AN EXCEPTION

A few states impose conditions on the employer's ability to change or modify enforceable manual or handbook promises. In such states, the employer may make such changes only if: (1) the employer provides additional consideration (such as a pay rise) to the employees in exchange for the modifications; or (2) the manual or handbook clearly states that the policies contained therein may be changed at any time.

---

ment with their employer. The effect and enforcement of such contracts will be discussed in chapter 13, which deals with unions in the workplace.

Wages and Hours of Work

As long as an employer complies with federal and state wage laws, it is free to set wage rates for its employees. Moreover, unless the employer has a written contract with the employee or a collective-bargaining agreement with the union, or has included a wage policy in an enforceable handbook, the employer can change the wage that it pays to its employees.

With the exception of those occupations whose hours are regulated by federal—and sometimes state—law (see the "Hours" section of chapter 5), an employer generally is allowed to establish its own rules with respect to both length of the workday and days of the workweek. So long as the employer is willing to pay the required overtime rate, it can require employees to work overtime.

There may, however, be circumstances in which the law requires the employer to accommodate its work schedule to the needs of particular employees. For example, Title VII requires that the employer accommodate the religious practices of employees, unless the accommodation would cause undue hardship. Thus, if an employee asks not to be scheduled for Sunday work because her religion prohibits work on the Sabbath, or an employee asks

( ) TALKING TO A LAWYER

Q. When I interviewed for my current job, I was told I would be eligible for stock options once I completed a year of work. It's been two years and I have not received the stock options. When I asked about it, I was told that my job didn't qualify for the benefit. I don't have anything in writing, but I know what I was promised. Don't they owe me the stock options?

A. If this was truly a negotiated part of the deal when you accepted your job, then your case becomes a difficult matter of proof. Otherwise, even if you could prove that your employer promised you the options, the employer could argue that its promise was an expression of unilateral intent—now rescinded—and was not a binding contract. The Statute of Frauds, which applies to oral agreements that cannot be performed within a year, may also apply to prevent enforcement of this promise.

—Answer by Theodore St. Antoine, Degan Professor Emeritus of Law, University of Michigan Law School

not to work overtime on Friday night because her religion prohibits work after sundown, the employer may be required to accommodate those requests. This might be accomplished by having another employee trade shifts and work on Sundays, or if another employee volunteers to work the overtime in her stead. But if the cost of the accommodation for the employer is more than minimal—for example, if the employer had to pay extra money for a substitute to fill in for the religious employee—then the employer is not required to grant the accommodation.

The Americans with Disabilities Act (ADA) also may require the employer to be flexible in its work schedule when dealing with individuals with disabilities. An employee whose disability may limit the number of hours he or she can work, or who needs a particular day off each week in order to obtain medical treatment, must be accommodated unless the accommodation would cause undue hardship. Under the terms of the ADA, whether the cost of an accommodation creates an undue hardship depends, among other factors, on the financial resources of the particular employer. Chapter 2 includes more information about compliance with these laws.

Health Insurance

No law requires an employer to provide health insurance. But if an employer does provide this benefit, it must be made available and administered to employees without unlawful discrimination.

If an employer provides health insurance, Title VII requires that the insurance cover pregnancy and pregnancy-related conditions. Moreover, pregnant employees and those with pregnancy-related conditions must be eligible for the same level of benefits as employees with any other covered medical condition.

(i) CONTRACEPTIVE COVERAGE

The Equal Employment Opportunity Commission (EEOC) has taken the position, and at least one court has agreed, that employers must cover expenses for prescription contraceptives under the same terms with which they cover expenses for prescription drugs used to prevent the occurrence of other medical conditions. According to the EEOC, employers must also offer the same coverage for contraception-related outpatient services as are offered for other outpatient services. If a woman visits her doctor to obtain a prescription for contraceptives, she must be afforded the same coverage that would apply if she—or any other employee—had consulted a doctor for other preventive or health maintenance services. On the other hand, if an employer limits coverage of comparable drugs or services (e.g., by imposing maximum payable benefits), those limits may be applied to contraception as well.

This is an area of law that is still developing—and, as yet, is unsettled.

What if an employer's health insurance plan covers not only employees, but also their spouses and dependents? In that case, benefits for the family do not have to be the same as the benefits provided to the employees themselves. But if the medical conditions of female employees' spouses are covered, then those of male employees' spouses—including pregnancy and pregnancy-related conditions—must also be covered. However, the pregnancy of dependents need not be covered.

Under the Age Discrimination in Employment Act (ADEA), employers must provide the same health insurance benefits to older employees that they provide to younger employees. **Medicare carve-out plans**, which allow an employer to deduct the value of Medicare benefits received by Medicare-eligible employees from health insurance benefits, do not violate the ADEA.

The ADA also affects health insurance benefits. An employer cannot deny employees with disabilities equal access to health insurance coverage. For example, if its employees are eligible for health insurance, an employer cannot deny those health insurance benefits to an employee who is blind.

The ADA does not, however, require that health insurance cover all medical expenses or all disabilities. Limitations are per-

---

(i) EQUAL TREATMENT FOR MENTAL ILLNESS

The Mental Health Parity Act applies to employers with more than fifty employees who offer health insurance plans that include coverage for mental health. Such plans must provide the same level of coverage for mental health care as is provided for physical illness, unless the cost of providing such parity would result in an increase in costs of at least 1 percent. While this law has a "sunset" provision that will cause the parity requirement to terminate on December 31, 2006, Congress has acted in the past to extend this requirement beyond previous termination dates.

missible if they equally affect both employees with disabilities and those without disabilities.

Preexisting-condition clauses are generally lawful. These clauses disallow coverage for medical conditions existing before an individual was employed by his or her current employer. (See the section below entitled "The Impact of Changing Jobs on Health Insurance Coverage" for a fuller discussion of preexisting condition clauses.) The law also allows limitations on coverage for certain procedures or treatments, so long as the limitations apply to a broad category of illnesses and not to a specific disability or group of disabilities. For example, a plan limiting reimbursement for psychiatric treatment to twelve sessions per year is lawful under the ADA, but limiting psychiatric treatment for schizophrenia to twelve sessions per year is not. Similarly, excluding coverage for eye care is lawful, but excluding coverage for glaucoma is unlawful. Lastly, the law allows caps on reimbursement, unless a plan distinguishes among specific diseases. Thus, a plan that caps reimbursement for cancer or AIDS treatment at $50,000, but that has a $1-million lifetime limit for other treatment, violates the ADA.

A health insurance plan featuring a disability-based distinction may be lawful if the employer can prove that the plan is a bona fide benefit plan that is not a subterfuge for violating the ADA. The EEOC has stated that a distinction may be justified by proof "that the disability-based disparate treatment is attributable to the application of legitimate risk classification and underwriting procedures to the increased risks (and thus increased cost to the health insurance plan) of the disability, and not to the disability per se."

The Impact of Changing Jobs on Health Insurance Coverage

Many employer group health insurance policies have clauses (called **preexisting-condition clauses**) that limit or exclude coverage for medical conditions that were diagnosed before an individual enrolled in the health plan. With the passage of the

Health Insurance Portability and Accountability Act of 1996 (HIPAA), the impact of such preexisting-condition clauses has been limited. Individuals with a preexisting medical condition that was diagnosed, or for which treatment was received, within six months before enrolling in a new health insurance plan would not be covered for that condition for the first twelve months. Thereafter, however, the preexisting condition would be covered for as long as the employee kept the insurance. Moreover, the twelve-month exclusion is reduced by the length, if any, of the individual's prior coverage under another health insurance policy. Lastly, a preexisting-condition clause can never be applied in cases involving pregnancy, newborns, or adopted children.

As an example, suppose an employee worked for Employer A for five years, during which time he was covered under the employer's group health insurance plan. Then assume the employee

(i) THIS COBRA DOESN'T BITE

A federal law with an unlikely acronym gives employees important rights when they have lost their jobs or health insurance. The **Consolidated Omnibus Budget Reconciliation Act of 1985 (COBRA)** applies to employers with twenty or more employees who offer group health insurance plans. (Churches and the federal government are not covered.) An employee who loses health insurance because his employment is terminated or his hours are reduced can choose to continue coverage for a period of up to eighteen months. However, the employee can be required to pay the full premium cost (even if the employer previously had paid for all or part of the premium cost), and can be charged an administrative fee of no more than 2 percent of the premium cost.

The **Uniformed Services Employment and Reemployment Rights Act (USERRA)** requires that the same health insurance continuation rights granted by COBRA be available to employees on uniformed service leave. Unlike COBRA, USERRA applies to all employers, even those with fewer than twenty employees.

⚠️ KEEPING EMPLOYEE HEALTH INFORMATION CONFIDENTIAL

The ADA requires that employers maintain in separate medical files—and treat as confidential—any employee medical information that they obtain as a result of employee medical examinations or medical inquiries. Employers may only disclose such information to supervisors, managers, or first-aid personnel on a need-to-know basis.

Additionally, self-insured employers must also comply with confidentiality regulations established under the Health Insurance Portability and Accountability Act (HIPAA). Except in limited circumstances, these regulations prohibit the disclosure of any individually identifiable health information that relates to an individual's past, present, or future health condition. However, employers may disclose such information to health-care providers in connection with treatment or payment, or pursuant to a valid authorization from the individuals involved.

---

quits his job and starts work for Employer B, which provides group health insurance for its employees. Employer B's health insurance plan could not apply any preexisting-condition clause to that employee, because he was covered under Employer A's plan for more than twelve months. If, however, an individual who had not previously been covered under a health insurance policy began working for Employer B, then Employer B's health insurance plan could apply its preexisting-condition exclusion clause to that employee for a twelve-month period.

PENSIONS

The law does not require employers to provide pension benefits. But if they do, they cannot discriminate against members of a protected class. In particular, even though actuary tables show that women live longer than men, employers cannot provide different pension plans based on gender. In **defined-contribution**

plans, employers must contribute the same amounts for both males and females. In **defined-benefit plans**, both males and females must receive the same benefit payouts.

Even if employers decide to provide pension plans, the law does not require them to provide pensions to all employees.

The Employee Retirement Income Security Act

The **Employee Retirement Income Security Act of 1974 (ERISA)**, a federal statute, is by far the most important pension law. While ERISA covers most pension plans operated by private-sector employers, it does not cover those operated by government employers. Specifically, ERISA applies to private-sector employers who have "qualified" plans under the federal tax laws. Contact your plan administrator to find out if ERISA applies to your pension plan. The tax laws provide important advantages to employers whose plans qualify.

ERISA protects employees if they participate in pension plans. It also covers employees' beneficiaries. ERISA preempts any state law that seeks to regulate pension plans, which means that states have no power to regulate such plans. States can, however, regulate how parties divide pension benefits in the context of divorce.

ERISA sets minimum standards that pension plans must meet in the following areas: 1) participation; 2) benefit accrual, vesting, and breaks in service; 3) funding; 4) administration of funds; 5) reporting and disclosure; 6) joint and survivor provisions; and 7) plan termination. Employers may, however, provide more expansive terms than those mandated by ERISA if they choose.

Participation

If an employer has chosen to offer a pension plan to its employees, ERISA generally requires that an employee be allowed to participate if he or she is at least twenty-one years of age and has completed one year of service with the company. ERISA defines one year of service as a twelve-month period during which the employee has worked one thousand hours (in which case he or she would be considered a half-time employee) or more.

Benefit Accrual

Employees begin to accrue benefits under pension plans once they qualify for participation. How those benefits accrue depends on the type of plan. A **defined-contribution plan** establishes a separate retirement account for each participating employee. A common kind of defined-contribution plan is the **401(k) plan**, though there are others. In these plans, the employer (and sometimes the employee) makes a contribution to the account at least annually. Benefits are based on how investments have fared. As a result, these accounts are riskier than defined-benefit plans, where an employee can be sure of a particular benefit. The benefit due to an employee upon retirement depends on the amount of money in the account and the payout method selected.

A **defined-benefit plan** is a traditional pension plan that promises an employee a specific level of payment upon retirement. The employer pays money into a fund, and contributions to and investment gains from that fund are used to pay the retirement benefit. Benefits are based on an employee's total years of participation in the plan—and, usually, on his or her final salary or average salary for the last several years of employment.

Vesting

Employees are not entitled to pension benefits until their rights to those benefits have vested. The term **vesting** refers to a point in time after which employers cannot take away an employee's accrued benefits. Once an employee's benefits are vested, he or she is entitled to payment upon reaching retirement age, even if he or she subsequently leaves the job. ERISA prohibits employers from terminating employees to avoid making benefit payments or to prevent vesting of benefits. However, employees can lose non-vested benefits if their employers fire them for other reasons, or if they quit.

ERISA provides for two different methods of vesting. In one method, employees are eligible for 100 percent of their retirement benefits after five years of service. A second method provides for a graduated system of vesting: after three years of service, employees are eligible for 20 percent of their pension benefits; after

(i) PRESERVING PENSION RIGHTS WHILE IN THE SERVICE

Under the Uniformed Services Employment and Reemployment Rights Act, employers must count the time during which employees were absent because of uniformed service as work with the employer for purposes of pension vesting and benefit accrual. Employers are liable for funding the resulting pension obligations. However, if an employer's liability to make contributions to a pension fund is based on matching an employee's contribution, the employer's funding obligation does not kick in until the employee's matching contribution is made. If the plan *requires* contributions from the employee, then the employee must be given, upon return to work, an opportunity to make up for any contributions missed due to military obligations.

---

four years, 40 percent; after five years, 60 percent; after six years, 80 percent; and after seven years, 100 percent.

If employees also contribute to their pension plans from their own salaries, their contributions always vest immediately—even if they have not worked long enough to vest in contributions made by their employers. In other words, if employees leave their employers before their pensions vest, they lose any benefits from their employers that accrued under those plans, but they do not lose any money that they contributed.

Because of vesting, an employee may be entitled to collect several pensions. Thus, if an employee worked in each of a series of jobs long enough for pension benefits to vest, he could receive a pension from each employer when he reaches **retirement age** (defined in most pension plans as age sixty-five, though many plans include the option of retiring earlier).

Breaks in Service

If a break in service occurs before benefits become vested, employees lose any entitlement to those benefits. A **break in service** occurs when employment is interrupted—specifically, when an employee works fewer than five hundred hours in a calendar year, plan year, or other consecutive twelve-month period. Thus, layoffs and unpaid leaves can cause a break in service. However, leave for military service does not constitute a break in service. (See the above box titled "Preserving Pension Rights While in the Service" for more information about the effect of USERRA on pensions.)

Funding

ERISA's funding requirements obligate employers (and perhaps employees, depending on the type of pension plan) to contribute enough money to cover pension payments when they become due, as determined actuarially. This part of the law aims to improve the stability of pension funds and prevent abuses. The law obligates employers and fund administrators to ensure that funding requirements are met.

Administration of Funds

ERISA also establishes rules aimed at preventing misuse of pension funds. Those who manage pension funds are fiduciaries whom the law obligates to act with "care, skill, prudence, and diligence" in conducting the pension plan's affairs. This means that fiduciaries must diversify the assets of pension plans among groups of investments in order to minimize the risk of large losses. The law also prohibits plan administrators from using pension assets to make investments in which they have a financial interest, and from borrowing money from the fund for personal use or for making loans to the employer. Participants have the right to sue administrators who breach their fiduciary duties.

Joint and Survivor Provisions

This part of the law affects employees who are married. Under a traditional pension plan, single employees will most likely receive a monthly pension for the rest of their lives—or, in some cases, a lump sum.

Married employees who pass away *before retirement* may provide that their spouses receive their vested benefits. The law entitles surviving spouses to qualified preretirement survivor annuities, which provide that spouses receive at least 50 percent of the amount of the vested benefits. The law automatically provides this benefit *unless* the spouse consents in writing to waive it.

ERISA also requires that a plan pay regular retirement benefits to a participant's spouse when the participant dies *after* beginning to receive retirement benefits. This is called the **qualified-joint-and-survivor-annuity benefit**. Under this benefit, the plan participant's monthly check is reduced while he or she is alive. When the participant dies, the spouse must receive a pension equal to at least 50 percent of the reduced pension. This benefit is automatically provided under the pension plan, *unless* the spouse consents in writing to waive it.

Whether a divorced spouse is entitled to a share of a participant's pension benefits depends on state law. Most states consider a pension to belong jointly to the employee and the employee's spouse. Thus, even though it may have been earned by one member of the couple, for legal purposes it probably belongs to both. If a state court orders that part of a participant's vested benefits be paid to an ex-spouse, ERISA requires the plan administrator to honor the court decree.

Terminating a Plan

ERISA does not prevent an employer from ending its pension plan, but it does provide some protection for employees if the employer does so. If an employer voluntarily terminates its plan, it must notify both the plan participants and the **Pension Benefit Guaranty Corporation** (**PBGC**)—a federal agency established by ERISA—of its intent to terminate. There must be sufficient assets in the plan to meet all benefit liabilities at the time of termination. The pension plan must first pay out to plan participants all benefits due under the pension plan. Any excess assets may revert to the employer, but such reversions are subject to a high excise tax to be paid by the employer.

ERISA also requires defined-benefit pension plans to pay insurance to the PBGC. In return, the PBGC guarantees the vested benefits of participants if a plan is terminated, up to a certain limit. The PBGC provides this protection only for certain benefits in specific types of funds. It also may not protect benefits for plans that are not defined-benefit plans, benefits above a certain dollar amount, and benefits that are not vested. Some early retirement benefits are not covered, and if the plan provides medical and disability benefits, these too may not be covered.

Reporting and Disclosure

Since each pension plan is different, it is important for employees to know the specific terms of their plans. ERISA requires employers to give a **summary plan description (SPD)** and a summary of the plan's annual financial report to every participant in the pension plan. The SPD is a nontechnical explanation of how the plan works and how benefits are paid out. It explains the benefit accrual rules, vesting requirements, and procedures for filing a claim for benefits. The summary of the annual finan-

( ) TALKING TO A LAWYER

Q. My company has always paid health insurance premiums for its retirees. I retired two years ago and the company has been paying my premiums. I just received a letter stating that as of July 1st the company will no longer provide health insurance coverage for retirees. Can they do that?

A. It depends. Health insurance benefits do not automatically vest. This means that employers can generally change or eliminate those benefits as they please. However, it may be the case that your employer promised not to reduce or eliminate your health insurance coverage (e.g., in a collective-bargaining agreement or in a benefit plan document). If this is the case, that promise may be binding upon the employer and may prohibit the employer from eliminating your insurance benefits.

—Answer by members of the ABA Section
of Labor and Employment Law

cial report is a nontechnical explanation of the financial data relevant to the operation of the plan. ERISA also requires that employers make available to the plan participants, upon request, copies of the plan itself and the annual report.

THE WORLD AT YOUR FINGERTIPS

• For more information about how ERISA affects employees' pension rights, peruse the selection of topics for consumers at the Department of Labor website at *www.dol.gov/ebsa/consumer_info_pension.html*.
• The Department of Labor website also includes information about health insurance portability at *www.dol.gov/dol/topic/health-plans/portability.htm*.
• The Legal Information Institute at Cornell offers a general description of federal pension law, with links to statutes, regulations, and recent court decisions, at *http://straylight.law.cornell.edu/topics/pensions.html*.
• The Workplace Fairness website features questions and answers about pension rights at *www.workplacefairness.org/index.php?page=pension*.
• *Employee Benefit Plans in a Nutshell* by Jay Conison (2003) provides a good explanation of how the law affects employer-provided pension and health benefits.

REMEMBER THIS

• Written employer policies promising benefits may be enforced as contracts.
• Employers may need to be flexible regarding the hours worked by employees when there are conflicts due to employees' religious beliefs or disabilities.
• If the employer provides health insurance, the employer cannot discriminate with respect to scope of coverage based on an individual's membership in a protected class.

• Upon separation from employment, employers must give employees the option to continue coverage under their existing health insurance plans for up to eighteen months, but employees may be responsible for the payment of full premium costs.

• Employers must maintain the confidentiality of all employee health information, with limited exceptions.

• Federal law provides for detailed regulation of employer pension plans.

CHAPTER 7

Time Off From Work

*Leaves for Sickness, Military Service, and
Other Reasons*

*The number of families in which both parents work, as well as
the number of working single parents, is larger than ever. Over
the past several years, more and more reservists and members of
guard units have been called into active service. And as longevity
has improved, more adults than ever have become caregivers for
elderly parents.*

*Employees have lives outside the workplace, and the de-
mands of their work lives and personal lives increasingly come
into conflict. This chapter addresses to what extent the law tries
to accommodate these conflicts.*

S everal federal laws directly address an employer's duty to
provide leave in specific circumstances. At the state level, a
broad array of laws addresses the issue of time off from work.

FEDERAL LAWS

Family and Medical Leave Act

The **Family and Medical Leave Act (FMLA)** requires employers to grant eligible employees up to twelve weeks of unpaid leave
within a twelve-month period, with the right to be reinstated to
their jobs. Employees are eligible for leave if they have worked at
least 1,250 hours for their employers for at least one year, and if
there are at least fifty employees at their work site or within
seventy-five miles of their work site.

Under the FMLA, leave is available only for the following
reasons:

- because of the birth of a child, and in order to care for the child;
- because of adoption or foster-care placement of a child;
- because of a serious health condition that makes the employee unable to perform his or her duties; or
- in order for the employee to care for a spouse, child, or parent with a serious medical condition.

Leave time is limited to twelve weeks of unpaid leave during a twelve-month period. The twelve weeks of leave do not necessarily have to be taken all at once; under certain circumstances, an employee is eligible for intermittent leave or leave on a reduced schedule. When the leave is for the birth, adoption or placement of a child, the twelve weeks generally must be taken consecutively. However, if the leave relates to a serious medical condition of either the employee or a family member, intermittent leave or a reduced schedule is available.

↻ TALKING TO A LAWYER

Q. My employer only has twenty employees, so the FMLA does not apply to my situation. I'm pregnant and will need time off when I give birth. Is the employer required to give me the time off and hold my job for me?

A. You should find out whether your state has a family medical-leave law that applies to smaller employers. Even it if does not, your employer is still covered by Title VII, which means that it cannot discriminate against employees based on pregnancy, childbirth, or related medical conditions. Under Title VII, the employer must give you leave and hold your job if it does so for other employees who need non-pregnancy-related leaves. Also, if you are represented by a union, your collective-bargaining agreement may give you family leave rights.

—Answer by members of the ABA Section
of Labor and Employment Law

The employee must provide at least thirty days' advance notice to his or her employer before taking family leave, if such notice is practicable. The employee need not mention the FMLA or even say that he or she needs leave, so long as some information regarding a qualifying situation is communicated. If thirty days' notice is not possible because of unforeseen or emergency circumstances, the employee must notify the employer as soon as possible. The employer may require the employee to provide medical certification when leave is requested for a serious medical condition, whether his or her own or that of a relative.

The FMLA does not require an employer to pay an employee during his or her leave period. However, an employee may elect—or an employer may require the employee—to use accrued paid vacation, personal-leave time, or sick-leave time during the FMLA leave period. In addition, if an employer provides health insurance coverage, it must continue that coverage during the leave with no additional charge to the employee. At the end of the leave period, the employer must reinstate the employee to his or her previous position or an equivalent position.

WHEN IS A MEDICAL CONDITION "SERIOUS"?

The FMLA regulations define a **serious medical condition** as a physical or mental illness, injury, or impairment that involves one of the following:

1. any period of incapacity or treatment in connection with inpatient care at a health-care institution;

2. a period of incapacity requiring absence from work, school, or daily activity in excess of three days that also requires continuing treatment by a health-care provider; or

3. continuing treatment by a health-care provider for a chronic or long-term health condition that is either incurable or so serious that, if not treated, it would result in a period of incapacity in excess of three days.

State laws also require employers to allow leave for family and medical reasons. These laws are important for two reasons. First, some of the laws regulate employers that are not subject to the FMLA; for example, Oregon's law applies to employers with twenty-five or more employees. Second, some states may grant more generous leave time to employees than is provided under federal law. For example, Connecticut provides for sixteen weeks of leave during a two-year period, but the law only applies to employers with at least seventy-five employees. California law provides for paid family leave. California's state disability insurance benefit system provides partial wage replacement for employees who take time off for non-work-related injuries or conditions (including pregnancy), to care for a sick or injured relative, or to bond with a new child.

A few states, such as Illinois, Massachusetts, Vermont, and Minnesota, have expanded the concept of family leave by providing that employees may take time off to participate in their children's school activities. Massachusetts and Vermont also provide time off for employees to attend routine medical appointments for their children or family members. Illinois also mandates unpaid leave time for the spouse or parent of an individual called to active duty in the military.

PREGNANCY LEAVE VS. FAMILY LEAVE

Family leave and pregnancy leave are not the same thing. **Pregnancy leave** is medical leave taken because pregnancy or a pregnancy-related disability makes a woman unable to perform the functions of her job. An employee may be eligible for pregnancy leave under Title VII under the same terms on which the employer covers other disabilities.

Family leave, on the other hand, is not necessarily related to the medical condition of pregnancy. Its purpose includes caring for a newborn, an adopted child, or a foster child. As such, it is available to both men and women.

Title VII

Under Title VII, an employer must treat time off from work due to pregnancy the same as it treats time off for any other medical condition. Therefore, if an employer's policy provides for paid sick leave, paid leave must also be available to employees who are absent due to pregnancy. If an employer reinstates an employee who is absent from work because of surgery, the employer must also reinstate a worker after childbirth.

Title VII also requires an employer to reasonably accommodate the religious practices of its employees. An employee who needs time off from work to attend a religious convention, or who cannot work on Saturdays because it is the employee's Sabbath, may be entitled to leave time or modification of his or her work schedule. The question is whether the modification or time off will create an undue hardship for the employer's business. If the modification or time off creates an undue burden for the employer, then the employer is not required to provide the accommodation. (For further discussion, see the "Refusal to

( ) TALKING TO A LAWYER

Q. A married couple works for my company. The wife is about to give birth, and both employees have asked for leave under the FMLA. Do I have to give them both time off, or can I tell them they have to choose which one of them will take leave?

A. You cannot tell them they have to choose. Following the birth, the wife may take up to twelve weeks of leave for her own serious health condition, if circumstances warrant. (She also may be entitled to leave prior to the birth.) The husband is eligible for up to twelve weeks of "bonding leave." Combined, however, the couple may take a total of no more than twelve weeks of leave in a twelve month period.

—Answer by members of the ABA Section
of Labor and Employment Law

Accommodate" section under "Prohibited Discrimination" in chapter 2.)

Americans with Disabilities Act

Under the Americans with Disabilities Act (ADA), an employer may be required to give leave time to a disabled employee as a reasonable accommodation. The ADA lists both flexible leave policies and modified work schedules as examples of reasonable accommodations for employees with disabilities. Once again, the law provides for an exception if these practices would cause an undue burden on the employer's business. Thus, if the practice causes an undue burden upon the employer, then the employer is not required to provide the leave. What might constitute a reasonable accommodation? The employer may be required to modify the work schedule of an employee with a mental disability to enable him or her to attend psychiatric sessions during the workday. Or an employer may be required to grant an employee unpaid leave time to undergo medical treatment related to a disability.

Uniformed Services Employment and Reemployment Rights Act

The Uniformed Services Employment and Reemployment Rights Act (USERRA) requires employers to grant an unpaid leave of absence of up to five years to any employee serving in the uniformed services. The **uniformed services** include the full-time and reserve components of the Army, Navy, Marine Corps, Air Force, Coast Guard, and National Guard, and the commissioned corps of the Public Health Service.

Upon honorable discharge, employees are entitled to reinstatement to their former positions, with the same seniority and other rights and benefits they had on the date they began uniformed service. They are also entitled to additional seniority-based rights and benefits they would have attained had they remained continuously employed. While on uniformed service, they are to be treated as if on leave of absence, and are entitled

⚠ EXCEPTIONS TO USERRA

Eight categories of service are exempt from coverage by USERRA, do not count towards the five-year limit, and require the employer to provide leave time that may exceed five years. The most common examples of such service are:

- service required to complete an initial period of obligated service;

- two-week annual training drills and monthly weekend drills for reservists and National Guard members; and

- service required under an order to remain on active duty during a war or national emergency.

---

to any non-seniority-based benefits that are available generally to employees on leave of absence.

Jury System Improvements Act

The **Jury System Improvements Act** is a federal law that prohibits an employer from disciplining or discharging an employee because he or she has been called to serve on a federal jury. Additionally, about thirty-seven states have laws prohibiting employers from firing workers called to perform jury service in the state court system. In effect, these laws require employers to grant unpaid leave to employees performing jury service and reinstate employees to their jobs when jury service is over.

STATE LAWS

State law may require employers to grant time off for reasons other than those provided by federal law.

Though there is no federal law governing time off for voting, about thirty states—including California, Maryland, New York, and Ohio—have laws requiring employers to give employees time off to vote in elections. These laws try to ensure that employees aren't prevented from voting by the fact that they need to be at work. For purposes of applying these laws, the relevant considerations are the hours during which polls are open and the hours during which employees are required to be at work. If an employee's work shift is from 3:00 P.M. until 11:00 P.M., the employer would not have to give the employee time off to vote, because polls in every state are open early in the day. But if the employee worked from 8:00 A.M. until 6:00 P.M., the employer might be required to grant time off. Most of these laws apply with respect to all elections—whether federal, state or local—although a few are limited to particular types of elections. Most do not allow employers to reduce employees' wages in exchange for granting time off.

About twenty states have provisions requiring leave time for employees called to serve as witnesses or to attend court proceedings. For example, California, Connecticut, and Pennsylvania mandate time off for crime victims to attend court hearings.

⚠️ MAKE IT KNOWN AND UNIFORM

Any leave policies created by an employer must not violate basic principles of antidiscrimination. Decisions whether to grant or deny employee leave requests should not be based on an employee's race, sex, religion, color, national origin, or membership in any other protected class.

Employers are at risk when supervisors and managers respond to employee requests for time off in an ad hoc manner. Suppose Pete gets a telephone call when his boy gets sick at school, and his supervisor lets him out of work to pick up his son. Two days later, when Mary's little girl is sick, her supervisor won't let her leave. The stage is set for a discrimination charge.

To prevent this problem, employers should have clear, well-communicated policies establishing uniform guidelines for leave requests, and should make sure their supervisors follow them.

Many states also have laws that govern time spent away from work for a variety of different activities. For example, Illinois and Maine require employers to grant unpaid leave to victims of domestic or sexual violence in order to seek medical care or to obtain remediation services. Other states provide leave for employees who are elected to public office, or for employees who are volunteer firefighters to respond to emergency calls. Illinois requires employers with fifty or more employees to provide one hour of paid leave every fifty-six days to employees who want to donate blood.

THE WORLD AT YOUR FINGERTIPS

• *Family and Medical Leave in a Nutshell* by Kurt H. Decker (2000) provides a good explanation of the FMLA, including issues relating to coverage and enforcement.

• For more information on the FMLA, visit the Department of Labor's website at *www.dol.gov* and click on "Family and Medical Leave Act (FMLA)."

• The Department of Labor also provides information on employee rights and employer obligations under USERRA at *www.dol.gov/vets/*.

• The Workplace Fairness website provides access to information on state and federal leave laws at *www.workplacefairness.org/index.php?page=leaves*.

• Findlaw provides links to information on both the FMLA and state leave laws. Visit *www.employment.findlaw.com* and click on "Family and Medical Leave."

REMEMBER THIS

• Federal laws require covered employers to give employees time off for the following reasons:
  • to care for a newborn child;
  • because of the adoption or foster placement of a child;

- because of an employee's serious medical condition;
- because of a spouse's, child's, or parent's serious medical condition;
- because of military service; or
- to serve on a federal jury.
- State law may require an employer to grant time off for reasons other than those addressed by federal law, such as:
  - voting in elections;
  - serving on state juries;
  - attendance at court proceedings; or
  - performing public service.
- Employers should make sure that all decisions concerning leave requests are made without regard to an employee's membership in a protected class.

CHAPTER 8

Terms and Conditions
of Employment

Rules Governing the Workplace

*Beta Office Supplies posted the following notice on its employee
bulletin board:*

NO SMOKING ALLOWED ON THE PREMISES.
EMPLOYEES ARE NOT PERMITTED TO DATE
    EACH OTHER.
EMPLOYEES ARE SUBJECT TO RANDOM DRUG
    TESTS.
NO CURSING OR OFF-COLOR LANGUAGE
    ALLOWED.
NO CELL PHONES ALLOWED ON PREMISES.
ALL EMPLOYEES MUST BE NEATLY DRESSED—
    NO T-SHIRTS OR FLIP-FLOPS.

Can companies really enforce these rules?

The law affects workplace rules in two ways. First, some statutes require employers to establish workplace rules. Second,
many statutes limit the types of workplace rules an employer can
impose.

WORKPLACE RULES REQUIRED
BY STATUTE

Occupational Health and Safety Legislation

The **Occupational Safety and Health Act (OSH Act)** is a federal law, the purpose of which is to "assure so far as possible
every working man and woman . . . safe and healthful working

conditions." It applies to almost all private-sector employers, but not to government employers.

The OSH Act imposes three obligations on employers. First, employers must furnish a workplace "free from recognized hazards that are causing or are likely to cause death or serious physical harm" to employees. Employees believing there is a health or safety hazard at work can either notify their supervisor or the company safety director, or contact the **Occupational Safety and Health Administration (OSHA)** and request an inspection. OSHA is the federal agency charged with enforcing the law. (Issues relating to OSHA inspections are discussed in Appendix II.) An employer cannot retaliate against an employee for making such a notification or request.

Second, employers must comply with the safety and health standards promulgated by OSHA. An example of such a standard is the **Hazard Communication Standard**. This standard requires that employees who work with hazardous chemicals be informed of the types of chemicals they are working with, and be trained in handling them. Chemical manufacturers and distributors must label containers, identifying any hazardous chemicals and providing appropriate hazard warnings. Any employer who uses such hazardous chemicals in the workplace must develop a written hazard communication program for its employees. As part of this program, the employer must compile a list of all hazardous chemicals used in the workplace; identify the physical and health hazards associated with these chemicals; state precautions to be used in handling the chemicals; and indicate emergency and first-aid procedures to be used in the event of a problem. This information must be made available to employees. Employees must also receive training in detecting the presence of chemicals in the workplace and protecting themselves from the attendant hazards. Other OSHA standards limit employees' exposure to toxic substances, require that employees wear personal protective equipment (like hardhats or respirators) when performing certain types of work, and require fire protection systems in the workplace.

The third OSH Act requirement is that employers with

⚠ IMMEDIATE DANGER!

Sometimes a workplace hazard poses such an immediate threat to employees' health or safety that there is no time to contact OSHA. The OSH Act protects a worker who refuses to perform a job that is likely to cause imminent death or serious injury. Generally, employees do not have a right to refuse to perform work, and normally an employer can discipline or discharge an employee for such a refusal. However, under the OSH Act, an employer cannot discharge or discipline an employee who refuses to perform work that the employee believes in good faith poses a real danger of death or serious injury, *if* all of the following factors are present:

1. a reasonable person in the employee's position would also conclude that there is a real danger of death or serious injury;

2. there is insufficient time to eliminate the danger through regular OSHA channels; and

3. the employee has unsuccessfully asked the employer to fix the problem.

eleven or more employees must keep a log and summary of all occupational injuries and illnesses, along with supplemental records detailing each illness and injury.

States may also regulate workplace health and safety in two ways. First, they may regulate workplace conditions that are not addressed by OSHA standards. Second, they may adopt state safety and health plans that, at minimum, duplicate the requirements of the OSH Act (they may also provide for higher standards). If such plans are approved by OSHA, the states are then responsible for enforcing safety and health regulations within their borders. About twenty-five state health and safety plans have received such approval. In the absence of approval by OSHA, however, a state may not regulate any safety and health issue that is already regulated by the OSH Act.

( ) **TALKING TO A LAWYER**

Q. I'm a secretary at a public-relations firm. My boss often comments on my appearance and clothing. He's never negative or crude; in fact, most of his comments would be considered compliments. A few times he has put his hand on my shoulder when he's at my desk. He's never asked me for a date or said anything sexual, but he makes me feel uncomfortable. Is this sexual harassment?

A. It may be. Your boss's comments and touching are unwelcome to you, and they appear to be motivated by your gender. For purposes of Title VII, the question is whether your boss's behavior is severe or pervasive enough that a reasonable person in your position would find the work environment hostile. If your employer has an anti-harassment policy, then it generally will not be held legally responsible for your boss's harassment unless you make a complaint through the proper channels and give the employer a chance to correct the problem. (The anti-harassment policy must allow you to make the complaint to someone other than the harasser.) You should consult a lawyer about the specific facts of your situation.

—Answer by members of the ABA Section of Labor and Employment Law

Antidiscrimination Law

Federal and state antidiscrimination law is the second statutory scheme that requires employers to establish workplace rules. Such laws require that workplaces be free from harassment based on any individual's membership in a protected class (see chapter 2 for more information about protected classes). Thus, Title VII prohibits harassment based on race, religion, sex, national origin, or color; the Age Discrimination in Employment Act (ADEA) prohibits harassment based on age; the Americans with Disabilities Act (ADA) prohibits harassment based on disability; and various state laws prohibit harassment based on certain other protected categories, such as sexual orientation or weight.

There are two types of prohibited harassment in the workplace: hostile-environment harassment, and quid pro quo harassment.

Hostile-environment harassment involves denigrating individuals based on their race, religion, gender, national origin, age, disability, or other protected status through the creation of an intimidating, hostile, or offensive working environment. It can consist of unwelcome verbal or physical conduct. A single isolated incident or comment generally will not be considered sufficient to create a hostile environment, unless the conduct is egregious; usually a series of incidents or a pattern of conduct is required in order to establish that the harassment creates a hostile environment. Examples of conduct that may constitute hostile-environment harassment include: vulgar or lewd comments about women; obscene or sexually suggestive posters; jokes relating to ethnicity; offensive racial or ethnic comments or gestures; graffiti written in bathrooms containing sexually or racially offensive statements; and physical groping, pinching, or slapping. In many cases, harassing conduct occurs via e-mail—for example, through the circulation of jokes, lewd pictures, or derogatory personal comments. Whatever the means through which the alleged harassment occurs, the issue is whether the comments and conduct are severe or pervasive enough to create a work environment that a reasonable person would find hostile or abusive.

In order to constitute hostile-environment harassment, comments and conduct must also be unwelcome to their target, in the sense that the target must not have invited the comments or conduct. However, the mere fact that an employee tolerates racial or sexual remarks, or attempts to laugh them off in order to fit in with other employees, does not necessarily mean that he or she has invited the conduct, or that the conduct is welcome.

Supervisors, managers, coworkers, and even customers can create a hostile environment. An employer can be held liable for the actions of its employees as well as its customers if their con-

ⓘ WHAT ABOUT THE WORKPLACE BULLY?

Antidiscrimination laws only address harassing conduct aimed at victims because of their membership in a protected class. But what about a supervisor who is "merely" abusive or obnoxious? In certain narrow instances of workplace bullying, a few states recognize a cause of action for intentional infliction of emotional distress. Generally speaking, such a claim cannot encompass ordinary employment disputes, such as hurt feelings over a lost promotion or a discharge from one's job. Rather, in order to make such a claim, an employee must show that the conduct is extreme and outrageous—beyond mere insults or insensitive or rude behavior. Grossly vulgar language, degrading conduct, or physical or verbal threats intended to abuse or terrorize employees may constitute intentional infliction of emotional distress. Moreover, when a supervisor engages in such conduct in the course of supervising the employees under his or her direction, the employer may be found liable for the supervisor's conduct.

duct creates a hostile environment. However, employers can protect themselves against liability. The key is to have a policy against harassment with an effective enforcement mechanism and adequate training to reinforce the policy. (See the "Preventing Harassment" sidebar below for further information.)

A company will not be liable for a supervisor or manager's conduct creating a hostile environment if the company can prove that it exercised reasonable care to prevent and promptly correct the harassing behavior, and that the employee unreasonably failed to take advantage of any preventive or corrective opportunities provided by the employer. A company will not be liable for its workers or customers creating a hostile environment unless it knew or had reason to know that the harassment occurred and it failed to take the proper corrective actions.

The second type of prohibited workplace harassment occurs only in relation to sex discrimination. It is known as **quid pro quo harassment**. The Equal Employment Opportunity

▶ PREVENTING HARASSMENT

Employers can take several steps to prevent harassment in the workplace. They can:

1. develop a written policy dealing with harassment, indicating that it is against the law and violates company policy;

2. provide an effective complaint mechanism for employees who have been subjected to harassment, including a procedure allowing employees to bypass their supervisor when the supervisor participates in the harassment or fails to address a complaint;

3. promptly undertake a complete and confidential investigation as soon as they are made aware of a problem, and impose appropriate disciplinary action if the complaint has merit;

4. prevent harassment before it occurs by circulating or posting the company anti-harassment policy and the Equal Employment Opportunity Commission (EEOC) guidelines on harassment, express strong disapproval of such conduct, and tell employees of their right to be free from harassment; and

5. implement an effective training program that reinforces the terms of the policy.

Commission (EEOC) defines quid pro quo harassment as "unwelcome sexual advances, requests for sexual favors, and other verbal or physical conduct of a sexual nature . . . when . . . submission to or rejection of such conduct is used as the basis for employment decisions." In other words, when an employee's job benefit is directly tied to an employee's submission to unwelcome sexual advances, the employee is a victim of quid pro quo harassment. An example would be a supervisor promising an employee a raise in exchange for going out on a date with him, or firing an employee who refuses to have sex with him.

Quid pro quo sexual conduct is prohibited whenever it is

unwelcome. If an employee shows through his or her conduct that sexual advances are unwelcome, it does not matter whether he or she eventually succumbs to the harassment "voluntarily." Why? Because the law assumes that the employee's actions are the result of coercion—fear of the employment consequences if he or she continues to reject the advances.

Only a person with supervisory or managerial authority can engage in quid pro quo harassment, since such harassment requires that the harasser have authority to grant or withhold job benefits. In general, an employer is **strictly liable** when a supervisor engages in quid pro quo harassment. This means that the employer is *always* held responsible for quid pro quo harassment by supervisors, even if it has no knowledge of the conduct and has a policy forbidding harassment.

Unwelcome sexual remarks or advances directed by men at women are prohibited, as are unwelcome remarks and advances

( ) TALKING TO A LAWYER

Q. I'm a receptionist at a law firm. Yesterday my boss told me I had to lose twenty pounds and start wearing makeup. He said that because I'm the "public face" that clients first see when they enter the office, I have to make a good impression. Can he fire me if I don't agree to his demands?

A. Probably not. Discharging you for refusing to wear makeup would be sex discrimination, because your boss would be requiring you to conform to a societal stereotype regarding feminine appearance. Although maximum-weight requirements are permissible where they are applied evenhandedly to both sexes, it sounds as though you are the only employee being required to lose weight, and that your boss is again acting on a stereotype regarding what a woman should look like in order to "make a good impression."

—Answer by members of the ABA Section of Labor and Employment Law made by women to men. Same-sex harassment is also prohibited when the difference in treatment—i.e., the harassment—is motivated by gender. For example, a male supervisor's unwelcome sexual advances toward a male subordinate may constitute sexual harassment. The issue is whether members of one sex are exposed to disadvantageous conditions of employment to which members of the other sex are not exposed—not whether the harasser and the victim are of the same or different genders.

Although Title VII's prohibition against sex discrimination does not include discrimination on the basis of **sexual orientation**, many courts interpret Title VII to prohibit discrimination against an individual because he or she does not conform to certain socially expected behaviors associated with his or her gender. Such stereotyping is held to be unlawful discrimination "because of sex." For example, discrimination has taken place if a woman is harassed because she doesn't wear makeup and jewelry, or because she is considered "too aggressive"; or if a man is ridiculed by coworkers because his appearance and mannerisms are "not masculine enough."

(i) IF YOU'RE THE VICTIM OF HARASSMENT

If you've been subjected to discriminatory harassment, you should immediately notify your supervisor. If your supervisor is the harasser, notify his or her superiors. Your employer cannot solve your problem if it does not know about it.

If there is a grievance procedure, you should use it. You can also express your disapproval of the conduct to the perpetrator, and tell him or her to stop.

You should keep a written record of all incidents of harassment, detailing the place and time of the harassing conduct, the persons involved, and any witnesses.

LEGAL LIMITATIONS ON EMPLOYER WORKPLACE RULES

As discussed in the section above, employers may impose rules to regulate employee conduct at the workplace. Generally speaking, most workplace rules aimed at regulating employee conduct in the workplace are within the employer's discretion. However, there are limits. Federal and state antidiscrimination laws prohibit employers from discriminatory enforcement of any workplace rules. Of course, that doesn't mean that an employer needs to have the same set of rules for, say, production line employees as it has for workers in the accounting department. If differences in the content or enforcement of workplace rules are not motivated by an employee's membership in a protected class (such as race, sex, etc.), then such differences are not illegal.

In addition, if employees are represented by a union, the employer generally has to bargain with the union before it can change workplace rules (see chapter 13 for further discussion of this topic).

Drug Testing

Employers sometimes require employees to undergo drug tests. Such tests can either be random or motivated by an employer's suspicion regarding certain employees. Generally, the same rules that apply to drug testing in the preemployment phase (see the "Drug Tests" section of chapter 4) apply to drug tests for current employees. However, a number of states have set different standards for drug tests of current employees. In some states, for example, an employer must have a reasonable suspicion that an employee is impaired before it can require a drug test. This requirement of reasonable suspicion generally applies to government employers as well. (See the "Constitutional Protections" section of chapter 14 for further discussion of drug tests for government employees.) Of course, in a unionized workplace an employer must bargain with the union before implementing drug tests for current employees.

Restricting Smoking at Work

Generally, an employer may restrict smoking at work, though in a unionized workplace the employer must bargain with the union before implementing such a policy. Indeed, many state laws, such as those in California and Rhode Island, *require* employers to establish no-smoking policies for certain work areas, such as hospitals and restaurants. At the same time, more than half the states prohibit discrimination against employees who use tobacco off duty, away from the workplace.

English-Only Rules

Employers restricting their employees' ability to speak any language but English on the job may run afoul of Title VII. An English-only rule could have an adverse impact on persons of certain ethnic or national origins, though it could be justified if the employer can show that the rule is job-related and consistent with business necessity. For example, a rule may be allowable if it requires employees to speak English when dealing with customers, but could be discriminatory if it requires employees to speak English during breaks and lunch times. Generally, in order to comply with Title VII, an English-only policy should be narrowly tailored to achieve a legitimate business need, and should be applied in a nondiscriminatory manner.

Dress Codes

Dress and grooming policies are generally allowed, but occasionally can run afoul of Title VII. Some employers, for example, impose a dress code on female employees but not on male employees; or impose more stringent appearance standards for women than for men. Such rules could violate Title VII because they constitute disparate treatment based on sex. Enforcement of a dress code also may, in some circumstances, violate the

⚠ DON'T FORGET ADVERSE IMPACT

A dress code may also have a more severe impact on a particular protected class. For example, an employer's policy concerning required
uniforms may not allow an employee to wear a head covering. This restriction could adversely impact members of certain religious groups.
The same may be true of a grooming code—for example, a rule requiring
employees to be clean-shaven could adversely affect members of certain religious groups or races. In such cases, the employer would have to
show that the policy was based on a business necessity and that accommodating the employee's religious beliefs would cause an undue
hardship to the employer.

National Labor Relations Act (NLRA). (For information regarding union insignia, see the "Showing Your Colors at Work"
sidebar in chapter 13.)

Off-Duty Conduct

Employers generally have narrow latitude to regulate employees'
off-duty conduct. Employers governed by collective-bargaining
agreements ordinarily have to show some reasonable relationship between off-duty conduct and job performance before they
can regulate such conduct.

A few states, such as Colorado and New York, prohibit employers from discriminating against employees for their lawful
off-duty conduct. More than half the states prohibit employment
discrimination for employees' off-duty use of tobacco. Several
other states prohibit discrimination because of the off-duty use
of any lawful substance (which, of course, includes alcohol
consumption).

Over twenty states prohibit employment discrimination based
on marital status, and about sixteen states prohibit discrimination based on sexual orientation.

About a dozen states prohibit certain types of employer inter-

◯ TALKING TO A LAWYER

Q. I work for a large brewery. I was in a tavern after work drinking an imported beer (not made by my employer). My supervisor saw me, and the next day I was fired for drinking a competitor's product. Can my employer do that?

A. Yes, unless you are covered by a collective-bargaining agreement that restricts your employer's ability to fire you (see chapter 13), or unless you live in a state that prohibits firing employees for lawful off-duty conduct.

—Answer by members of the ABA Section
of Labor and Employment Law

ference with employees' political activity. Some states—like California, Louisiana, and Missouri—prohibit employers from limiting employees' political activity. A few states, like Florida and Wisconsin, make it unlawful for an employer to threaten or coerce an employee to vote or not vote. Massachusetts prohibits employment discrimination aimed at influencing a voter to give or withhold a vote or make a political contribution. New York prohibits employment discrimination based on an employee's political activities.

Finally, an employer's attempts to learn about employee off-duty conduct can subject the employer to liability under state law for **invasion of privacy**. An invasion of privacy can occur when an employer's conduct constitutes an unreasonable and offensive intrusion into matters concerning which an employee has a reasonable expectation of privacy. Moreover, public dissemination of private facts that would be offensive or objectionable to a reasonable person can also constitute an invasion of privacy.

Employee Credit Ratings

An employee's debts or financial condition can sometimes result in the garnishment of the employee's wages (see the "Wage Payments and Garnishments" section of chapter 5 for a discussion of limits on garnishment), or may cause the employee to file for bankruptcy. Federal law prohibits employers from discharging employees because their wages have been garnished once, and also prohibits an employer from discriminating against employees solely because they have filed for bankruptcy.

Confidentiality Policies

Rules that restrict an employee's ability to disseminate documents or information about his or her employer or the employer's policies may run afoul of both the NLRA and some state laws. While an employer has an interest in maintaining the confidentiality of proprietary information, trying to restrict employee discussion about wages and/or terms and conditions of employment interferes with employee rights under the NLRA. (See chapter 13 for a discussion of the NLRA.) In particular, prohibitions on exchanging information about wages, benefits, or problems in the workplace impede the rights of employees to engage in concerted activity for mutual aid, which violates the NLRA. State law may also prohibit such policies. For example, California prohibits employers from maintaining pay secrecy policies or disciplining employees who discuss their wages.

Regulating Solicitation and Distribution

Policies that restrict the ability of employees to engage in solicitation and distribution in the workplace may also violate the NLRA, and are discussed in detail in chapter 13.

THE WORLD AT YOUR FINGERTIPS

• How is an employer supposed to keep up with all the different OSHA regulations? The Occupational Safety and Health Administration maintains a comprehensive website with information geared toward helping employers comply with the law. To access this information, go to *www.osha.gov* and click on "Compliance Assistance."

• The Workplace Fairness website provides links to websites of all the state government agencies dealing with workplace health and safety issues, at *www.workplacefairness.org/index. php?page=health*. This site also answers questions about discriminatory harassment at *www.workplacefairness.org/index.php?page= harassment*.

• The Legal Information Institute at Cornell provides a brief overview of the OSH Act—with links to the law, regulations, and recent court decisions—at *http://straylight.law.cornell.edu/topics/ workplace_safety.html*.

• The Findlaw website provides more information about the OSH Act. Visit *www.employment.findlaw.com*, click on "More Topics," then "Workplace Health & Safety."

• The website of the U.S. Equal Employment Opportunity Commission provides a general overview of harassment law, with a link to the federal regulations on that topic, at *www.eeoc.gov/ types/sexual_harassment.html*.

REMEMBER THIS

• Employers need to be aware of, and comply with, OSHA safety regulations.

• Employers should adopt and enforce policies prohibiting harassment.

• Employers should be aware of state laws that may restrict the application of certain rules. For example, state law may regulate drug testing, or limit the employer's ability to establish rules regulating employee off-duty conduct or activities.

• Restrictions on employees' ability to communicate amongst themselves about workplace issues may violate federal and state law.

CHAPTER 9

Monitoring and Surveillance

Big Brother May Be Watching You Type

Cathy maintains a weblog (or "blog"), ChattyCathy.com, where she records her feelings and opinions about life. She had a particularly bad day at work on Tuesday, and wrote in her blog that her supervisor was a jerk who only got his job because his uncle was the plant manager. When she arrived at work on Wednesday morning, her supervisor fired her. "Too bad your uncle doesn't work here," he said. Moral of the story? Big Brother may be watching you.

As technology has improved, so have employers' methods for monitoring employee performance and activities on or off the employers' premises. Such monitoring can take the form of listening in on conversations, video monitoring, reading e-mail, tracking employee movements, or monitoring employee access to websites. Conversely, employee access to technology enables employees to communicate ideas and opinions through e-mail and blogs, and to gather information for professional or personal use. This proliferation of technology raises issues concerning limitations on employers' rights to monitor employee activity, and to discipline employees for their use of technology. This chapter will address these issues.

AUDIO MONITORING

The **Federal Wiretap Act** prohibits employers from eavesdropping on or wiretapping employee telephone calls. There are two limited exceptions to this prohibition. The first applies to employers who act in the "ordinary course of business." This exception allows an employer to listen to any business-related communication without an employee's knowledge or consent, as long as the employer uses a telephone extension. An employer may not, however, monitor communications of a purely personal nature. Once the private nature of a telephone conversation is ascertained, any continued eavesdropping by the employer is not considered to be in the ordinary course of business, and may subject the employer to liability. A second exception applies where the employer has the consent of one party to the communication.

The Federal Wiretap Act also applies to the tape recording of telephone conversations. Recording a call that is not in the ordinary course of business, or in which employees were not expressly notified of the taping, would violate the law.

Most state laws relating to telephone monitoring and taping are modeled after the Federal Wiretap Act. A few states have more stringent restrictions on monitoring employees' phone calls. For example, California requires an audible beep on the line to alert the caller that the conversation is being monitored. Other states prohibit eavesdropping without the consent of both parties to the conversation.

The Federal Wiretap Act also prohibits the recording of oral communications when the speaker has a reasonable expectation that the conversation will not be overheard or recorded. This prohibition applies to both employees and employers. However, the interception of oral communications is not unlawful where the person recording the conversation, or consenting to the recording, is also a party to the conversation. In order for this exception to apply, the interception may not be for the purpose of committing any criminal or tortious act in violation of federal or state law. Some state laws prohibit the taping of conversations without the consent of all parties to the conversation.

The National Labor Relations Act (NLRA) prohibits employer surveillance of union activity and union meetings. Thus, any monitoring of employees that has the effect of closely observing union conduct violates the law. Moreover, if a union represents the employees for purposes of collective bargaining, the employer cannot unilaterally decide to install surveillance

( ) TALKING TO A LAWYER

Q. *My boss has been making sexually suggestive remarks to me that I find offensive, and I've told him so. Should I tape his remarks so I have proof of his conduct in case he fires me?*

A. Under federal law, you can surreptitiously tape record your conversations with your boss to protect yourself and gather evidence of his improper conduct. This is called the **one-party-consent exemption**. However, some states require the permission of both parties in order to record an otherwise private conversation.

—Answer by members of the ABA Section
of Labor and Employment Law

equipment to monitor employee conduct, but must first negotiate this issue with the union.

VIDEO MONITORING

Generally speaking, an employer may photograph or videotape employees in plain view or at their workstations. If the videotape includes audio, however, the audio portion of the tape is subject to the restrictions imposed by the Federal Wiretap Act.

Problems can also arise if the video surveillance is covert. State tort law may protect employees against highly offensive intrusions upon privacy in places where they have a reasonable expectation of privacy. For example, monitoring employee bathrooms may be considered an invasion of privacy.

Some states have also passed legislation regulating employer monitoring of employees. Connecticut, for example, prohibits surveillance or monitoring "in areas designed for the health or personal comfort of the employees or for the safeguarding of their possessions, such as rest rooms, locker rooms or lounges."

( ) TALKING TO A LAWYER

*Q. My company installed a video camera outside the ladies' room to keep
track of everyone coming in and going out. I feel embarrassed when I
use the restroom. Is this kind of spying allowed?*

A. Although the Federal Wiretap Act does not apply to silent videotaping,
the employer nevertheless may be liable under state law for invading its
employees' reasonable expectation of privacy. Even if the employer
puts its employees on notice that they will be videotaped, the employer
may be liable for invasion of privacy if the videotaping is found to be
per se unreasonable. In addition, some states have passed legislation
regulating employer monitoring of employees in certain situations.

—Answer by members of the ABA Section
of Labor and Employment Law

Similarly, California prohibits any audio or video recording in
restrooms or locker rooms without a court order.

COMPUTER MONITORING

The Federal Wiretap Act was amended by the **Electronic Communications Privacy Act of 1986 (ECPA)** and the **Stored
Communications Act.** The ECPA regulates the interception of
electronic communications such as e-mail. The Stored Communications Act protects against unauthorized access to "electronic
communication while it is in electronic storage"—for example,
when such communications are stored on a computer's hard drive.
    As currently interpreted by the courts, the ECPA only pro-
hibits the interception of e-mail during transmission. Conse-
quently, an employer that "captures" e-mail content before it is
delivered to the recipient has violated the ECPA. The employer's
retrieval of e-mail stored in its own system, however, is not prohibited. Thus, e-mail that has been temporarily stored in the em-

ployer's system following transmission, as well as e-mail in electronic storage in the employer's system for backup protection, can be accessed and read by the employer without violating the ECPA or the Stored Communications Act. The employer could also access a stored cache of website addresses, allowing it to determine which websites an employee has visited, without violating the law.

Moreover, since the ECPA only applies to communication that affects interstate or foreign commerce, intracompany e-mail systems in which messages do not cross state lines, that are not connected to an interstate network, would not be regulated by the ECPA. The ECPA also allows employer access to e-mail if there is employee consent. If employees are given clear notice that the employer has a policy or practice of monitoring electronic communications on its computers or computer system, its employees will be deemed to have consented to monitoring when they use that system. In such circumstances, the employer could monitor the content of e-mail during transmission, as well as monitor the content of websites visited by employees, without violating the ECPA.

As a general rule, an employer is not prohibited from disciplining or discharging employees based on the content of their e-mail. There are two exceptions to this general rule: 1) if the content of the e-mail is specifically protected by state or federal law, in which case the discipline or discharge would violate that law; and 2) when the employee is protected against discipline or discharge, except for just cause.

Some examples of the first exception may include: an e-mail sent to a government agency informing the agency of the employer's violation of a law (see the "Whistle-Blower Protection" section in chapter 11); an e-mail sent to a labor union requesting information about joining a union (see chapter 13 for further discussion of unions in the workplace); or an e-mail sent to a coworker complaining about discrimination at work and suggesting that the worker talk to the human resources department about the problem (see the "Anti-retaliation Laws" section in chapter 11).

Situations involving the second exception arise when the employment relationship is not at will, and the employee can be fired only for just cause. Just-cause protections are found in collective-bargaining agreements, and may be detailed in employee handbooks. If so, the employer may discipline or discharge an employee only if the content of an e-mail is sufficient to create just cause. (See the "Being Fired" section of chapter 11 for a discussion of just cause.)

Federal law does not regulate computerized monitoring of work that is performed on a computer—i.e., monitoring of error rates, log-in times, or key strokes. Only a few states have directly addressed the issue of computer monitoring. For example, both Connecticut and Delaware require that employers provide prior notice of computer monitoring, but such monitoring is not prohibited so long as notice is given.

Employees who maintain a public-access webpage or web log should also be mindful that their employers may access the information contained therein and discipline or discharge them based on the content. Once again, unless the content itself is protected by law or the employee is covered by just-cause protection, disciplinary action or discharge by the employer would not violate the law.

"Anonymous" communications in Internet chat rooms and

⚠ AVOIDING PROBLEMS WHEN MONITORING EMPLOYEES

To avoid liability when monitoring employees, employers should take the following steps:

- access files and e-mail only for legitimate business reasons;

- make sure employees know that the office computer and telecommunications systems are owned by the business;

- adopt written policies governing the use of computer and telecommunications equipment; and

- inform employees that the company reserves the right to monitor the use of office computers and telecommunications equipment.

↻ TALKING TO A LAWYER

Q. *I maintain a personal website. On it I provide links to other sites that interest me. One of the links is to the website of the Lambda Legal Defense Fund, an organization that works to protect the rights of gay people. I think my employer fired me because of my website. Is that legal?*

A. There are several possible sources of protection in this situation. First, is there a state statute or local ordinance prohibiting discrimination on the basis of sexual orientation? If so, you may be able to prove that the reason for your termination was related to the Lambda link, which raises the possibility that your employer fired you because it thought you were gay. Of course, if the employer fired you simply for maintaining a personal website, or because of other content on the website, then you would not be able to prove that your termination was motivated by your sexual orientation.

Second, are you represented by a union and covered by a collective-bargaining agreement? If so, that agreement likely requires that your employer have just cause in order to fire you, and the fact that an employee maintains a personal website generally does not constitute just cause.

Third, do you live in one of the few states—like Colorado or New York—that prohibits employers from terminating employees for legal off-duty conduct? If so, the firing would likely violate the law.

Fourth, does your employer have a written handbook or manual that limits its discretion in discharging employees? If so, a state court may enforce that limitation.

Lastly, does your state have a law—as Montana does—requiring good cause before an employer can discharge an employee? If so, your employer's conduct may be unlawful, since an employee's maintenance of a personal website generally is not considered good cause for termination.

However, if none of these factors is present in your case, you are
an at-will employee and the termination would be legal.

—Answer by Barbara Fick, Associate Professor of Law,
Notre Dame Law School

on bulletin boards may not be as anonymous as you might think.
Employees who have defamed their employer or disclosed confidential business information via chat rooms or bulletin boards
have been fired for such remarks. An employer that believes a
particular employee has made such remarks can sue the employee as a Jane or John Doe, and then subpoena the Internet
service provider (ISP)—thus requiring it to provide the employee's name. Disclosure by an ISP of a subscriber's name to a
private-sector employer is not prohibited by the Federal Wiretap
Act or its amendments, although courts generally will seek to
balance the First Amendment rights of an anonymous online
poster against a company's right to protect its proprietary interests and reputation.

Employers that attempt to regulate employee use of e-mail
should also be aware of the ways in which the NLRA applies to
situations involving e-mail. If an employer allows employees to
send non-business-related e-mails, it cannot prohibit employees
from using the e-mail system to discuss union activities or issues
relating to employment policies or conditions. Moreover, a blan-
ket prohibition on the use of e-mail for any non-business-related
purposes may constitute an unlawfully overbroad no-solicitation
rule, which may violate the rights of employees to communicate
with each other about work issues. (For a discussion of no-
solicitation rules, see the "Employers and the NLRA" section of
chapter 13.)

THE WORLD AT YOUR FINGERTIPS

• The Findlaw website contains additional information on privacy rights in the workplace. Visit *www.employment.findlaw.com*,

EMPLOYEE TRACKING

Employers are increasingly using technology to trace employee movements, both inside and outside the workplace. For example, employers can use global positioning systems (GPS) in work vehicles to track employee movements off premises, and "swipe" cards to control access to interior workplace locations and trace employee movements. Currently no federal or state legislation addresses the use of such technology; however, tracking an individual's movements may raise questions of invasion of privacy under state common law doctrine, particularly when employees have a reasonable expectation of privacy and are unaware that such monitoring is occurring.

click on "More Topics," and then click on "Privacy in the Workplace."

• *Employee Privacy Rights and Wrongs* by Philip Dickinson (2001) provides a detailed discussion of issues related to workplace privacy.

REMEMBER THIS

• An employer cannot intercept telephone calls unless it listens in on an extension used in the ordinary course of business, has the consent of one of the parties to the communication, or has expressly notified the employee that monitoring will occur.

• Where a speaker has a reasonable expectation of privacy, individuals cannot record conversations without the speaker's consent—except where a party to the conversation has either intercepted the conversation or consented to the interception, and where the interception is not for the purpose of committing any criminal or tortious act in violation of federal or state law.

• An employer cannot monitor employee union activity.

• Covert video surveillance may constitute an invasion of privacy.

- Employers cannot intercept electronic computer transmissions without employee consent.
- Information stored on an employer's own computer system may legally be accessed by the employer.
- Disciplinary action taken by employers against employees based on the content of employees' electronic communications may be illegal if the content of those communications is protected by either federal or state law.

CHAPTER 10

Employee Discipline

Investigating Employee Misconduct

Inventory has been disappearing from the company's warehouse, and the plant manager wants to find out who is responsible. He would like to give all the employees lie detector tests, search their cars and lockers, and frisk them as they leave the plant. He wonders, however, whether he needs some kind of search warrant like he has seen on Law and Order.

As a general rule, employers can use their discretion in deciding what types of employee conduct should be disciplined, and the type of discipline to impose. Employees' rights in this area are protected mainly through federal and state antidiscrimination laws. These laws prohibit employers from imposing discipline because of an employee's membership in a protected class. In addition, workers may be protected under collective-bargaining agreements (discussed in chapter 13).

In addition to antidiscrimination laws, there are other legal protections for workers. Some state laws prohibit employers from imposing discipline for certain reasons—mostly relating to off-duty conduct of the employee, such as off-duty use of tobacco or other lawful substances. As mentioned earlier, some states forbid employers to discipline employees because of their off-duty political activities. Also, almost all federal and state employment laws specifically forbid employers from disciplining employees because they have tried to enforce rights provided to them under the law. (These provisions are discussed in the "Anti-retaliation Laws" section of chapter 11.)

Otherwise, employers generally are free to discipline employees as they see fit. Employers often inform employees of punishable offenses, either through employee bulletin boards or employee handbooks, but employers are not required to do so.

Employers are free to make case-by-case determinations regarding workplace offenses.

Also, employers generally are free to decide the punishment imposed for each workplace offense. One employer may decide that sleeping on the job merits a week's suspension, whereas another employer may issue a written warning. Employers do not have to issue warnings before imposing discipline. Employers can fire employees for committing a workplace offense—even for the first violation, and even if employees have good performance records.

Sometimes, however, employers may impose limitations on themselves. As discussed in chapter 6, if employee handbooks contain specific enforceable promises concerning employee discipline, failure by the employer to observe the promised procedures or conditions could constitute a breach of contract. In addition, when an employee handbook sets forth an employer's disciplinary procedure relating to a given offense, some courts may deem the employer to have created an implied-in-fact con-

---

(i) HOW CLEAR IS CLEAR?

Handbook language that is not highly specific—for example, language stating that "the following list of offenses may subject the employee to discipline"—generally is not considered sufficient to delineate, for legal purposes, the offenses for which discipline may be imposed. However, more specific language—for example, a statement that "employees will be disciplined *only* for the following offenses"—may be sufficient to warrant legal enforcement. A statement that the employer will treat employees fairly during the disciplinary process may also be too vague to be enforced. But a more specific statement—for example, that "no employee will be discharged unless he or she first receives a written warning"— could be sufficient to prevent an employer from legally firing an employee without written notice.

tract, pursuant to which an employee may only be disciplined or terminated for just cause. (See chapter 11 for a discussion of implied contracts.) For such contracts to be enforceable, however, the handbooks must have been given to employees, and the language relating to discipline must be clear and unambiguous.

Whatever offenses employers decide are punishable, and whatever the punishments they impose, Title VII and other antidiscrimination laws require that rules and punishments be uniformly applied in a nondiscriminatory manner. The basic rule is that similarly situated people should be treated the same. Thus, if a white employee is given a warning for cursing at a supervisor, a Hispanic employee with a similar employment record

( ) TALKING TO A LAWYER

Q. I was given a disciplinary suspension under my company's "three-strike" rule for being late to work. It's only happened twice in the last two years, and I had valid reasons both times: once my car broke down, and once my child was sick. I was also late one other time, but that was five years ago. Isn't there a time limit on my employer's right to impose discipline? And doesn't it count for something that two of my "tardies" were beyond my control?

A. There is no law establishing a time limit for imposing employee discipline. Moreover, employers are permitted to establish no-fault attendance policies and to discipline employees for lateness or absences, even if such infractions are not the fault of the employee. Such policies are permitted unless a collective-bargaining agreement or federal or state law imposes restrictions on the employer's ability to discipline under these circumstances.

—Answer by members of the ABA Section
of Labor and Employment Law

committing the same offense should also be given a warning; he or she may not be fired. Such a difference in treatment would be considered discrimination on the basis of the employee's national origin, and therefore a violation of Title VII.

Similarly, an employer would violate Title VII by disciplining a woman who missed work, but not a man who was similarly absent. Differences in treatment are allowed, but not if the employees are similarly situated. Suppose the man who was absent from work presented his supervisor with a doctor's note justifying his absenteeism, while the woman did not have a legitimate excuse. In that case, the employer may be able to discipline the woman (and not the man) without running afoul of Title VII, because the difference in treatment would be motivated by a difference in the employees' circumstances—i.e., the employees would not be similarly situated.

PERSONNEL FILES

Employers usually keep personnel files containing records relating to employees. Personnel files may contain information on an employee's background, workplace history, and work performance. Employers often consult these files before deciding whether to discipline an employee and what type of discipline to impose, as well as when making decisions regarding promotions or wage increases. Federal and state laws address both the confidentiality of personnel files and employees' access to these files.

The Family and Medical Leave Act (FMLA) and the Americans with Disabilities Act (ADA) both contain confidentiality provisions relating to the medical information retained by employers about employees. Both laws require employers to keep employee medical records confidential and separate from personnel files. The ADA states that the only persons who may be informed about an employee's medical conditions are first-aid or safety personnel (if the medical conditions in question may require emergency treatment) and government officials investigating compliance with the ADA. The employer may also inform supervisors and managers about restrictions on work duties or necessary accommodations required by a disability.

The federal Privacy Act of 1974 forbids federal government employers from disclosing any information contained in an employee's files without the employee's written consent. The Privacy Act grants employees of the federal government the right to access their personnel records, and permits them to make copies of any portion of the documents contained therein. It also sets forth a procedure by which federal employees may challenge the information contained in their files. Many states have similar laws regulating access to the files of state employees.

Some states also protect certain information about private-sector employees. For example, California and Pennsylvania prohibit disclosure of employee medical records. At least one state, Connecticut, prohibits the disclosure of any personnel information without the written consent of the employee in question. Moreover, unnecessary disclosure of information that an employee reasonably expects will be kept private may create employer liability under state tort law for invasion of privacy or intentional infliction of emotional distress.

The Occupational Safety and Health Act requires private-sector employers to give employees access to medical records that employers must maintain when employees are exposed to potentially toxic materials at work. The National Labor Relations Act (NLRA) requires private-sector employers to give unions information that is necessary and relevant for collective-bargaining purposes. This can include access to employee personnel files. There is, however, no duty to disclose such information directly to the employees in question.

Many states grant employees the right to access their personnel files. Some of these laws also provide procedures enabling employees to challenge information contained in those files.

( ) TALKING TO A LAWYER

Q. *My supervisor called me into his office this morning and told me I was being suspended for sleeping on the job. I was stunned—I've never done such a thing. Don't I have the right to a hearing to prove that I didn't violate the rules?*

A. In most states, the general answer to your question is "no." **At-will employees**—that is, employees not covered by an employment contract or collective-bargaining agreement—may be disciplined or terminated for good cause, bad cause, or no cause at all, so long as the reason for the termination is not otherwise discriminatory. In some states, however, employers must have good cause for terminating an employee. What constitutes good cause varies from state to state.

Absent a disclaimer to the contrary, in many states employers must follow the disciplinary procedures set forth in their employee handbooks.

—Answer by members of the Publications Committee,
ABA Section of Labor and Employment Law

INVESTIGATORY METHODS

Federal and state laws limit the methods an employer may use to investigate whether employees have violated workplace rules. (See chapter 9 for a discussion of the legal issues arising from the use of monitoring techniques.)

Lie Detector Tests

The Employee Polygraph Protection Act (EPPA) regulates the use of lie detectors to investigate employee misconduct. This federal law establishes protections that apply nationwide. Many states, however, impose even tighter restrictions on employer use of polygraph tests for current employees. For example, Alaska and Connecticut prohibit employers from giving tests, and even from asking employees to take such tests.

Under the EPPA, lie detectors may only be used "in connection with an ongoing investigation that involves economic loss or injury to the employer's business." Thus, an employer could use a polygraph to determine if an employee had embezzled money, but not to find out if he had cursed at his supervisor. Employers involved in making or distributing controlled substances (i.e., drugs) are allowed to administer polygraphs to employees with direct access to controlled substances who are the subject of an ongoing investigation.

The EPPA provides that in order to be subjected to polygraph tests in the context of an ongoing investigation, employees must have had access to the missing or damaged property that is the subject of the investigation. Also, an employer must have a reasonable suspicion that an employee is involved in the incident in question. Mere access to the property in question is not enough to support reasonable suspicion. However, if an employer manufactures, distributes, or dispenses controlled substances, that employer does not have to prove reasonable suspicion of the employee's involvement; mere access to the property is sufficient.

Even if an employer complies with these two requirements, procedural limitations are still placed on the use of a polygraph. Before the test is given, the employee to be tested must be given reasonable written notice of the time at which the test will be administered, and of his or her right to consult an attorney before the test. The employee must also be informed that he or she cannot be required to take the test as a condition of employment, and that he or she can terminate the test at any time. The employer must also explain the nature of the test and provide the employee with an opportunity to review the questions to be asked during the test.

The EPPA prohibits an employer from using the results of a polygraph test as the sole basis for imposing discipline; the employer is required to have additional supporting evidence. Before

⚠ DON'T ASK, DON'T TELL

During a lie detector test, an employee cannot be asked any questions about:

- his or her religious or political beliefs;
- his or her opinions regarding racial matters;
- his or her opinions or activities involving labor unions; or
- any matter relating to his or her sexual behavior.

taking any disciplinary action, the employer must interview the employee based on the test results, and provide the employee with a written copy of the analysis of the test results.

Credit Reports

The Fair Credit Reporting Act (FCRA) sets forth notification requirements that apply when an employer obtains a consumer report or an investigative consumer report either: (1) in connection with the investigation of suspected misconduct relating to employment; or (2) to determine compliance with any preexisting written employer policies. (See the "Two Different Types of Reports" sidebar in chapter 4 for definitions of "consumer report" and "investigative consumer report.") If the employer takes an adverse action against an employee based on information obtained from such reports, then it must inform the employee and make available a summary of the report, excluding the names of any sources from whom information was obtained. The employer does not, however, have to obtain an employee's consent or give notice before obtaining a report.

A few states have more stringent limits on employer use of investigative and consumer reports. For example, Massachusetts and New York require employers to notify and receive authorization from employees before obtaining such reports.

Some states limit the type of information that an employer can obtain about an employee's non-employment-related activities. For example, an employer may be prohibited from gathering information on non-employment-related activities, whether through credit reports or other means, unless the employee provides the employer with written authorization to obtain the information.

Investigatory Interviews

A typical employer investigatory method is to question the employee to get his or her side of the story. Employee interrogations can raise several issues under both federal and state law.

If the employee in question is represented by a union, the NLRA provides for employee representation during investigatory interviews. An employee has the right to request the presence of a union representative before he or she participates in an investigatory interview that could result in discipline. Employers cannot require employees to participate in the interview without the union representative present, but they can decide to forego the interview and make a decision about discipline without talking to the employee.

Employee interrogation can also create liability under state tort law. An interrogation that is conducted in an outrageously abusive manner that violates community standards may constitute an intentional infliction of emotional distress. If employers use force or coercion to prevent an employee from leaving an investigatory interview, then they may also be liable for false imprisonment. However, telling an employee that he or she will be fired if he or she leaves the interview is not considered coercive for purposes of claiming false imprisonment.

Employee Searches

Lastly, employers may want to search employees or their belongings during a workplace investigation. While such searches

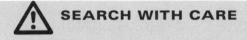

⚠ SEARCH WITH CARE

Employers should be extremely careful about how they conduct searches, or they could be liable for a long list of torts—including assault, battery, false arrest, intentional infliction of emotional distress, and invasion of privacy.

First, an employer should have a work-related reason for the search. However, this does not mean that the employer has to prove probable cause. (**Probable cause** is the standard that applies in criminal cases, and it only applies to the government—not to individuals or private employers.) Second, the employer should conduct any search using the least-intrusive means possible. Third, the employer should inform employees that searches might be conducted. Fourth, the employer should not physically harm employees in the course of a search, or threaten employees with physical harm. Last, employers should not attempt to prevent employees from leaving the premises by threat of harm or other coercive means, although employers are usually allowed to tell employees that they may be disciplined or discharged if they leave.

can raise problems for government employers (see chapter 14 for more information on government employment), there are few restraints on private-sector employers in this regard. Unless a collective-bargaining agreement restricts an employer's right to search employees, reasonable searches are generally allowable.

Questions sometimes arise about searches of areas or belongings with respect to which employees may have a reasonable expectation of privacy; in such cases an employer's search may constitute an invasion of privacy. For example, opening employee mail that has been marked "personal," searching employee lockers where employees are allowed to use their own locks to secure the contents, or searching employee automobiles may all give rise to claims for invasion of privacy.

( ) TALKING TO A LAWYER

Q. *My supervisor accused me of theft. He yelled at me in front of my coworkers and took me into his office where he berated me, called me names, and demanded that I admit I stole the money. Then he took my purse and looked through it. He never found any proof that I did anything wrong, but he gave me a two-week suspension anyway. Can he do that?*

A. The suspension as such is probably legal, but the rest of the employer's behavior may constitute an intentional infliction of emotional distress. In addition, the searching of your purse may constitute an invasion of privacy.

—Answer by Theodore St. Antoine, Degan Professor
Emeritus of Law, University of Michigan Law School

THE WORLD AT YOUR FINGERTIPS

• The Department of Labor website contains links to information regarding the law, regulations, and compliance assistance relating to lie detector tests, at *www.dol.gov/dol/compliance/comp-eppa.htm.*

• A quick reference guide to admissibility, licensing laws, and statutory provisions of each state's polygraph laws is published by the American Polygraph Association at *www.polygraph.org/intro.htm.*

• *Dealing with Problem Employees: A Legal Guide* by Amy Delpo and Lisa Guerin (2003) provides advice on how to handle matters of employee discipline.

REMEMBER THIS

• Disciplinary procedures contained in employee handbooks may be enforceable.

- An employer may not base disciplinary action (or the severity thereof) on an employee's membership in a protected class.
- Some state laws allow employees to access the information contained in their personnel files.
- With few exceptions, employers cannot require employees to undergo lie detector tests.
- State law may limit the type of information an employer can gather about employee conduct.
- Employees represented by a union are entitled to union representation during an investigatory interview that could lead to discipline.
- To avoid liability under state tort law, searches should be conducted for work-related reasons only, by the least-intrusive means possible, and with limited physical contact.

CHAPTER 11

Ending the Employment Relationship Involuntarily

What You Need to Know About Firing and Layoffs

"You're fired!"

Many Americans have heard these harsh words bellowing from the mouth of Donald Trump. Is The Apprentice, *one of today's most popular reality-TV shows, really "reality?" Is it that easy for someone to be fired? Does an employer have to have good cause to fire someone? Does an employer have to treat employees fairly? These questions are important to most employees.*

While it may be fun and games on The Apprentice, *the words "You're fired" are dreaded and feared by most employees. Many employees report that they believe they are entitled to fair treatment at work and cannot be fired without good cause. However, as many employees learn to their surprise, there is no enforceable legal right to fair treatment.*

No job lasts forever. Employment can be terminated either voluntarily or involuntarily. Some employees voluntarily separate from their employment through retirement or voluntary resignation. Other employees are involuntarily separated through discharge or layoff. This chapter examines the concept of **employment at will** and how the law affects discharges and layoffs.

BEING FIRED

In the U.S., most employees are considered **employees at will**. What does it really mean to be an at-will employee? Simply stated, employment at will means that an *employer or employee* can terminate the employment relationship at any time, for any reason, with or without notice. Applied to employers, the at-will doctrine means that an employer can terminate, except as otherwise restricted by an express or implied agreement, the employment of any employee at any time for a good reason, a bad reason, or no reason at all—but never for an *illegal* reason. Applied to employees, the nature of the at-will employment relationship means that an employee is free to quit the job at any time for any reason or no reason at all.

There are three major categories of employees, however, who are not employed at will. The first group consists of the relatively small number of workers who have written employment contracts setting forth the length of their employment relationships and prohibiting discharge except under specified circumstances. These contracts are enforceable in state courts. While employment contracts can be entered into at any level of employment, such contracts typically are used with executives and highly skilled professionals. Offer letters should not be confused with employment contracts. (An offer letter typically offers an individual a job and sets forth some of the specifics of the position, such as duties and pay.)

The second group consists of employees represented by unions and covered by collective-bargaining agreements. These agreements normally provide that employees can be discharged only for **just cause**. The precise meaning of this phrase might vary from contract to contract, but it certainly limits the employer's unfettered right to fire. (See the "Just-Cause Clauses" section of chapter 13 for a discussion of just-cause standards.) Moreover, collective-bargaining agreements typically set forth grievance mechanisms. These give unionized employees a way to challenge their firings. (Collective-bargaining agreements are discussed in detail in chapter 13.)

The third group consists of government employees who are protected by civil-service laws. These laws normally require the employer to have just cause to terminate an individual's employment. Government employees can appeal discharge decisions through civil-service commissions. Government employees also enjoy constitutional protections from certain types of discharge.

(Civil-service laws and constitutional rights are discussed in more detail in chapter 14.)

There are two other exceptions to the general rule that employees can be terminated at will. One state has passed a law giving workers protection from being arbitrarily fired. Montana has enacted the **Wrongful Discharge from Employment Act**, which expressly prohibits firing of non-probationary employees, except for good cause. **Good cause** is defined as "reasonable job-related grounds for dismissal" for legitimate business reasons. The other exception arises when federal or state law imposes a specific restriction on the employer's power to fire. Such restrictions, which are described below, only apply to a limited category of cases. If there is no specific restriction, however, the employer can fire an employee for any reason or no reason at all.

( ) TALKING TO A LAWYER

Q. *I just got fired. I worked at the company for ten years, and always had excellent evaluations and received annual raises. I was not given an explanation for my termination or an opportunity to defend myself. Isn't this unlawful?*

A. While the circumstances surrounding your termination appear to have been handled unfairly, unless you can find evidence that you were terminated for an illegal reason—i.e., based on your membership in a protected category as defined by federal or state antidiscrimination statutes, based on your participation in reporting alleged misconduct relating to your employer, etc.—then your termination is not unlawful. That is, of course, unless you work for the government, have an express or implied employment agreement, are covered by a collective-bargaining agreement, or work in a state that recognizes the implied-covenant-of-good-faith-and-fair-dealing exception to the doctrine of at-will employment.

—Answer by members of the ABA Section
of Labor and Employment Law

Antidiscrimination Laws

Title VII, the Age Discrimination in Employment Act (ADEA), the Americans with Disabilities Act (ADA), the Uniformed Services Employment and Reemployment Rights Act (USERRA), and the National Labor Relations Act (NLRA) all prohibit employers from firing workers if the firing is motivated by an employee's membership in a protected class. (For further information, see the discussion on antidiscrimination laws in chapter 2.) The Employee Retirement Income Security Act (ERISA) also protects employees from being fired if the aim of the firing is to prevent the employees from accruing pension and welfare benefits.

Many state laws extend the definitions of protected classes and activities in this area. For example, states like California, Michigan, and Wisconsin prohibit firings based on weight, height, sexual orientation, marital status, and arrest record. As discussed in chapter 8, many state laws also prohibit employment discrimination, which includes discharge for off-duty conduct such as smoking, drinking, or political activity.

▶ FIRING MEMBERS OF A PROTECTED CLASS

In determining whether a discharge violates antidiscrimination laws, the issue is whether the firing was motivated by the employee's membership in a protected class. Merely belonging to a protected class does not grant an employee immunity from being fired. But being in a protected class means that, when employers decide what types of conduct warrant discharge and when to enact such discharge, the employee must be treated the same as similarly situated employees not in the protected class. As with employee discipline, the basic rule is that similarly situated people must be treated the same.

USERRA

USERRA provides certain employees special protection against firing. The broad prohibition against terminating employees who are or have been members of the uniformed services is supplemented by a special provision dealing with employees reinstated to their jobs after a leave of absence for military duty. USERRA provides that a person who is reemployed cannot be fired *except for cause* within one year after reemployment, as long as the employee's period of military service was more than 180 days. An employee whose period of military service was more than thirty but less than 181 days may not be fired except for cause within 180 days after reemployment.

Anti-retaliation Laws

Effectively enforcing labor and employment laws requires help from employees themselves. Often employees are in the best position to know what happens in the workplace and whether their rights have been violated. Many enforcement agencies depend on complaints from employees to alert them to potential violations of the law.

Employees may feel particularly vulnerable, however, when it comes to making complaints. Their economic livelihood depends on their employers, which have the authority to discipline and discharge them. Understandably, employees may be reluctant to stand up for their rights or make complaints, for fear that they will lose their jobs.

Because of the potential for retaliation against employees who enforce their statutory rights, all federal labor and employment laws (with the exception of the Worker Adjustment and Retraining Notification Act, discussed in the sidebar on page 173), and most state labor and employment laws, specifically prohibit employers from disciplining or discharging employees because they have attempted to enforce their rights under the law. Enforcing their rights includes filing a complaint with the

( ) TALKING TO A LAWYER

Q. My supervisor fired me because he found out I was having an affair with a married man. "As a Christian," he said, "I am deeply offended by such disregard of the seventh commandment." Isn't this religious discrimination? At the very least, it's none of my employer's business.

A. Title VII does prohibit an employer from firing employees because of their religion. The focus of the statute is generally on the *employee's* religious beliefs, and not on the fact that a conflict exists between an employee's conduct and the religious beliefs of others. At least one court, however, has found a violation of Title VII when an employee was fired because her off-duty conduct disturbed the religious sensibilities of other employees. Your question raises a separate issue related to how the employer learned of your affair. If the employer utilized means that were invasive of your personal privacy, you might have a tort claim for invasion of privacy.

—Answer by Barbara Fick, Associate Professor of Law, Notre Dame Law School

agency that enforces a law, helping the agency to investigate a complaint, and participating in a proceeding to enforce rights under the law (such as testifying or filing a lawsuit).

The anti-retaliation clauses featured in Title VII, the ADEA, and the ADA offer a broader scope of protection than most standard anti-retaliation provisions. These three laws protect not only employee **participation activity** (activity that constitutes enforcement of rights), but also **opposition activity**. This means that employers cannot discriminate against an employee because he or she "has opposed any practice made unlawful" under Title VII, the ADEA, or the ADA. Employees who complain to their employers about discrimination in the workplace, or who take part in demonstrations protesting employment discrimination, are protected from retaliation under these laws.

Whistle-Blower Protection

Employees in most states receive protection for whistle-blowing—i.e., protection from retaliation and discharge in the event the employees report fraudulent or illegal activities or conduct threatening to the public welfare. This whistle-blowing protection typically is provided either by statute or judicially. Over thirty states have passed **whistle-blower laws**. These laws prohibit employers from firing employees who report suspected violations of state or federal laws, rules, or regulations.

Whistle-blower laws are much broader in scope than anti-retaliation laws. Anti-retaliation provisions are limited to the enforcement of specific rights set forth in the applicable statute. For example, the anti-retaliation provision in Title VII protects employees who file complaints alleging that their rights under Title VII have been violated. The protection provided by whistle-blower laws, on the other hand, is not limited to instances in which employees report violations of particular laws. Under many state whistle-blower laws, as long as employees are reporting a suspected violation of *any* law, they are protected.

In addition, anti-retaliation laws are linked specifically to laws dealing with the workplace. For example, the OSH Act's anti-retaliation clause protects employees who make complaints regarding safety and health issues at work. Whistle-blower laws,

(i) ONE SIZE DOES NOT FIT ALL

The scope of the whistle-blower laws varies considerably by state. Most states protect only government employees, but a significant number also protect private-sector workers. Also, sometimes these laws protect employees only when they report violations to particular persons. Some laws protect employees who disclose information either to their employers or to an appropriate government agency. Other laws protect employees only when the report is made to a government agency.

on the other hand, are not limited to the workplace. Thus, a construction worker who reports that his employer is paying off a housing inspector will be protected under these laws.

There is also a whistle-blower law that protects employees of the federal government. The **Whistleblower Protection Act** prohibits employers that are federal government agencies from retaliating against an employee for disclosing any information that the employee reasonably believes provides evidence of a violation of any law, rule, or regulation.

In addition, Congress in 2002 passed the **Sarbanes-Oxley Act** to address issues relating to corporate corruption and accounting fraud. One of the law's provisions provides whistle-blower protection to employees of publicly traded companies when they provide information concerning securities or shareholder fraud to federal law enforcement officials, Congress, or their supervisors.

STATE COMMON-LAW EXCEPTIONS TO EMPLOYMENT AT WILL

As mentioned at the beginning of this chapter, the employment-at-will doctrine governs most cases of employee termination. Most state courts, however, have identified certain situations in which an employer's otherwise complete right of discharge is limited. The two major common-law exceptions to at-will employment that are recognized by courts are: (1) public-policy exceptions; and (2) implied contracts of employment based on an employer's oral or written assurances.

The Public-Policy Exception

Over thirty state courts have adopted the **public-policy exception** to the employment-at-will doctrine. This exception allows an employee to bring an action for wrongful or retaliatory discharge against his or her employer if the employee's termination is contrary to the underlying public policy of the state. The meaning of the phrase "contrary to underlying public policy" differs by state; however, states that recognize this exception usually require the employee to prove that his or her termination was motivated by the exercise of a clearly established statutory right or the performance of a clearly established statutory duty.

The public policy of a state is generally grounded in the state's constitution, laws, and regulations, and sometimes in its state court decisions. Courts justify the public-policy exception by reasoning that employers should not be allowed to use their economic power over employees in a way that undermines the interests of the community as a whole, or that is injurious to the public good. For example, one of the first cases dealing with this exception involved an employer that instructed one of its employees to testify falsely before a state legislative committee. When the employee refused to commit perjury, he was discharged. The court held that the employer's use of its authority to undermine the policy of the state could be punished by allowing an employee to pursue an action for wrongful discharge.

Four types of firing have been deemed by courts to raise public-policy concerns. The first such type is the firing of an employee who **refuses to perform an illegal act**. A company that fires an employee for refusing to commit perjury is an example of an employer that wrongfully engages in this type of termination.

A second type of firing that offends public policy is the termination of an employee who **reports a violation of the law**. Protection provided to employees under this public-policy exception is similar to the protection extended under state whistleblower laws. In one case, for example, an employee of an eyeglass company was fired after reporting to the federal Food and Drug Administration that his company was not performing legally required tests to determine the shatter resistance of lenses. A court held that the employee could sue his employer for wrongful discharge in violation of public policy.

A third type of case involves firing an employee for **engaging in acts that public policy encourages**. For example, an employee who voluntarily cooperates with government authorities investigating possible antitrust violations would be protected from

( ) TALKING TO A LAWYER

*Q. My employer, a grocery store chain, fired me because my spouse filed
a negligence lawsuit against the store after slipping on a banana peel
in the produce department and hurting her back. This had nothing to
do with me. Is my employer allowed to punish me for what my wife
is doing?*

A. In the past, your employer certainly would have been within its rights.
Now, however, some courts might entertain a public-policy claim
against the employer on the grounds that its actions interfered with
your wife's legal right to sue.

—Answer by Theodore St. Antoine, Degan Professor
Emeritus of Law, University of Michigan Law School

discharge. There is no law requiring the employee to cooperate
in such a situation; thus, failure to do so would not constitute an
illegal act. Also, the employee would not actually be reporting violations of antitrust laws, so the second type of public-policy exception to the employment-at-will doctrine would not apply.
However, helping the government enforce its laws is

(i) THE STATES PICK AND CHOOSE

States recognizing the public-policy exception to the employment-at-will
doctrine do not necessarily recognize it in all four types of cases that are
described above. A few states do recognize the exception in all four
types of cases, and most recognize both the exception for refusing to
perform an illegal act and for exercising a statutory right. But several
states—including Alabama, Florida, and Georgia—have rejected any attempt to modify the strict common-law employment-at-will doctrine, and
do not recognize any public-policy exception under any circumstances.

considered good for the public as a whole. Thus, an employer's attempt to stop an employee from cooperating would be viewed as contrary to the public good.

The fourth type of case involves firing an employee for **exercising statutory rights**. The protection offered under this public-policy exception is very similar to the protection offered under the anti-retaliation provisions of the labor and employment laws. For example, an employer that fires employees for filing workers' compensation claims is deemed to have undermined the employees' statutory rights to receive workers' compensation benefits, and is therefore said to be acting contrary to the state's public policy.

Implied Contracts

The second exception to the employment-at-will doctrine relates to **implied contracts**. Most state courts have recognized that employers' promises to limit the circumstances under which they will terminate their employees can be binding and enforceable. Such promises can be the result of statements found in manuals and handbooks, or of oral statements made directly by an employer to an employee.

Many employers have created personnel manuals or handbooks that outline policies and procedures governing the

▶ SPECIFICITY COUNTS

Vague statements in personnel manuals or handbooks—for example, a statement that "all employees will be treated fairly" or that "in most cases employees will be warned before they are discharged"—may not be enforceable. More-specific language is more likely to be enforceable— for example, a statement that "no employee will be discharged without good cause; employees will only be fired if they violate one of the following rules," followed by a list of specific rules that may not be violated.

employment relationship. These may include acceptable reasons for discharge and the procedures to be followed in the event of such discharge. As discussed in chapter 6, the statements contained in these handbooks can be enforced if they are given to employees and contain clear and specific language regarding the circumstances required for discharge.

An employer can avoid creating binding promises by clearly and unambiguously informing its employees that the policies contained in its handbook are not intended to create a contract. Even when the requirements for a binding contract are present, employers remain free to revoke or revise the policies contained in such handbooks. Once they give notice to employees that a policy has been changed, the old policy is no longer enforceable with respect to situations arising after the change.

A few courts will enforce oral promises of job security, but such promises can be very difficult to prove. In order to be enforceable, promises of job security usually must be made specifically to the employee in question, and not in a statement or announcement made to employees generally. Also, such promises usually must be made during preemployment interviews, when an employer uses them as incentives to get an employee to accept the job. In other words, in order to enforce a promise of job security, an employee must have reasonably relied on the promise and accepted his or her job in part because of the promise. In addition, the wording of the promise must be very specific. Vague

⚠ THERE'S ALWAYS AN EXCEPTION

A few states do not allow employers to revoke or revise enforceable handbook promises, unless the employers provide additional consideration (i.e., some type of compensation) to employees in exchange for the modification, or have clearly stated in their handbooks that the policies outlined therein are subject to change.

⚠ PROTECTING AGAINST IMPLIED CONTRACTS

Many employers attempt to avoid the oral creation of implied just-cause contracts (i.e., oral promises of job security) by stating on their application forms (or elsewhere) that if an employee is hired, he or she is employed at will and can be discharged at any time for any reason, and that no individual within the company is authorized to make any promises to the contrary. Employers can take other precautions to ensure that written handbooks or statements of policies and procedures do not create implied contracts. Such steps include:

- stating that the employment relationship is an at-will relationship;

- providing at-will disclaimer language clearly and conspicuously—i.e., not in a small font or in an inconspicuous part of the handbook;

- reserving the employer's right to unilaterally change, alter, rescind, or modify all handbook provisions without notice;

- specifically including language stating that the handbook does not constitute either an express or implied contract, but merely provides general information and information relating to policies and benefits;

- not stating that termination requires just cause;

- not guaranteeing *any* specific policies or practices; and

- asking employees to sign a form indicating their receipt of the handbook, and acknowledging that the employment relationship is at will, that the handbook does not create an implied or express contract concerning any terms or conditions of employment, and that the employer has reserved the right to freely alter, modify, or rescind any provision of the handbook at any time without notice.

promises of "permanent" employment or vague statements—
such as "the job is yours so long as you perform"—typically will
not be enforced. It is extremely helpful in such cases for an employee to have additional objective evidence (such as memoranda
or handbooks) to support his or her arguments that an oral
promise was made.

MITIGATION

As a legal term, **mitigation** refers to steps taken to lessen damage resulting from wrongful conduct. For example, a landlord
whose tenant skips town with six months left on his lease generally must make an effort to rent the now-vacant property to another tenant—in other words, the landlord must mitigate the
damages caused by the first tenant's wrongful vacating of the
lease. If the landlord does not take steps to limit the loss caused
by the tenant's departure, a judge might find that the tenant is
not liable for the full amount of unpaid rent.

In the context of labor law, "mitigation" refers to the fact that
employees who think they've been illegally fired must take active
steps to seek new employment. They are required to **mitigate**
the damages suffered as a result of their unlawful termination.

⚠ **YOU CAN'T SIT BACK AND RELAX**

Failing to look for a new job can affect the amount of damages awarded
by a court to a terminated employee. Employees claiming they have
been unlawfully terminated must use reasonable diligence to find equivalent employment with another employer. Employees are not required to
go into another line of work, accept demotions, or take demeaning jobs.
But if they do not look for—or if they refuse—jobs substantially equivalent to the ones they had, they may forfeit their right to back pay.

(i) LOSING YOUR JOB TO OFFSHORE COMPETITION

The **Trade Adjustment Assistance (TAA)** program provides for compensation and training benefits to employees who lose their jobs due to increased foreign imports. Employees who are found to be eligible for the TAA program can receive assistance in finding new work (including employment counseling, job search and referral programs, and career assessment), reimbursement for job search expenditures, relocation allowances, job training, and income support, as well as a tax credit for health insurance premiums.

A group of three or more employees, a union representing employees, or an employer may all file a petition with the U.S. Department of Labor's Division of Trade Adjustment Assistance for TAA benefits. For more information, access the DOL website at *www.dol.gov/dol/topic/training/tradeact.htm*, or call the Department of Labor at (202) 693–3560.

BEING LAID OFF

While the effect of a discharge and a layoff may be the same— i.e., an employee is out of work—the reasons behind discharges and layoffs are usually different. A **discharge** is usually the result of some conduct of the employee—for example, the employee's performance was not up to standard; the employee violated company work rules; or the employee's personality conflicted with those of others in the workplace. A **layoff**, however, usually stems from some issue relating to the operation of the business—for example, sales are down and the employer does not need as many workers; a merger has resulted in duplication among workers; or the company has reorganized so that certain types of jobs are no longer needed. There is usually less stigma attached to a layoff than to a discharge. Also, a laid-off employee may be called back to work if business improves; a discharged worker will not.

▶ **FAIRNESS COUNTS**

Employers can limit their exposure to liability for discharges if they treat employees fairly. Employers should:

- clearly communicate guidelines and policies to employees and supervisors;

- ask key questions—such as, "Is there supporting documentation of the problems with the employee?" and "Have proper procedural steps been followed?";

- investigate allegations against employees, and not act rashly;

- not make arbitrary decisions; and

- be evenhanded when making decisions—consistency counts.

No specific law governs how employees may be laid off or the means by which employers must select who will be laid off. If there is no collective-bargaining agreement establishing layoff procedures, an employer generally is free to determine when layoffs are necessary and who is to be laid off. Contrary to popular belief, an employer—absent the requirements of a collective-bargaining agreement—is not required to use seniority (i.e., the principle of "last hired, first laid off") to determine layoffs. Nor does the law require employers to pay severance to laid-off workers.

Of course, as with all areas of employment, an employer's freedom to discharge or lay off employees is restricted by anti-discrimination laws. Thus, an employer may not decide which employees to lay off based on the membership of those employees in one or more protected classes.

During layoffs, concerns about age discrimination often arise. Mass layoffs disproportionately reducing the number of older workers may indicate that age discrimination is taking place. An employer may not base a layoff decision on the assumption that older workers are not as productive as younger workers, or on

(i) **FAIR WARNING**

The **Worker Adjustment and Retraining Notification Act (WARN Act)** requires covered employers to give employees sixty days' advance notice of mass layoffs and plant closings. The WARN Act is a federal law that applies to private-sector employers with one hundred or more employees. Employers must provide notice to employees, their unions, and state and local government officials. A **mass layoff** is defined as a workforce reduction that results in the layoff of at least 33 percent of the workforce (and at least fifty employees) or at least five hundred employees.

Failure to give sixty days' notice may make an employer liable for back pay, and for any benefits due under an employee benefit plan, for each day that the notice was not given.

In addition, some states have enacted state equivalents to the WARN Act that might contain different threshold coverage and eligibility requirements in addition to varying notice requirements.

the belief that "young blood" is necessary for new ideas. However, decisions can be made based on the performance and evaluations of the specific employees involved.

To encourage employees to voluntarily quit rather than face layoffs, employers sometimes offer incentive packages. These packages usually provide for economic inducements that are not generally available to laid-off employees. They also often require employees to waive their right to sue the company for anything that happened while they were employed. Such **waivers** are enforceable, as long as they are knowing and voluntary, and can prevent an employee from suing the company for any violations of labor and employment laws. There is one exception to the general enforceability of knowing and voluntary waivers: courts will not enforce a waiver of any claims that arise under the Fair Labor Standards Act (discussed in chapter 5).

⚠️ SPECIAL RULES FOR THE AGE DISCRIMINATION IN EMPLOYMENT ACT

If an employee waiver entails the waiving of rights under the ADEA, a very specific list of requirements must be satisfied. Besides the general requirements for a voluntary waiver that are discussed above, the ADEA also requires that:

- the waiver specifically refer to the ADEA;
- the waiver not waive rights arising after the waiver is signed;
- the employee be advised in writing to consult an attorney;
- the employee be given at least twenty-one days to consider the waiver before being required to sign; and
- the waiver be revocable within seven days after it is signed.

If more than one person is affected by the waiver, additional requirements apply regarding the provision of detailed information, and the twenty-one day consideration period is extended to forty-five days.

Courts usually ask several questions to determine whether a waiver is **knowing and voluntary**:

1. Is the waiver written in a way that can be easily understood by the employee?

2. Did the employee receive a benefit in exchange for the waiver that he or she was not already entitled to receive?

3. Did the employee have a reasonable amount of time to consider the offer?

THE WORLD AT YOUR FINGERTIPS

- The Findlaw website provides links to information concerning employees' legal rights when fired. Visit *www.employment.findlaw.com*, and click on "Losing a Job: Your Rights."

• See the end of chapter 2 for information on how antidiscrimination laws affect termination of employment.

• The Workplace Fairness website discusses whistle-blowing and anti-retaliation laws at both the state and federal level. Visit *www.workplacefairness.org*, click on "Know the Law," and then click on "Whistleblowing."

• The Department of Labor website provides links to the law, regulations, and pamphlets explaining the WARN Act, at *www.dol.gov/dol/topic/termination/plantclosings.htm*.

REMEMBER THIS

• An employee cannot be fired because of his or her membership in a protected class.

• Employees cannot be fired for trying to enforce their rights under federal or state employment laws.

• Many states protect employees from discharge for "blowing the whistle" on unlawful employer conduct.

• Many states prohibit employers from firing employees for reasons that violate public policy.

• Written limitations set forth in employer handbooks regarding the employer's right to discipline and discharge employees may be enforceable as implied contracts.

• Federal law requires employers to give sixty days' notice of certain mass layoffs or plant closings.

• Employee waivers of the right to sue an employer for illegal conduct must be knowing and voluntary.

• Employees who have been illegally discharged or laid off must mitigate their damages.

CHAPTER 12

Ending the Employment Relationship Voluntarily

The Lowdown on Retiring and Quitting

Acme Industries has just been bought out by Theta Electronics. The employees at Acme are worried, because rumors are circulating about layoffs and employee buyouts. Fred, who works in the accounting department at Acme, knows that his is one of the departments that is normally targeted for elimination during takeovers. Fred is nearing retirement and worries he may be forced out. Should he start looking for another job, wait to see if he's offered a buyout, or put in for early retirement?

This chapter examines how the law affects employees and employers when an employee is retiring from or quitting a job. It also discusses some issues that arise regardless of whether employment ends voluntarily or involuntarily.

RETIRING

The Requirements of the Age Discrimination in Employment Act

The Age Discrimination in Employment Act (ADEA) has outlawed mandatory retirement. This means that employees cannot be forced to retire at any age. There are, naturally, exceptions to this rule. Police and firefighters who are employed by either state or local governments can be forced to retire if:

- there is a state or local law in effect as of March 3, 1983, that establishes a mandatory retirement age or, if there is no law, if the employee is fifty-five years old; and
- retirement is pursuant to a bona fide retirement plan.

Another exception applies to individuals employed as bona fide executives or high-level policy-making employees for at least two years before their forced retirements. These executives can be forced to retire at the age of sixty-five (or later) if they are eligible to receive an immediate, nonforfeitable annual retirement benefit of at least $44,000. Small employers not covered by the ADEA are usually covered by state age discrimination laws prohibiting mandatory retirement.

Employers may, however, offer voluntary retirement packages to employees, as long as acceptance by the employees is truly voluntary. Employers usually make such offers as a way to downsize the workforce and avoid involuntary layoffs. The ADEA specifically allows an employer to offer such packages to classes of employees based on age. (Thus, the fact that a voluntary retirement package is offered only to employees who are fifty-five years of age and older is not illegal discrimination against individuals who are, say, fifty-two years old.) When the voluntary retirement package includes a waiver of the right to sue under the ADEA, the waiver must be knowing and voluntary and meet the requirements discussed in the sidebar on page 174.

Postretirement Income

When employees retire, they face the responsibility of ensuring an adequate source of continuing income. Two major work-related systems provide such postretirement income: pensions and Social Security. Many employees who work for private companies are covered by a pension plan, although the trend in recent years has been away from such plans and toward 401(k) plans. Additionally, more than 95 percent of American employees are eligible for Social Security retirement benefits.

Pensions
If your employer provided pension benefits during your employment (see the "Pensions" section of chapter 6 for a discussion of the rules governing employer pension plans), you will need to

file a claim in order to start receiving those benefits. The requirements that must be met in order to file a claim for pension benefits varies depending on the specific terms of the plan. Generally, if you are vested, you are eligible for payments from your fund when you reach the age of sixty-five (or the normal retirement age specified in the plan). Most pension plans require you to file a written claim for payments to begin. Within ninety days, the plan administrators must either begin payment to you or notify you in writing that the claim has been denied.

If a claim is denied, you are entitled to request a review of the decision. If, upon review, the claim is still denied, you can appeal that decision. Some plans provide for **arbitration** as the means of appeal. In arbitration, a dispute is heard and resolved by a private individual or panel; it's an alternative to the formal court system. When arbitration is required, you must use that mechanism. Eventually you can challenge the denial of a claim in court by filing a lawsuit under the Employee Retirement Income Security Act (ERISA).

Social Security

Not every employee has a private pension plan, but almost all employees are entitled to Social Security benefits. If you enjoy private pension benefits, you will receive Social Security benefits in addition to your pension benefits, though in some private pension plans your benefits will be reduced to take into account what you are receiving from Social Security. Almost every employee who has received credit for ten years of work is fully insured for retirement purposes under the Social Security laws. (Exceptions exist for some government employees and railroad employees.)

Unlike with a private pension plan, where you will lose any accrued benefits that have not vested if you change employers or have a break in service, receipt of benefits under the Social Security system is not dependent on an employee's relationship with any specific employer or on a certain number of consecutive years of service. Thus, for purposes of the ten-year work requirement, the Social Security system credits you for all qualified

CREDIT WHERE CREDIT IS DUE

To be eligible for Social Security, it's not enough just to work; you have to earn a minimum amount in order to get credit for benefits. The amount of earnings it takes to earn a credit changes each year. The maximum amount of credits you can earn per year is four. In 2005, you could earn one credit for each $920 in total wages. Once you earn four credits, the Social Security system will credit you with one year of work.

work that you perform, regardless of the number of employers for which you've worked. In addition, for purposes of the ten-year requirement, the years you work need not be consecutive. Thus, if you work for one year, are out of the workforce for two years, and then resume working, your initial one year of work will count toward the ten-year requirement.

Under the law, employees can receive full Social Security retirement benefits at the **normal retirement age**. The normal retirement age is determined using a graduated scale based on your year of birth. If you were born on or before 1937, normal retirement age is sixty-five; if you were born between 1943 and 1954, the normal retirement age is sixty-six; and for individuals born on or after 1960, the normal retirement age is sixty-seven.

LIMITS ON DOUBLE-DIPPING

What if you want to work and receive benefits at the same time? If you retire before reaching your normal retirement age, your Social Security payments will be reduced based on the amount that you earn. Once you reach the normal retirement age, however, there will be no such reduction.

You can opt to receive partial benefits at age sixty-two, regardless of your year of birth. Conversely, if you delay retirement beyond the normal retirement age, your benefits will be higher when you finally do retire. The amount of money that you'll receive upon retirement depends on how much money you earned over your lifetime, and your age at retirement.

To receive Social Security retirement benefits, you must file a written application with the Social Security Administration. You should file two or three months before your retirement date. Your first check should arrive soon after you quit working.

 ## DO SOME CHECKING BEFORE YOU RETIRE

To plan for your retirement, you'll want to know the benefits to which you'll be entitled when you retire at a given age. Many employers routinely provide such information regarding their pension plans.

To get this information regarding your Social Security benefit, pick up a Personal Earnings and Benefit Estimate Statement form at your local Social Security Administration office at any time (even years before) your retirement, or call toll-free at 1–800–772–1213.

The Personal Earnings and Benefit Estimate Statement form not only estimates your benefits, but also tells you how much you've paid in to the Social Security system, and verifies that your employers have been depositing into the system both your and their share of Social Security taxes. If your wages have been wrongly reported, you have three years from the date on which the wages were earned to correct the mistake. However, there is no time limit on correcting an error caused by an employer's failure to report your earnings. To correct such an error, you'll need proof—such as a pay stub, a written statement from the employer, or Form OAR-7008 (Request for Correction of Earnings Record).

You can also get more information on the Social Security system, calculate your benefits, or apply for benefits online at *www.ssa.gov*.

QUITTING

In the absence of a written contract limiting an employee's right to quit, the employee is free to quit at any time and for any reason. However, if there is a written contract, there may be notice and other requirements governing the right to quit.

Employees are not required by law to give any type of notice prior to quitting. It is usually a good idea to do so, however, as a matter of common employment courtesy.

Regardless of whether employment ends voluntarily or involuntarily, several issues commonly arise: payment of wages owed; references for future employment; covenants not to compete; and eligibility for unemployment compensation.

Getting What You're Owed

While no federal law regulates this subject, almost every state has passed a law that sets a deadline for paying accrued wages when employees leave a job. These laws are usually referred to as **wage payment statutes**. About half the states require that unpaid wages must be paid no later than the next regular pay period after an employee departs a job. In other states, payment must be made within a specific time period beginning on the date of separation—for example, within three days of termination. The time period specified in these laws varies in length from zero (i.e., employees must be paid immediately) to fifteen days.

▶ ## WAGES ARE MORE THAN HOURLY PAY

Wage payment laws take a broad view of wages. Most of them define as **wages** not only unpaid wages, but also unused accrued vacation pay and severance pay (when the employer's policy provides for severance pay as a benefit of employment).

References

Generally, employers are not legally required to provide references for employees. There are a few exceptions. For example, Indiana, Kansas, and Missouri have **service letter acts**. These acts require that, upon the request of a terminated employee, an employer must provide a letter that states the nature of the employee's former job, the length of his or her employment, and the reason for his or her separation.

Employers providing references should be aware of certain legal implications. Most states have blacklisting statutes. **Blacklisting** is the act of intentionally trying to prevent someone from obtaining employment. Violations of blacklisting statutes may result in fines or jail time. However, making truthful statements about someone's ability to perform the job in question is not considered blacklisting.

The anti-retaliation clause in Title VII prohibits giving a bad reference to a former employee because that person has filed a charge under Title VII.

The way a reference is made and its content also may give rise to employer liability under state **tort law**. Employees may be able to recover damages for defamation, intentional interference with a prospective employment contract, intentional infliction of emotional distress, or negligent misrepresentation.

Defamation occurs when one person's false statement injures the reputation of another person. Providing false information to a prospective employer with the intent of causing an applicant to lose his or her job constitutes **intentional interference** with a prospective employment contract. False statements that cause a loss of money (i.e., a wage-paying job) can be grounds for **negligent misrepresentation**. Each of these tort actions assumes that an employer's statement is false; making truthful statements concerning a former employee usually does not subject the employer to liability for defamation, interference with contract, or misrepresentation.

Disclosing even true information, however, may result in tort liability for **intentional infliction of emotional distress**. If

( ) TALKING TO A LAWYER

Q. I own a small business. I received a call today from another employer who asked for a reference for one of my current employees. This employee has been trouble since day one, and I'd love to get rid of him. So I told the caller that the employee was a terrific employee, very reliable, and that we'd hate to see him go. Now I'm feeling a little guilty that I misled the prospective employer and lied about my opinions of the employee. Can I get in trouble for this?

A. Yes. Providing a false recommendation can give rise to legal liability. Providing a negative reference may lead to claims by the former employee. Hence, providing a neutral reference or no reference at all is the better course of action.

—Answer by members of the ABA Section
of Labor and Employment Law

the information is private and personal, the employee may have a reasonable expectation that it will be kept private. If the information is unrelated to work, disclosing it may make the employer liable.

Because of the potential pitfalls involved, many employers refuse to provide any type of reference. Others provide only basic information, such as verification of the former employee's dates of employment, rate of pay, and job duties performed. Employers that do provide references can limit their exposure to liability by:

- limiting the number of individuals authorized to provide references;
- seeking the former employee's permission prior to providing a reference;
- avoiding statements based on hearsay or gossip; and
- discussing only issues that have a direct bearing on an individual's work.

(i) DEFENDING YOURSELF

Most states recognize a **qualified privilege defense** to charges of defamation, even if the information provided by an employer turns out to be false. This means that, if the employer was providing a reference in good faith to someone with a legitimate reason to ask for it, the employer will not be liable—even for a false statement. However, the employer will lose the qualified privilege if:

- it was motivated primarily by ill will in making the statement;

- it provided the information to individuals who did not have a legitimate reason to receive it; or

- the statement was made without grounds for believing it was true.

Covenants Not to Compete

Covenants not to compete are written contracts restricting an employee's ability to compete against his or her former employer for a certain period of time and in a certain geographic area. For example, this kind of contract might provide that a financial advisor will not provide financial services to customers within a twenty-five-mile radius of the employer's place of business for twelve months after leaving the company. These agreements are designed to prevent employees from unfairly competing with their former employers.

Covenants not to compete are enforceable only if the employer has a substantial right, unique to its business, that it is trying to protect. Thus, a covenant between a retail store and an in-store salesperson based on that employee's access to customers likely would not be enforced, because the customer list would not be a unique or substantial interest of the employer. However, a covenant between a securities firm and one of its salespersons may be enforced, because the securities salesperson may have received specialized training in the securities field, and may have had access to confidential customer lists and cus-

SUBSTANTIAL AND UNIQUE BUSINESS INTERESTS

The types of interests that courts have recognized as protected by covenants not to compete are:

- specialized knowledge unique to an employer, and obtained by an employee while working for that employer (e.g., trade secrets);

- access to customer lists that are not otherwise easily accessible; or

- specialized skills acquired while working for the employer.

tomer trading histories. The time and effort expended by the firm in acquiring and maintaining its customer base may be a protectable employer interest.

Even a covenant seeking to protect a unique and substantial business right must be reasonable in terms of geographic area and time limits. Reasonableness depends on the specific facts of each case. Time limits of one year are generally deemed reasonable by courts, but time limits of more than three years may not be deemed reasonable. In addition, geographic limitations

⚠ TIMING IS IMPORTANT

While most covenants not to compete are entered into when employees are hired, sometimes an employer may require employees to sign such a covenant as a condition of continued employment. Some states will only enforce covenants that are executed when an employee was hired. Other states will enforce a covenant executed as a condition of continued employment, as long as the employee actually works for a reasonable period of time after signing the covenant. Some states require independent **consideration** (i.e., something offered in return, such as improvements in salary and status) in addition to continued employment.

generally should apply only to the area in which an employee worked.

In assessing the validity of covenants not to compete, courts attempt to balance the restrictions necessary to protect an employer's unique and substantial business interests with the individual's need to earn a livelihood. Courts can enforce valid covenants either by issuing an **injunction** (a kind of court order) preventing the former employee from working in violation of the covenant, or by awarding money to the former employer for losses resulting from the unfair competition.

UNEMPLOYMENT COMPENSATION

States administer the unemployment insurance system to provide employees and their families with weekly income during periods of unemployment. When workers are unemployed due to plant closure, layoff, natural disaster, or other acts or circumstances that are not their fault, they may be entitled to receive **unemployment compensation**. The system is funded by state and federal taxes paid by employers.

Most employees are covered by the insurance system, but there are some exceptions. Generally excluded are: self-employed individuals, independent contractors, casual employees, and agricultural employees. To receive unemployment compensation, an eligible employee must meet certain requirements. These requirements vary among the states, but most states have four basic criteria:

1. the applicant must have earned a minimum amount of wages within a specified period and/or worked for a minimum period in the recent past (for example, at least twenty weeks of work at an average weekly wage of at least $20);

2. the applicant must register for work with the state unemployment office;

3. the applicant must be available for work; and

4. the applicant must be actively seeking employment.

Once employees meet the eligibility requirements, they may still be denied unemployment compensation benefits because of a **disqualifying event**. As a general rule, employees are disqualified if they voluntarily quit without good cause or if they have been fired for misconduct. In some states, the disqualification lasts only for a specified length of time, after which an employee can receive unemployment compensation.

Since one of the eligibility requirements for unemployment compensation is that the applicant actively be seeking work, an applicant who refuses a suitable job offer may become ineligible for benefits. In these situations, eligibility depends on why the employee refused the job. If the job did not involve suitable work, the refusal is acceptable. For purposes of retaining eligi-

GOOD CAUSE

Workers are ineligible for unemployment compensation if they voluntarily quit without "good cause." The meaning of "good cause" varies greatly among the states. Some states consider certain types of personal reasons to be good cause for quitting—for example, having to care for a sick relative, or following a spouse who has found work in another state. Most states, however, require that good cause arise from an employer's actions. For example, working conditions so bad that they would cause a reasonable person to quit would be considered good cause in some states. The **reasonable person** standard often is very important in determining good cause. It is not enough that a situation is intolerable to a specific employee; the conditions must be such that a reasonable person, in the same position as that employee, would feel compelled to quit.

Employees are also ineligible for unemployment compensation if they were fired for misconduct. The meaning of "misconduct" also varies by state, but generally incompetence alone is not considered misconduct. Violating known company rules and insubordination are examples of misconduct.

bility for unemployment compensation, a job is considered not suitable if an individual lacks the experience needed to perform it, if it is more hazardous than the employee's previous job, or if the physical condition of the employee prevents him or her from accepting it. States may also consider travel costs and time, bad working hours, community wage levels, and compelling personal problems in deciding if a job may be rejected. Finally, individuals usually cannot lose benefits for refusing a job offer that is made because the current workforce is on strike.

If wages and conditions of a new job are inferior to those of an employee's former job, he or she may not have to accept that job to remain eligible for unemployment benefits. For example, a skilled craftsperson is permitted to refuse a job as a janitor. After a certain period of time, however, most states require employees to "lower their sights" and accept lesser jobs.

To receive unemployment compensation, you must file a claim for benefits at your local state unemployment office. File as soon as possible after unemployment begins, since you won't

(i) STRIKES AND BENEFITS

Employees who are on strike and therefore out of work may be entitled to unemployment compensation, depending on state law. A few states allow employees to collect unemployment compensation if the strike is caused by an employer's violation of the National Labor Relations Act (NLRA) or an employer's breach of the collective-bargaining agreement. Some states also allow employees to receive benefits if the employer has "locked out" the employees.

Most states, however, do not permit striking employees to collect unemployment compensation benefits. The period of disqualification varies by state. In some states the disqualification lasts for the entire strike; in other states the disqualification lasts for a fixed period of time. If a striker is permanently replaced, however, the employee may then be eligible for benefits.

get benefits until all the paperwork is processed and eligibility for benefits is verified. Bring the following documents with you to the unemployment office to help verify your eligibility: your Social Security card, recent pay stubs, and any documents indicating the reason for your job loss.

After filing an initial claim, you usually must report regularly to the unemployment office to verify your continued eligibility for benefits. You can lose benefits if you do not report.

The amount of unemployment compensation benefits that an individual receives varies by state. The general formula provides that an employee receives 50 percent of his or her weekly wage, not to exceed a statutory cap on the amount paid. The cap is based on a percentage of the state's average weekly wages for all employees. Because of the cap on maximum benefits, most employees receive much less than 50 percent of their weekly wage.

Usually unemployment compensation benefits last for up to twenty-six weeks. In times of extended high unemployment, however, benefits may be paid for an additional thirteen weeks, and sometimes longer.

Employees moving to another state to look for work can still collect unemployment compensation, because all states belong to the **Interstate Reciprocal Benefit Payment Plan**. This plan allows employees to register for work and file for unemployment compensation in a new state. The law of the original state, however, determines eligibility for benefits. The employee must satisfy

 NO DOUBLE-DIPPING

If unemployed workers receive other benefits or income, those amounts are usually deducted from their unemployment compensation benefits. Some states ignore small amounts of money received, but most states will reduce or stop unemployment compensation benefits for weeks in which an unemployed worker receives disability benefits, severance pay, or other types of income.

TALKING TO A LAWYER

Q. *I fired an employee because he sexually harassed a coworker. I just received notice that he filed for unemployment compensation benefits. Can I take steps to stop him from collecting?*

A. Yes. If the employee sexually harassed a coworker in violation of company policy, this could be deemed employee misconduct under your state's unemployment compensation laws, and therefore could result in a denial of unemployment compensation benefits.

—Answer by members of the ABA Section
of Labor and Employment Law

A. You should respond to the notice you received by explaining to the state unemployment compensation agency the reason for the employee's discharge.

—Answer by Barbara Fick, Associate Professor of Law,
Notre Dame Law School

that state's requirements to receive unemployment compensation in the new state.

THE WORLD AT YOUR FINGERTIPS

• The Workplace Fairness website answers questions about covenants not to compete, at *www.workplacefairness.org/index.php?page=noncompete*.
• The same site also provides a brief introduction to unemployment compensation benefits, at *www.workplacefairness.org/index.php?page=insurance*.
• The Social Security Administration website, at *www.ssa.gov*, provides comprehensive information on the operation of the Social Security system.

REMEMBER THIS

- Employees need to file a written claim to receive their pension benefits.
- Employees are eligible for partial Social Security benefits at age sixty-two. Eligibility for full benefits begins no later than sixty-seven, depending on date of birth.
- In most states an employer must pay all unpaid accrued wages, including accrued vacation pay, within a relatively short period of time after employment terminates.
- Employers should be careful when providing references for employees. Information should be provided only to individuals with a legitimate need to know, and should be limited to work-related issues and statements that the employer reasonably believes to be true.
- A narrowly tailored covenant not to compete based on an employer's unique business interests will usually be enforced.
- Employees whose employment is terminated for reasons other than misconduct, or who quit for good cause, may be able to collect unemployment compensation benefits.

CHAPTER 13

Unions in the Workplace

The Rights of Both Employees and Employers

The employees at City Transportation are represented by the Teamsters Union. The union is in negotiation with the company for a collective-bargaining agreement. The union and employees are unhappy with the company's proposed wage increase, and are talking about going on strike.

The employees at Dave's Trucking Company are not represented by a union. They haven't had a wage increase for several years. Every time employees have asked Dave for a raise, he's refused even to discuss it. Now they think that if they picket Dave's terminal, they may be able to get him to give them a raise.

Should these employees go on strike or picket their employers? If they do, what actions can the employers take to deal with the situation? The answers to these questions can be found in the National Labor Relations Act.

In 2004, unions represented only 7.9 percent of the private-sector workforce, down from about 35 percent in the 1940s and 1950s. This has led some commentators to announce the death of organized labor and the irrelevance of the National Labor Relations Act (NLRA), a federal law that governs the labor-management relationship. But they may be wrong on both counts.

A fraction less than 8 percent of the workforce still constitutes more than 12 million people, a sizeable number of workers. And in recent years, labor unions have been engaging in self-examination to analyze their weaknesses and build on their strengths, hoping to revitalize their organizing energies. Furthermore, even if employees are not represented by a union, the NLRA can still affect their rights at work.

The NLRA grants employees the right to engage or not engage in "concerted activity" (which includes union activity) free from employer and union interference, restraint, and co-ercion. It also prohibits certain union activity such as secondary boycotts. (See the "Secondary Boycotts Outlawed" sidebar later in this chapter for an explanation of secondary boycotts.) It establishes procedures for determining when employees have chosen a union to represent them, and it regulates the relationship between unions and management in dealing with workplace issues. The NLRA is premised on the assumption that individual employees have very little leverage in bargaining with their employers over wages, terms of employment, and workplace problems. In practice, employers generally determine these issues unilaterally, without much discussion with workers. However, when workers pool their individual bargaining power and deal with their employer as a group, usually with a union acting as their representative, they can more effectively influence workplace conditions and resolve workplace problems.

If employers are covered under federal law, the NLRA generally preempts state regulation of their union-management relations. Most states have passed laws closely modeled on the NLRA to regulate private-sector employers exempt from federal law. Therefore, the discussion that follows will take into account some state law in addition to the NLRA.

EMPLOYER COVERAGE

Whether the NLRA applies to employers depends on their gross dollar volume of business. Retail and manufacturing are two major industries in which employees are often subject to coverage. Retail stores are covered if they gross $500,000 in annual sales. Manufacturers are covered if they annually ship or receive at least $50,000 worth of goods across state lines. The law also sets various dollar standards for other types of businesses.

EMPLOYEES AND THE NLRA

The assumption that the NLRA only applies to workplaces with unions is an unfortunate but common misperception of both employees and employers. On the contrary, the NLRA protects employees engaged in protected, concerted activity, whether they act with or without the assistance of a union. Nonunion employers act at their peril in ignoring the impact of this law on their companies.

The NLRA gives employees the right to:
- form and join unions;
- support and assist unions;
- choose a union to represent them for purposes of collective bargaining with their employer; and
- engage in group conduct that has as its purpose collective bargaining or helping each other regarding workplace issues.

The law also gives employees the right to choose *not* to engage in these activities. Having given employees these rights, the law then protects employees in exercising them. It prohibits both employers and unions from interfering with employees who are trying to exercise these rights.

The rights granted under the NLRA are not absolute. The rights are only given to employees who work for an employer covered by the NLRA. The NLRA regulates only private-sector employers engaged in interstate commerce, and excludes railroads and airlines. Moreover, even if you are a covered employee, you can lose the protection of the NLRA if you try to exercise your rights for an unlawful purpose, or in a way that unnecessarily interferes with a legitimate employer interest.

An exhaustive catalogue of employee activities protected by the NLRA is beyond the scope of this book, but the next few pages discuss the most common forms of protected activity.

The right to form and join unions includes the right to talk with union organizers and supporters, socialize with union organizers, attend union meetings, and become a member of a

⚠ NON-COVERED INDIVIDUALS

Certain categories of employees are not considered to be "employees" under the NLRA and, therefore, are not entitled to the Act's protections. Excluded individuals include domestic employees, farm workers, independent contractors, supervisors, and managers. A **supervisor** is someone with authority to hire, fire, discipline, promote, or address the grievances of other employees, or to effectively recommend to the company that such action be taken. A **manager** is a high-level employee who uses independent judgment in making and carrying out company policies.

union. Forming a union often involves engaging in organizing activity. Organizing activity may include discussing the benefits and disadvantages of unionization with other employees, soliciting employee signatures on **union authorization cards** (cards that authorize a union to act as the exclusive bargaining representative for employees), distributing union literature, serving on a union-organizing committee, or wearing union insignia.

Support and assistance to a union can take many forms, including circulating or signing a petition in support of a union, engaging in a work stoppage in support of a union position, picketing and distributing handbills, contributing money, or speaking to other employees advocating the union's position.

Employees have the right to decide whether they want a union to represent them, to change their representative from one union to another, or to change the composition of union leadership in accordance with the union's constitution and bylaws. The decision whether or not to be represented by a union belongs to the employees. Traditionally, the employer and union can campaign for the support and votes of the employees, but the employees ultimately choose whether they will be represented. More and more frequently, however, unions organize employees through employer neutrality agreements. Pursuant to such agreements, employers agree not to campaign against unions and to take a neutral (and often silent) position when it comes to the issue of union representation.

Employees have the right to strike (in the absence of a no-strike clause in a collective-bargaining agreement), to picket, to distribute handbills in support of a union's bargaining demands, and to advocate in a variety of ways their support for the union's bargaining position.

The NLRA also guarantees employees the right to refrain from engaging in any such activities. Employees who do not wish to participate in union activity, distribute handbills, or strike, or who don't want to participate in group conduct, can't be required to do so.

As mentioned earlier in this chapter, the rights granted by

CONCERTED ACTIVITY: ACTING TOGETHER WITHOUT A UNION

The right of workers to engage in **concerted activity**—that is, group conduct aimed at helping each other with respect to workplace issues—does not apply only in the presence of a union. Rather, employees have the right to engage in concerted activities even in the absence of a union. Employee activity in the absence of a union is considered protected concerted activity under the NLRA if it involves issues relating to workplace concerns and if there is group conduct. For purposes of the statute, activity relates to workplace concerns when its purpose is to improve wages, benefits, or other terms and conditions of employment. Obviously group conduct takes place when two or more employees act together, but even action by an individual employee can sometimes constitute group action if that person is speaking on behalf of fellow employees. For example, a single employee asking his employer to provide him with health insurance coverage is not engaged in protected concerted activity. However, if the employee is acting as the spokesperson for other employees, or if the employees as a group ask the employer for health insurance coverage, then the protections of the NLRA would apply.

the NLRA are not absolute. If the purpose or method of employees' activity is illegal, or if the method of such activity unduly interferes with a legitimate employer interest, the activity will not be protected. Suppose a group of male employees complains to their employer because it promoted a woman to a supervisory position. The male employees don't like working for a woman, and ask the employer to demote her. This activity is not protected under the NLRA, because the male employees are try-

( ) TALKING TO A LAWYER

Q. The workers at my warehouse are refusing to work. It's been extremely hot and humid this summer, and then the air conditioning at my plant broke down. I've got repair guys working on it, but it's not fixed yet. I'll admit it's really miserable in the warehouse—it must be 110 degrees—but I've got product that needs to be shipped or I'll be in breach of my contracts with my customers. Now my warehouse guys are sitting outside in the shade, drinking cold sodas, and have told me they're not coming back to work until the air conditioner is fixed. I told them if they don't get back to work I'd fire them all. I think we're at a standstill. What can I do?

A. Absent a prohibition in their collective-bargaining agreement, employees are permitted to withhold their services to protest their working conditions. Striking employees cannot be fired, but the employer can choose to replace striking employees to meet the company's business needs.

—Answer by members of the ABA Section
of Labor and Employment Law

A. Concerted activities are protected under the NLRA even when employees are not represented by a union. Poor working conditions are a legitimate basis for a strike.

—Answer by Theodore St. Antoine, Degan Professor
Emeritus of Law, University of Michigan Law School

ing to persuade the employer to discriminate based on sex—a violation of Title VII.

Even if their objective is lawful, the way that employees conduct themselves may remove them from the protection of the law. For example, suppose employees go on strike to get their employer to grant a wage increase, but in connection with the strike they vandalize the employer's property. Although the object of the strike (a wage increase) is lawful, the employees' activity in connection with the strike (vandalism) is unprotected, because it is unlawful and interferes with a legitimate employer property interest.

EMPLOYERS AND THE NLRA

When employees exercise rights protected under the NLRA, the employer can't interfere with the exercise of those rights. Employers also can't discriminate against employees with respect to hiring, firing, and terms and conditions of employment because the employees have engaged in such conduct.

Employers might try to interfere with their employees' rights through both words and actions. The NLRA prohibits employers from threatening employees with adverse employment consequences because they have exercised, or may exercise, their rights. It's against the law for employers to threaten employees with loss of their jobs or benefits, to threaten discipline or reduction of hours, or to threaten plant shutdown if employees join or support a union or otherwise engage in concerted activity.

Employers also can't bribe employees with promises. Thus, an employer promising employees a pay increase in return for voting against the union has violated the law. Questioning employees about their union sympathies or activities, or other types of protected activities, is also prohibited. In addition, spying on employees as they engage in protected activity constitutes unlawful interference.

Employer rules that unnecessarily interfere with the ability of employees to exercise their rights in the workplace also violate

( ) TALKING TO A LAWYER

Q. *For the past several months, the employees at my company have been hassling me for a raise. I told them that finances were tight, but if things improved I would be able to do something for them. Now they're starting to talk about bringing in a union, and I saw some of the employees distributing union literature. I'd like to nip this in the bud. My revenue stream has improved recently, so I can afford to give them some kind of raise. May I?*

A. Legally, you may not grant the raise unless this is the usual period of time during which your company grants pay increases. Otherwise the NLRB will infer that your motive was to deter union organization, and that is illegal.

——Answer by Theodore St. Antoine, Degan Professor Emeritus of Law, University of Michigan Law School

the law. Employees have the right to discuss union or workplace issues (**solicitation**), and to hand out leaflets or other printed material (**distribution**). Employers, on the other hand, have a legitimate interest in ensuring productivity and safety in the workplace. To accommodate these competing interests, certain types of rules are allowed; others are prohibited.

Employers may make and uniformly enforce rules that prohibit solicitation during working time. **Working time** is the time employees are being paid to work; it does not include all time spent at the workplace. Thus, an employer may not prevent employees from discussing union issues during paid or unpaid break times and meal times, or before or after work. A further exception exists for retail businesses and hospitals. In those work environments, an employer may prohibit solicitation not only during working time, but also on the selling floor and in immediate patient care areas.

Distribution of literature may be prohibited not only during

⚠ KEEPING OUT TRESPASSERS

The NLRA's rules about solicitation and distribution at work apply only to employees. Thus, the employer generally can close its property to non-employees, even if their purpose is to solicit employees on behalf of a union. Such a trespass rule must, of course, be uniformly enforced against all outside solicitors.

If a union has no other reasonable means of reaching employees—say, at a remote lumber camp or on an oil rig—then employers may have to allow nonemployee organizers onto their property.

working time, but also in work areas. Work areas do not, however, include such areas as employee cafeterias, locker rooms, and parking lots.

Of course, even lawful rules must be uniformly enforced. Thus, if an employer forbids only union discussion during working time, yet permits other types of discussion and solicitation during working time—for example, allows employees to sell Girl

ⓘ SHOWING YOUR COLORS AT WORK

Employees sometimes wear union T-shirts, buttons, or other insignia to show their support for a union. This conduct generally is protected conduct under the law; having a dress code or requiring uniforms isn't enough to justify a ban on union insignia. In certain situations, however, an employer may be able to justify a restriction based on a legitimate business interest. For example, restrictions may be justified to prevent alienation of customers (where employees come in contact with customers) or to prevent adverse effects on patients in health-care institutions. While a total ban may not be justified, employers in such circumstances may be permitted to ban all but "tasteful and inconspicuous" insignia.

Scout cookies or solicit contributions for and talk about other causes—then the employer will likely have violated the law.

The NLRA also prohibits an employer from taking **adverse employment actions** against employees because they have participated in conduct protected by the law. This means that employers can't fire, demote, lay off, or refuse to hire employees, or deny them a raise, because they have supported a union or engaged in other protected, concerted activity. Just as an employer cannot threaten to fire employees because they have joined a union, the employer cannot carry out such a threat and actually fire someone for that reason.

The fact that an employee has engaged in protected conduct does not, however, insulate him or her from discipline or discharge for other reasons. Employees who support a union may

▶ **LOOKING FOR MOTIVE**

How do you determine whether an employer took action against an employee because of protected activity? The National Labor Relations Board (NLRB) and the courts typically ask the following questions:

- Did the employer know that the employee engaged in the protected activity?

- Has the employer made any statements indicating hostility about the rights granted to employees under the NLRA?

- Has the employee been treated differently, without any satisfactory explanation for the difference in treatment?

- Was the employer's adverse action close in time to the employee's protected activity?

- Was the employer's action disproportionate to the offense that the employee is alleged to have committed?

- Has the employer given conflicting reasons for its actions?

lawfully be disciplined for tardiness, absenteeism, poor performance, or insubordination, provided that employees who do not support a union are similarly disciplined. As with antidiscrimination laws, the key is to treat similarly situated employees the same. If employees who exercise their rights under the NLRA are singled out for different treatment based on their protected activities, the employer has violated the law.

UNIONS AND THE NLRA

The NLRA also prohibits union conduct that coerces employees regarding the exercise of their rights. Like management, unions are prohibited from bribing employees. Some examples of unlawful conduct by unions include:

- threats of violence, as well as physical violence directed at employees;
- acts of vandalism directed at an employer's property when enacted in the presence of employees; or
- mass picketing that interferes with access to an employer's premises.

Election Procedures

A union-organizing campaign can start either because employees have contacted a union or because the union, on its own, seeks to organize the employees.

Organizing campaigns sometimes begin when union organizers discuss with employees what they perceive to be the benefits and advantages of union representation. The goal is to determine whether the employees have any interest in the union representing them in their dealings with their employer. Employees may be invited to attend union meetings and may receive leaflets containing information about the union. At some point, union authorization cards are circulated. The cards authorize the union to act as the employees' exclusive bargaining

⟨ ⟩ TALKING TO A LAWYER

Q. I work for a company that has facilities in several separate locations. Employees at my plant are represented by a union, but the other locations are not organized. I wanted to speak with the employees at the other locations to talk about the advantages of union representation, but my employer told me that I could not enter the facilities. Can the employer keep me out and prevent me from talking to my fellow workers?

A. Employees are entitled to access the parking lots and other exterior nonworking areas of their employer's separate facilities in order to exercise their rights under the NLRA. However, they can be prevented from entering the interiors of plants or any exterior areas that are working areas.

> —Answer by Theodore St. Antoine, Degan Professor
> Emeritus of Law, University of Michigan Law School

representative. If at least 30 percent of the employees in an appropriate unit sign a card (see the "Representation" section below for a discussion of bargaining units), the union can petition the **National Labor Relations Board (NLRB)** for a secret-ballot election so employees can vote on whether to be represented by the union.

It also is possible (and increasingly more common) for a union to be recognized by an employer without a secret-ballot election. An employer can agree to a card check, in which the union presents the employees' signed authorization cards to a neutral third party. If a majority of employees in the unit have signed cards, the employer agrees to recognize the union as the employees' exclusive bargaining representative. Often, however, employers still insist on an election.

Under the NLRB's traditional processes, an employer has the opportunity to talk to its employees about the disadvantages

of union representation. It has the right to express its views and
opinions about unionization, and to present arguments and information in an attempt to persuade the employees against voting for the union. But an employer cannot threaten or coerce
its employees or promise them benefits; any such threats or
promises violate the law.

When an election is held, it is conducted by secret ballot;
employees are given the opportunity to vote for or against union
representation. The election is generally held at the employer's
place of business so that all eligible employees have the opportunity to cast a ballot. The election is conducted by the NLRB to

(i) GETTING RID OF THE UNION

An election procedure, called a **decertification election**, also exists for
voting out a union that currently represents a group of employees. The
decertification process can only be implemented at certain times and can
only be initiated by employees; if any managerial or supervisory personnel are involved in supporting or assisting the decertification, it is not
valid. As mentioned previously, the decision whether to be represented
by a union is to be made by employees only; any employer instigation or
encouragement of the decertification process is prohibited interference
with employee rights.

Employees generally initiate the decertification process by circulating a
petition, and by asking employees to sign their names if they are inter-
ested in voting out the union. If at least 30 percent of the employees sign
such a petition, it can then be filed with the NLRB. If the timing of the petition is not otherwise limited by the NLRB's rules, the NLRB will schedule a secret-ballot election among employees, who will then have the
opportunity to vote on whether or not to retain the union as their representative. As a practical matter, the number of employee groups that
successfully decertify their unions is relatively low.

ensure that it is fair, and employees can freely decide whether they want the union to represent them. A majority of the valid votes cast in the election decides the outcome.

If the union wins the election, it becomes the bargaining agent for the employees, and the union and the employer generally begin negotiations for a collective-bargaining agreement.

Representation

When a union wins an election, it doesn't necessarily represent every worker employed by a company. Rather, a union election is held only among those employees who are considered to have a "community of interest" at a given workplace. These employees form a **bargaining unit**—that is, a group of workers represented by the union.

Employees have a community of interest when they share similar working conditions, jobs, hours of work, and supervision. For example, employees who work on an assembly line

---

(i) REPRESENTING EVERYBODY IN THE UNIT

Once selected, a union is the exclusive bargaining agent for all the employees in a bargaining unit. In effect, the union represents all the bargaining-unit employees on all workplace issues. This means that, instead of each individual employee attempting to improve conditions or resolve problems at work by dealing with the employer on a one-to-one basis, the union acts on everyone's behalf.

Once selected, the union represents all the employees in the bargaining unit—even those employees who did not vote for the union. As is the case with national politics, this arrangement is based on a democratic majoritarian principle: that an elected representative represents and makes decisions affecting all the people in a political unit, including those who did or did not vote for that representative.

---

probably do not share a community of interest with office workers, but salespersons in a department store would probably share a community of interest with one another—even if they worked in different departments and sold different types of goods.

In addition to having authority to act as exclusive representative of the bargaining unit employees, the union has the obligation to use that authority in a fair and nondiscriminatory manner. Thus, the NLRA imposes a duty of fair representation on all unions, requiring them to act in the best interests of all the bargaining-unit employees. Decisions that the union makes in dealing with workplace issues cannot be arbitrary, discriminatory, or made in bad faith. Unions are, however, given broad discretion in exercising their authority to act on behalf of employees. As the

(i) RESOLVING CONFLICTS IN GOOD FAITH

Unions have a duty to exercise their authority in good faith. For example, when negotiating with an employer, a union may have to decide whether to ask for an increase in wages or an increase in pension benefits, knowing that the employer will not agree to allocate additional money to both. The younger employees in the bargaining unit may want higher wages, but the older employees may be more concerned about pension benefits. Obviously, whatever decision the union makes will leave some employees dissatisfied. Nevertheless, as long as the union's decision is not arbitrary, discriminatory, or made in bad faith, the union has not violated its duty of fair representation.

In this example, if the union chooses to bargain for improved pension benefits because it thinks that a healthy pension plan is important, this is an allowable decision. But if the union chooses to fight for improved pension benefits simply because most of the older employees supported the union while younger employees campaigned against it, then its decision could be deemed discriminatory and in bad faith.

Supreme Court stated in the 1953 case of *Ford Motor Co. v. Huffman*: "The complete satisfaction of all who are represented is hardly to be expected. A wide range of reasonableness must be allowed a [union] in serving the [employees] it represents, subject always to complete good faith and honesty of purpose in the exercise of its discretion."

Collective-Bargaining Agreements

As the exclusive bargaining agent for employees, the first important duty for a newly certified union is to attempt to negotiate a collective-bargaining agreement with the applicable employer. The NLRA requires both the employer and the union to bargain in good faith with regard to wages, hours, and other terms and conditions of employment for purposes of reaching an agreement. A refusal to bargain in good faith violates the law.

The duty to bargain in good faith means that once a union has been selected, the employer loses the ability to make unilateral changes in wages, hours, and other terms and conditions of employment. Before any changes can be made in the workplace relating to these issues, the employer must bargain with the union and try to reach an agreement.

For example, suppose that in a newly unionized workplace the employer wants to institute a work rule banning smoking in the workplace. Before the union arrived, the employer could simply have announced that it was implementing such a rule. Now, in the presence of the union, the employer must notify the union about the proposed rule. The employer must sit down and bargain in good faith with the union about the issue of smoking in the workplace, whether a rule is needed, and, if so, what the rule should be.

Sometimes an employer and a union negotiate in good faith, but are unable to agree about an issue. At this point, the employer is allowed to put into effect the last proposal that it made to the union.

The fact that the union is the exclusive representative of employees for purposes of bargaining means not only that the employer has the duty to bargain with the union, but also that the employer is forbidden to negotiate with anyone else. Thus, the employer cannot negotiate workplace issues directly with the employees or with other unions.

Instead of bargaining over workplace issues as they arise (i.e., one at a time), unions and employers often negotiate **collective-bargaining agreements** that set out the terms and conditions of employment. Essentially, such agreements reduce to writing the "law of the shop." An employer and union often agree on the benefits, duties, and rules that will govern the relationship between employees and the company for a set period of time. (Many collective-bargaining agreements are three years in length.) The collective-bargaining agreement is an enforceable contract binding on the employer, the union, and the bargaining-unit employees.

In negotiating a collective-bargaining agreement, the employer and union are obligated to attempt to reach agreement

---

(i) MANDATORY SUBJECTS

For purposes of negotiating collective-bargaining agreements, mandatory subjects include:

- rates of pay;
- hours of work;
- health insurance;
- pension benefits;
- vacations;
- seniority rights;
- job assignments;
- work rules; and
- procedures for promotions, layoffs, discharges, recalls, and transfers.

regarding **mandatory subjects**—that is, all issues relating to wages, hours, and other terms and conditions of employment.

However, this same *duty* to bargain does not apply to issues that do not involve wages, hours, and other terms and conditions of employment—for example, what type of products the company will manufacture or how much money the company will spend on advertising. The employer retains its unilateral decision-making authority on these types of issues.

Because they are very important to unions, three types of provisions are found in many collective-bargaining agreements: just-cause clauses, grievance and arbitration clauses, and union security clauses.

Just-Cause Clauses

A **just-cause clause** limits an employer's ability to discipline and fire employees at will. Unlike the employment-at-will situation, in which an employer is free to discipline and discharge employees for any reason or no reason at all (see chapter 11 for exceptions to this rule), the just-cause clause in a union contract requires that the employer have **just cause** (or **proper cause**) for disciplining or firing an employee.

The just-cause requirement limits not only the reasons for which an employer may impose discipline, but also the types of discipline that may be imposed. Where a just-cause requirement is in place, the reason for discipline usually must be related to legitimate work issues. For example, an employer might have just cause to discipline an employee for absenteeism, but not for listening to rock music. (Though in an employment-at-will situation, the employer could discipline for either of these reasons.) Just cause also requires that the punishment "fit" the crime. Thus, an employer would likely be deemed to have acted without just cause if it fired an employee for being three minutes late to work on a single occasion, since the severity of the punishment would seem out of proportion with the infraction. (Although, once again, the employer would be free to fire the employee for that same reason in an employment-at-will situation.)

ⓘ THIS CAUSE IS JUST

An employer generally has just cause for taking a disciplinary action if:

- it has notified its employees that the conduct in question could be cause for discipline;

- the reason for the disciplinary action is reasonably related to the efficient operation of the business;

- the employer undertook a fair and impartial investigation prior to imposing discipline and had reason to believe the employee committed the violation;

- the disciplinary action is applied uniformly to all similarly situated employees; and

- the discipline is not disproportionate to the offense involved, and takes into account the past record of the employee.

Grievance and Arbitration

The grievance-and-arbitration provision of a collective-bargaining agreement is the usual mechanism for enforcing the terms of the agreement. It also provides the means by which the union can challenge an employer's discipline or discharge of a represented employee. If employees or the union (or, in some cases, the employer) believe that the contract has been violated, they can file a complaint using the grievance procedure set forth in the agreement. The **grievance procedure** usually involves a multistep process in which the union and the employer attempt to resolve their dispute over the application of the terms of the contract. If they cannot reach an agreement between themselves, the dispute may be submitted to an arbitrator for a decision.

The **arbitrator** is a neutral third party: an individual, a panel or (in some industries) a joint committee comprised of both labor and management. The arbitrator holds a hearing at which both the union and employer present evidence and testimony in support of their interpretations of the disputed contract provision. After considering the evidence, the arbitrator issues a decision stating which party's interpretation is correct. This decision is final and binding on both the union and the company.

Not every grievance goes to arbitration. Often a company and union can agree on how to resolve a problem. Other times the union, after reviewing the disputed situation, believes that the employer acted correctly and did not violate the contract. Sometimes the union may think that it does not have a strong enough case to win at arbitration, even though it still thinks the employer is wrong.

Just because an employee files a grievance does not mean that the union must pursue that grievance through the entire grievance-and-arbitration process. As long as the union does not

(i) A TYPICAL GRIEVANCE

Here is an example of how the grievance-and-arbitration process might work: Suppose a collective-bargaining agreement provides that, in a situation where two employees of equal skill and experience are eligible for a promotion, the person with more seniority receives the promotion. The employer awards a promotion to Employee Jones. However, Employee Smith has more seniority than and thinks she is as good an employee as Jones, so she believes that she should have been promoted instead. Smith files a written grievance and gives it to the union shop steward to notify the union that she thinks her employer violated the contract. The shop steward then notifies the company of the grievance, and a meeting is set up to discuss the grievance with a supervisor.

If the steward and supervisor cannot agree on how to resolve this problem, then "higher ups" within the organizational structure (such as the business agent or union president and the plant or human resources manager) will discuss the issue, in the manner set forth in the contract's grievance procedure. If they still cannot agree after following all of the internal grievance steps specified in the agreement, then the union may submit the case to an arbitrator for decision.

act arbitrarily, discriminatorily, or in bad faith in deciding how to handle an employee's grievance, it has fulfilled its duty of fair representation. Thus, in the example presented in the sidebar above, if the union decides not to pursue Employee Smith's grievance because it does not agree that she is as skilled as Jones, it has acted lawfully; however, if its decision is based on the fact that Smith is a woman and Jones is a man, then it has violated its duty of fair representation by behaving discriminatorily.

Union Security Clauses

A **union security clause** requires *all* employees in a bargaining unit to make periodic payments to their union as a condition of

(i) YOU CAN'T MAKE ME PAY!

Not all collective-bargaining agreements contain union security clauses. And even if they do, employees aren't always required to be dues-paying union members as a condition of employment. About twenty states (mostly in the South and western-mountain regions) have laws prohibiting the inclusion of union security clauses in collective-bargaining agreements. These states are known as **right-to-work states**.

In addition, individuals whose religious beliefs prohibit them from supporting labor unions are exempt from paying money to such unions, but they can be required to pay an amount equivalent to the value of union dues and fees to a nonreligious, non-labor-related charitable organization. This accommodation to an employee's religious beliefs is required under both the NLRA and Title VII.

Finally, individuals can object to paying any dues and fees that are spent for purposes unrelated to collective bargaining and representation of the workforce. Objecting individuals must notify their union of their objection. In such a situation, they are entitled to a reduction in the amount they are required to pay. For example, if 20 percent of dues money is used to support political candidates, objecting individuals could have their union dues (or service fee or fair-share payment) reduced by 20 percent.

employment. Union members are required to pay certain dues and fees. The other employees in the bargaining unit are not required to join the union, but they can be required to pay for the work that the union performs on their behalf in negotiating and administering the collective-bargaining agreement. These are called **service fees** or **fair-share payments**. An employee who refuses to pay the required dues, fees, or payments can be fired. In effect, this is the workplace equivalent of taxes that we pay to support the operation of the government: We may not like the government's policies and may not have voted for our current leaders, but we still are required to pay taxes to support the work performed by the government on our behalf.

Strikes

The NLRA specifically protects employees' right to strike. But, as with other rights granted by the statute, the right to strike is not absolute; some restrictions apply.

Whether a strike is protected under the NLRA depends on the purpose of the strike, the conduct of the strikers, and the timing of the strike.

The Strike's Purpose

If employees strike to obtain economic benefits and improved terms and conditions of employment, or to support union bargaining demands, the strike is considered an **economic strike**. Economic strikes are lawful. Economic strikers retain their status as employees, and firing them for striking is a violation of the NLRA.

If the object of the strike is to protest unfair labor practices committed by the employer, then the strike is an **unfair-labor-practice strike**. Unfair-labor-practice strikes are not only lawful, but also allow more protection to strikers than other types of strikes. An unfair-labor-practice striker cannot be permanently replaced, and has the right to be immediately reinstated upon his or her unconditional offer to return to work. An employer that refuses to reinstate unfair-labor-practice strikers violates the NLRA.

(i) REPLACED BUT NOT FIRED

An employer has the right to hire replacement workers to continue its operation during an economic strike. If the employer has hired **permanent replacements**, striking workers whose jobs have been filled by permanent replacement workers will not be entitled to their jobs when the strike ends. The striking employee has the right to be recalled to the first vacancy that later occurs, whether because a replacement worker resigns or is fired, or because the employer expands its business. Refusal by an employer to recall an economic striker to the first substantially equivalent job vacancy violates the law.

If the employer has hired only **temporary replacement workers** during the economic strike, then striking workers have the right to get their jobs back as soon as the strike ends.

Whether a replacement worker is permanent or temporary depends on what the employer told the replacement worker at the time he or she was hired. If the employer told the worker that he or she was only being hired until the strike ended, then the worker is considered a temporary replacement; if the worker was told that he or she would have the job regardless of when the strike ended, then the worker is considered a permanent replacement.

Sympathy strikers are employees who are not directly involved in a labor dispute, but are acting in solidarity with striking employees. For example, suppose assembly line workers at a manufacturing plant strike to support their bargaining demands. The clerical workers at the plant are not part of the bargaining unit and are not represented by the union, but nonetheless refuse to cross the picket line. In this example, the clerical workers are sympathy strikers against a common employer. As long as the strike itself is lawful, sympathy strikers are engaged in protected conduct and cannot be fired or disciplined.

Sympathy strikers who support a strike by another group of employees against a common employer are entitled to the same reinstatement rights as the strikers themselves. Employees who refuse to cross an economic picket line have the same reinstatement rights as economic strikers; employees who refuse to cross an unfair-labor-practice picket line are entitled to the same reinstatement rights as unfair-labor-practice strikers.

Sympathy strikers can also support a strike by a group of employees who have a different employer. As an example, suppose truck drivers are supposed to make a delivery to a manufacturing plant where assembly line workers are on strike. When they see the picket line, the truck drivers refuse to cross the picket line to make their delivery. They are sympathy strikers supporting a strike by a different employer's workers. They cannot be fired for refusing to cross the picket line, but they may be replaced. This is true whether the employees they support are unfair-labor-practice strikers or economic strikers.

Conduct of the Strikers

Striking workers who engage in certain types of conduct during a strike are unprotected by the NLRA and can thus be disciplined

---

(i) SECONDARY BOYCOTTS OUTLAWED

Secondary boycotts are illegal under the NLRA. A **secondary boycott** is picketing aimed at a company (the **secondary employer**) with which the applicable union does not have a dispute, but that does business with an employer with whom the union *does* have a dispute (the **primary employer**). The purpose of a secondary boycott is to put pressure on a secondary employer to cease doing business with a primary employer. For example, suppose truck drivers are engaged in an economic strike against their employer, Acme Trucking Company. Beta Manufacturing Company has a contract with Acme to deliver material and supplies to Acme's factory. If the truck drivers picket Beta Manufacturing Company as a means of pressuring Beta to stop doing business with Acme, then their activities will constitute an illegal secondary boycott.

(i) **SPECIAL CARE FOR HOSPITALS**

The NLRA requires unions representing employees of health-care institutions to give ten days' notice before they go on strike. If the union fails
to give such notice, or if the employees go out on strike before the ten-
day period elapses, then the employees are not protected and can be
lawfully disciplined or fired.

or fired. However, only strikers who actually engage in unprotected conduct can lawfully be punished; not all striking workers
are responsible.

Threat of force or actual violence by striking workers is conduct unprotected by the NLRA. Vandalism and sabotage of an
employer's property also is unprotected, as are sit-down strikes
and intermittent strikes. A **sit-down strike** occurs when striking
workers refuse to leave their employer's property. An **intermittent strike** occurs, for example, when employees engage in a five-
hour work stoppage on alternate days, but not every day.

Timing of the Strike

Many collective-bargaining agreements contain **no-strike clauses**.
Under such a clause, employees agree that they will not strike for
the duration of the contract. If they go out on strike in breach of
a no-strike clause, they are unprotected by the NLRA and their
employer can discipline or fire them.

Hiring Halls

Hiring halls are essentially union-run employment agencies. They
are prevalent in the construction and maritime industries and, to
some extent, are used in the trucking industry. The employers in
these industries tend to be mobile, and employment is often
short-term or irregular, making conventional hiring methods in-
efficient. In some circumstances, unions comprised of employees in these industries operate as employment clearinghouses.

TWO KINDS OF HALLS

Whether by written agreement or practice, if an employer agrees to use a hiring hall as the exclusive means for hiring workers, then the hall is considered an **exclusive hiring hall**. If the employer merely uses the hiring hall as one source among many for recruiting workers, it is considered a **nonexclusive hiring hall.**

Employees who are available for work register at the hiring hall. Employers then contact the hall and request a specific number of employees for a certain job, and the union dispatches registered workers. The employer and union may formalize this arrangement in a collective-bargaining agreement, or may pursue such an arrangement informally.

In an exclusive-hiring-hall arrangement, the union must allow any employee to register for referral, whether the individual is a union member or not. Refusing to allow nonunion employees to register violates the NLRA. Nonunion employees may, however, be charged a fee for the use of the referral service. A union can refuse to allow nonmembers to use a nonexclusive hiring hall.

In referring workers from a hiring hall, whether it is exclusive or nonexclusive, the union must fulfill its duty of fair representation. Thus, it cannot decide which employees to refer based on arbitrary, discriminatory, or bad-faith reasons. A union that refers white employees before African-American employees has acted in a prohibited discriminatory manner and violated its duty of fair representation. It has also violated Title VII, which prohibits labor unions from discriminating in referrals based on race.

Internal Union Affairs

The **Labor-Management Reporting and Disclosure Act of 1959 (LMRDA)** (also known as the **Landrum-Griffin Act**) deals mainly with the relationship between unions and their members.

The law grants union members certain basic political rights within the union organization:

- the right to free speech;
- the right to vote on union business and in union officer elections;
- the right to a secret-ballot election before dues are increased;
- procedural safeguards against union discipline; and
- protection from retaliation for enforcing their rights.

The law also requires unions to file annual reports with the Department of Labor disclosing information about their fiscal operations. In addition, it contains procedural requirements that must be satisfied in order for a national or international union to impose a trusteeship on a local union. A **trusteeship** occurs when a national union takes over the operations of a local union because the local officers have been involved in criminal activity or financial mismanagement. The law also imposes requirements for ensuring fair election of union officers. Lastly, the law imposes fiduciary obligations on union officers to exercise their authority in the best interests of the union members and the union as a whole.

(i) THE RAILWAY LABOR ACT

Union activity engaged in by employees of airlines or railroads is regulated by the Railway Labor Act (RLA). Most of the rights granted to employees under the RLA, as well as the restrictions imposed on employers and unions, are similar to those found in the NLRA. But the enforcement procedures differ, because different federal agencies were created to deal with each law.

There are three major differences worthy of note. First, secondary boycotts are not illegal under the RLA. Second, the law imposes a "cooling-off" period after bargaining breaks down before a union can go on strike. Third, disputes over the application and interpretation of collective-bargaining agreements are usually submitted to an **adjustment board** (rather than to private arbitration) for resolution.

Unlike the NLRA, which grants rights to all employees, the LMRDA only grants rights to union members. An employee who is in a bargaining unit that is represented by a union, but who is not a member of that union, does not obtain any rights under the LMRDA.

THE WORLD AT YOUR FINGERTIPS

• For more information about the rights granted and restrictions imposed by the National Labor Relations Act (NLRA), visit the site of the National Labor Relations Board at *www.nlrb.gov*.

• *Labor Law in a Nutshell* by Douglas Leslie (2000) provides a good introduction to the topic of unions.

• *Organizing and the Law* by Stephen Schlossberg (1991) addresses employee, union, and employer rights and responsibilities as they relate to union activity and organizing drives.

• *The Developing Labor Law*, edited by Patrick Hardin et al. (2001), and its *Cumulative Supplement* (2005) comprise a comprehensive guide to law under the National Labor Relations Act and related labor laws.

REMEMBER THIS

• Employers cannot interfere with, restrain, or coerce employees in the exercise of their rights to engage in union activity or concerted activity.

• Employers cannot threaten employees to prevent them from joining a union.

• Employers cannot discriminate with regard to hiring, termination, or terms and conditions of employment because of employee union activity.

• The NLRA protects employee group activity related to workplace issues, even if no union is present.

• The NLRA limits the employer's authority to restrict employees' rights to communicate at the workplace about work issues.

• Employees can lose the protections of the law by engaging in unlawful conduct—such as vandalism, violence, or sabotage—when engaging in concerted activity.

• If a majority of a company's employees choose a union to represent them, the employer must bargain with the union about wages, hours, and other terms and conditions of employment.

• The terms contained in a collective-bargaining agreement are enforceable, usually through a grievance-and-arbitration procedure.

• Employers generally cannot fire employees for going on strike, and can permanently replace employees only if they are engaged in an economic strike.

• Secondary boycotts are unlawful under the NLRA.

CHAPTER 14

Government Employment

Civil Service, Constitutional Protections, and Other Special Features

The director of quality management at the county psychiatric hospital is fired after writing an internal report. The report is critical of the hospital's decision to allocate more space for administration offices, which has had the effect of further reducing much-needed space for the overcrowded facility's patients.

Elsewhere, a public high-school teacher is suspended for wearing a black armband in protest of the war in Iraq.

Had these employees been employed in the private sector, their chances of successfully challenging their employer's actions would have been slim. But these employees successfully regained their jobs—and this chapter will explain why.

Government employment is different from private-sector employment. Government employees are people who work for the federal, state, or local government. Private-sector employees are nongovernmental employees. The law sometimes recognizes a distinction in the way government employees versus private-sector employees are to be treated.

Many labor and employment laws apply to both government and private-sector employers. In particular, most of the antidiscrimination laws apply to both. There are a few notable exceptions: the Occupational Safety and Health Act (OSH Act), Employee Retirement Income Security Act (ERISA), the Employee Polygraph Protection Act (EPPA), and the National Labor Relations Act (NLRA) do not apply to government employers. (In addition, the Americans with Disabilities Act (ADA) does not apply to federal employees.) In most states, the exemption of government employers from the NLRA is counterbalanced by laws regulating union issues in government employment. The federal

(i) CONGRESSMEN AND SENATORS ARE EMPLOYERS, TOO

Generally, the OSH Act, ERISA, the EPPA, and the NLRA do not apply to government employers at the local, state, or federal levels. However, an exception exists for employees who work for the legislative branch of the federal government. They are guaranteed the protections afforded by the Fair Labor Standards Act (FLSA), Title VII, the Americans with Disabilities Act (ADA), Age Discrimination in Employment Act (ADEA), Family and Medical Leave Act (FMLA), OSH Act, FLRA, EPPA, Worker Adjustment and Retraining Notification Act (WARN Act), Rehabilitation Act, and Uniformed Services Employment and Reemployment Rights Act (USERRA).

government has also passed a similar law to regulate its employees at the federal level.

Government employees have some additional protections not available to private-sector employees. Civil-service laws and rights guaranteed under the U.S. Constitution and state constitutions limit what government employers can do vis-à-vis their employees.

GOVERNMENT LABOR-MANAGEMENT RELATIONS

Both the **Federal Labor Relations Act (FLRA)** and various state labor-relations laws draw heavily on the legal principles established under the NLRA. In fact, the FLRA and many state laws incorporate various sections of the NLRA verbatim. As a result, many of the protections that were discussed in the previous chapter, which addressed unions in the workplace, also apply to government employees.

There are, however, three major differences between the NLRA and the various public-sector union laws. First, the categories of employees covered by these laws are sometimes broader than those covered by the NLRA. The NLRA exempts supervisory employees from its protection, but some states (such as Hawaii,

⚠ NON-COVERED EMPLOYEES

In addition to supervisors, the FLRA excludes employees of certain government agencies and departments—such as the General Accounting Office and the FBI—from its coverage. Moreover, approximately twenty states do not grant state employees the right to engage in collective bargaining.

Michigan, and New York) include government supervisory employees within the protection of state laws. Like the NLRA, however, the FLRA expressly excludes supervisors.

Second, the workplace issues that are subject to negotiation with unions tend to be more limited in government employment than in private-sector employment. Under the broad terms of the NLRA, employers and unions may bargain over issues relating to wages, hours, and other terms and conditions of employment. Many state laws also allow bargaining over issues in these subject areas, but then go on to prohibit bargaining over certain specific issues. Sometimes they prohibit bargaining on any issue relating to managerial prerogatives. For example, the school curriculum, length of the school day, and scheduling of extracurricular activities are issues that may not be negotiated under some state education laws. Issues that are already regulated under a state civil-service or merit system law are often excluded from bargaining. The FLRA also prohibits federal agencies from bargaining over wages; it limits bargaining to issues touching on "conditions of employment."

Third, the FLRA and many state laws prohibit government employees from going on strike. A strike exerts pressure on an employer to agree to the employees' bargaining demands. Without the ability to strike, employees have no leverage for persuading a recalcitrant employer to change its bargaining position and agree to their proposals. Accordingly, laws that prohibit strikes frequently provide for **impasse resolution procedures** to help the parties reach an agreement when they are deadlocked. Such

EXECUTIVE ORDERS

Over a series of administrations, U.S. Presidents have issued Executive Orders addressing certain aspects of the employment relationship for federal executive agencies such as the Department of Defense, the Department of Health and Human Services, and the Department of Justice. **Executive Orders** are official orders issued by the President that direct the operations of the federal government. For example, Executive Order 11478 prohibits discrimination in employment on the basis of race, color, religion, sex, national origin, age, sexual orientation, or parental status. Executive Order 13145 prohibits discrimination based on genetic information. And Executive Order 11935 requires that all employees who take the competitive civil-service exam or who are hired for competitive service be U.S. citizens.

procedures range from mediation to fact-finding and arbitration. In some cases, if an employer and a union are unable to agree to the terms of a contract, a third-party arbitrator will decide the contract terms.

CIVIL-SERVICE LAWS

Every state, as well as the federal government, has enacted **civil-service laws**. These laws require that employment policies be based on merit, and are designed to eliminate political considerations in the government employment process. Typical features of civil-service systems include: guidelines for recruiting applicants, testing programs for screening applicants, impartial hiring criteria based on merit, job classifications based on duties and responsibilities, and protection of employees against arbitrary discipline and discharge.

A civil-service employee who has completed a probationary employment period usually may be fired only for **good cause.**

(i) NOT EVERYONE IS CIVIL

Not all jobs within the government are considered civil-service jobs; some types of jobs are exempt from civil-service laws. For example, high-level policy-making positions are rarely covered under civil-service rules, nor are jobs involving a high level of specialized skill for which examination would be difficult—such as legal jobs performed by attorneys.

Generally, good cause requires that a firing be based on work-related considerations that promote the efficiency of government operations.

Commissions usually are established to ensure that government employers are following the civil-service rules. Such commissions hear employees' complaints and decide whether the employees' rights under the civil-service regulations have been

(`) TALKING TO A LAWYER

Q. I work in my state's budget office. Recently my supervisor found out that I was gay and told the director of my office. Now I'm afraid my employer might take some kind of personnel action against me. There is no law in my state prohibiting employment discrimination based on sexual orientation. But don't I have a right to privacy?

A. As a state employee, you will likely be protected by your state's civil-service law. If you are fired, your employer will likely have to prove that you were fired for cause. Furthermore, some state laws may provide for a privacy-related claim, such as a claim for publication of private facts. Federal law generally does not protect you against sexual orientation discrimination.

—Answer by members of the ABA Section
of Labor and Employment Law

violated. The particulars of civil-service laws and the role and operation of the applicable commissions vary from state to state.

CONSTITUTIONAL PROTECTIONS

The rights guaranteed to individuals by the U.S. Constitution are guaranteed against *government* restrictions. Because public employers are considered "arms" of the government, public employees are protected in the workplace by the Constitution, whereas private sector employees are not. For example, because the First Amendment provides that "Congress shall make no law . . . abridging the freedom of speech," a government employer that disciplines an employee for speaking out may run afoul of the Constitution.

Though the Constitution limits the behavior of public employers, it places no such restraints on the behavior of *private* persons. Thus, a private-sector employer who refuses to hire someone because he or she is a member of the American Civil Liberties Union (ACLU) has not done anything prohibited by the Constitution. Likewise, if a private company prevents an employee from speaking out, it does not violate the Constitution.

While government employees have greater protection in certain instances than private-sector employees, they do not enjoy the full protection of the Constitution that is enjoyed by ordinary citizens. This is because when the government acts as an employer, it has a special interest in providing effective and efficient service. This, in turn, may necessitate certain restrictions on employees that the government could not impose on ordinary citizens. Thus, in striking a balance between effective government service and the constitutional rights of government employees, courts sometimes have allowed employment rules that infringe on government employees' constitutional rights.

Freedom of Speech

The First Amendment protects government employees' freedom of speech in the workplace. However, government employees do not have an absolute right to free speech, and courts recognize that an employee's right to freedom of speech must be balanced against the need of government employers to efficiently perform their services. In order to accommodate these two competing interests, the Supreme Court has developed a balancing test for determining the limits of governmental employees' free-speech rights.

Initially, courts will consider the content of an employee's speech: Is the content of the speech a matter of public concern, or merely of personal interest? Courts have held that employees' speech about public matters is entitled to First Amendment protection, while speech relating to purely private concerns is not. For example, a schoolteacher criticizing the curriculum developed by her school board speaks about a matter of public concern, and her statements are likely protected. However, a teacher's complaints about not getting a raise will likely be considered purely personal, and will not be protected.

If the speech involves public issues, the courts then balance the employee's free speech rights with the government's interest in promoting the efficiency and integrity of its business. In doing so, the manner, time, and place of the employee's speech is relevant. In the 1987 case of *Rankin v. McPherson*, the Supreme Court stated that courts should also consider:

> whether the statement impairs discipline by superiors or harmony among coworkers, has a detrimental impact on close working relationships for which personal loyalty and confidence are necessary, or impedes the performance of the speaker's duties or interferes with the regular operation of the enterprise.

Without sufficient interest, the government cannot discipline or fire government employees based on speech that involves matters of public concern.

Freedom of Association

In addition to protecting freedom of speech, the First Amendment also protects government employees' freedom of association. This means that individuals have the right to associate with other individuals or belong to groups and organizations (such as

ⓘ MAINTAINING THE GOVERNMENT'S NEUTRALITY

In order to secure a politically neutral civil service, the **Hatch Act** restricts certain types of political activity by employees of the federal government. Specifically, the Act prohibits employees from using their official authority to interfere with or affect the result of an election, limits the role that employees may take in partisan political management or campaigns, and limits political activity in the workplace. Employees may participate in politics as individuals, and can express opinions about political matters. But employees who violate the Hatch Act can be disciplined or fired.

In many cases, employees' political activities are also regulated at the state level. Many state laws duplicate the Hatch Act. A few states' laws are more restrictive, in that they prohibit both nonpartisan and partisan political activity. Some state laws are less restrictive, prohibiting political activity only during work hours or if it interferes with work duties.

---

the Nation of Islam, the ACLU, or the Ku Klux Klan) without fear of government interference or retaliation.

Generally, a government employer cannot consider an applicant's membership in organizations or the identity of the applicant's friends and acquaintances in making employment decisions. As with free-speech rights, a government employer cannot infringe on employees' freedom to associate without a significant employment-related justification.

However, restrictions on political affiliation are permitted in certain situations. For example, a government employer may make employment decisions based on political affiliation if political affiliation is an appropriate requirement for the job in question, or if the job requires the employee to carry out the political agenda of elected officials. Thus, cabinet members and their top assistants can be hired and fired based on their political affiliations, while most clerical and administrative employees, as well as professional-level employees without policy-making duties, cannot be fired or disciplined for the same reason.

Employee Searches

The Fourth Amendment prohibits the government from conducting unreasonable searches and seizures. In the employment context, this limits a government employer's right to drug test its employees, as well as to search its employees' possessions.

Drug Testing

Drug testing of government employees is generally allowed in two circumstances. First, if the government employer has a reasonable suspicion that an employee is involved in drug use, it can require the employee to undergo a drug test. **Reasonable suspicion** must normally be based on specific facts implying drug use, and not on assumptions or rumors.

Second, even without reasonable individualized suspicion, a drug test may be allowed if the government employer can demonstrate a special need for the test. By way of example, courts have found sufficient governmental need in cases involving:

1. post-accident testing of transportation employees involved in serious accidents;

2. testing of employees involved in the war against drugs, such as customs agents;

3. testing of employees in positions requiring them to carry firearms;

4. testing of employees in positions with access to sensitive government information; and

5. testing of employees with duties that have an immediate impact on public safety.

Once an employer has demonstrated reasonable suspicion or a special need for a test, courts will balance the government's interest in administering the test against the employee's privacy interests.

Searches

The Fourth Amendment also protects government employees against unreasonable searches. However, this protection is limited to areas in which employees have a **reasonable**

expectation of privacy. For example, an employee probably does not have a reasonable expectation of privacy in a desk or filing cabinet shared with coworkers, or in a work area exposed to the public. However, the employee's expectation of privacy would be much higher in the case of a locked drawer in an unshared desk.

When an employee can establish a reasonable expectation of privacy, an employer's ability to search is subject to some restrictions. As with an employee's right to freedom of speech, an employee's right to be free from unreasonable searches must be balanced against the government interest used to justify the intrusion. Typically, the government employer justifies such intrusions based on its need for supervision, control, and efficient operation of the workplace.

The general rule is that a government employer may conduct an investigatory search in response to work-related misconduct or a work-related non-investigatory search, in limited circumstances. In the 1987 case of *O'Connor v. Ortega*, the Supreme Court stated that such a search may be conducted only if there are "reasonable grounds for suspecting that the search will turn up evidence that the employee is guilty of work-related misconduct, or that the search is necessary for a non-investigatory work-related purpose such as to retrieve a needed file." Moreover, any search must be conducted in a manner that is "reasonably related to the objectives of the search and not excessively intrusive."

Although the law on this point is unsettled, some cases suggest that government employers may need probable cause to suspect workplace misconduct before they can search personal items—such as a briefcase, luggage, or a purse that an employee brings into the workplace. (**Probable cause** is a legal standard in search-and-seizure law; it requires facts sufficient to make a reasonable person believe that contraband is likely to be found in the area to be searched.) On the other hand, most courts reviewing the issue have found no reasonable expectation of privacy in an employee's use of an employer-owned computer system.

Thus, neither government employer searches of employee hard drives and e-mail nor monitoring of employees' Internet use has generally been found to violate the Fourth Amendment. This is clearly the case when an employer specifically notifies employees that their computer use is subject to monitoring.

Right Against Self-Incrimination

The Fifth Amendment protects persons from being compelled in criminal cases to act as witnesses against themselves. Thus, government employees can refuse to answer their employer's questions when the answer might subject them to criminal prosecution. The privilege against incrimination applies, for example, if a government employer questions employees about illegal drug use, or asks whether they received a bribe.

Since the Fifth Amendment protects against compulsion in these types of situations, a government employer may not threaten to fire an employee who refuses to answer incriminating questions, nor may it refuse to hire such an employee. However, if a government employer grants employees immunity from criminal prosecution based on any information they disclose, employees can be required to answer such questions or face discipline or discharge.

It is important to note that this Fifth Amendment protection extends only to answers that would subject an employee to criminal liability. Thus, if a government employer were to question employees about whether they were sleeping on the job, the employees would be required to answer (because sleeping on the job is not a criminal offense).

Right to Privacy

The Supreme Court has interpreted the Constitution as granting to individuals a right to privacy against government intrusion. The Court, however, has narrowly defined the scope of this privacy right, limiting it to conduct related to traditional family concerns such as marriage, contraception, child rearing, and abortion. Government employers, therefore, are prohibited from asking questions about, or basing employment decisions on, these fundamental privacy interests.

Right to Due Process

The **Fifth Amendment** also prohibits the government from depriving an individual of liberty or property without due process. In the employment context, discipline or discharge can (in some circumstances) constitute a deprivation of an employee's liberty or property interests. In such cases, a government employer may not fire or discipline an individual without due process. It is important to note, however, that not all discipline and discharge decisions involve liberty or property rights.

Discharges or disciplinary actions implicate the **liberty interests** of government employees in their jobs if:

1. the way in which employees are disciplined or dismissed impugns their character as the result of a false characterization; and

2. the stain on the employees' character is made public.

 **TALKING TO A LAWYER**

Q. I work in my state's department of agriculture as an extension officer. A group of us spoke to our supervisor the other day to voice several complaints: we hadn't had a raise in eighteen months and we requested a cost-of-living increase; we also complained that one of the employees in our department (who happens to be the son of the department's head) wasn't pulling his weight—not coming into work on time, leaving early, and generally goofing off on the job. Not only did our supervisor fail to resolve any of the issues we raised, but now he's also scrutinizing closely everything we do. We fear that we're being set up to get fired. What can we do?

A. As a state employee, you will likely be protected from discharge by your state's civil-service law. In the event of your termination, your employer would likely have to prove that you were fired for cause. In addition, your supervisor's conduct may provide you with several claims. If your supervisor is subjecting you to additional scrutiny or takes an employment action against you because of your statements, the supervisor may violate state or federal labor law that protects concerted activity. Your statements about the favoritism shown to the department head's son may also be a matter of public concern implicating the First Amendment.

—Answer by members of the ABA Section
of Labor and Employment Law

In determining whether government employees have a **property interest** in their jobs, courts ask whether there is a written or implied contract or a statute granting the employees such an interest. For example, teachers with tenure are considered to have a property interest in their jobs, because there is an express understanding that "tenure" means that one cannot lose a job without just cause.

When liberty or property interests are at stake, the government may not take away that interest from an employee without due process. **Due process** requires that:

• discharged employees be given notice of the reason for discharge;

• a hearing be held at which employees have the opportunity to present evidence in their defense and to hear the evidence presented against them; and

• a decision be made by an impartial third-party decision maker based on the evidence presented at the hearing.

THE WORLD AT YOUR FINGERTIPS

• The website of the U.S. Merit Systems Protection Board provides information on merit hiring in the federal civil-service system at *www.mspb.gov/*.

• The home page of the Federal Labor Relations Authority, at *www.flra.gov*, provides information about the FLRA and its enforcement procedures.

• *The Rights of Public Employees* by Robert O'Neil (1993) is a handbook developed by the ACLU that answers questions about the constitutional rights of public-sector employees.

REMEMBER THIS

• Whether state government employees have collective-bargaining rights is based on state law. Not all states give employees these rights.

• Many employees of the federal government have collective-bargaining rights under the FLRA.

• Many government employees are covered by civil-service laws that protect them from discharge without good cause.

• Government employees enjoy constitutional protections in the workplace that are not available to private-sector employees.

• Government employers can restrict employees' constitutional rights when necessary to ensure effective and efficient government service.

• In some situations, government employees are entitled to a hearing before being disciplined or discharged.

CHAPTER 15

Enforcing Workplace Rights

Some Guidelines for Resolving
Workplace Problems

I applied for a promotion at work and was turned down. I was told that the other applicant for the job was more qualified, but I wonder whether this is really the case. I've read about my rights, and I think my rejection for the promotion may have been motivated by my national origin (I'm originally from the Middle East), by the fact that I tried to organize a union in my department (I was unsuccessful), or by my politics (I engaged in a heated debate with my supervisor during the last presidential election).

So what do I do now? Do I get myself a lawyer and go to court?

There is no single uniform method for enforcing the rights discussed in this book. Given the same set of facts, you could well have multiple avenues for enforcing a particular right.

Often you might choose to enforce a right by means of private grievance-and-arbitration systems. Other times, you'll file a complaint with a government agency that has the authority to investigate and prosecute violations of the law. Sometimes you'll need to file a lawsuit in court. If you go to court, you are technically not required to have a lawyer. But lawsuits are complicated, and the other side will most likely be represented by legal counsel. To have a real chance of winning, you'll probably need a lawyer. In many circumstances, you may be required to use a combination of these or other procedures to enforce your rights.

This chapter discusses the mechanics of the various alternatives for enforcing workplace rights. Appendix II identifies which specific mechanisms are available under each particular federal law.

NEGOTIATION

Generally it's a good idea to discuss any workplace problems directly with your employer as they arise. Only if such discussion proves futile does it make sense to involve a third party, whether that party is a government agency or a lawyer. Many employers have policies for bringing workplace issues to the employer's attention. These policies may be outlined in employer handbooks or manuals, posted on bulletin boards, or may simply be common knowledge in the workplace. Observing such policies often results in a quick, easy, and inexpensive resolution of the problem.

Even if an employer does not have an established procedure for enforcing workplace rights, it's a good idea to contact someone within your organization to discuss the relevant issues and obtain information prior to seeking further relief outside the employer. Your immediate supervisor or your employer's human resources/personnel department often is a logical starting point.

 PREPARE YOURSELF

Before meeting with your employer's representative, it is a good idea to prepare for the meeting by briefly outlining what you perceive to be the problem or issue you want the employer to address, and what solution(s) you are proposing to resolve the issue. Once you have the information clearly in your own mind, you will be in a better position to present it to your employer. Give the employer's representative a chance to respond to your concerns and listen to his/her perspective on the issue. It is often a good idea to take notes during the discussion—this helps to keep you focused on the issues. Try to stay calm; being highly emotional may cloud your judgment and detract from accomplishing your objective.

MEDIATION

Mediation is another way of resolving workplace problems. When an employee and the employer's representative are unable to reach an agreement on how to deal with a problem, in some situations a neutral third party may be able to help them work it out. This neutral third party (the **mediator**) does not provide an answer, but helps the parties arrive at their own mutually agreeable solution. The mediator can clarify the issues, reduce tensions between the parties, and act as a sounding board for testing out possible solutions. The final resolution of the problem remains, at all times, with the employee and the employer. But the help of this neutral third party sometimes is the catalyst that will produce a final resolution.

 HOW TO FIND A MEDIATOR

Many communities have local mediation centers that keep lists of available and trained mediators. The American Arbitration Association has a list of mediators with experience in employment disputes and will assist the parties in appointing an acceptable mediator and scheduling a meeting. There also are private companies and individuals listed in the telephone book that offer mediation services. Some local mediation centers offer their services for free, but most mediators charge an hourly fee that varies based on the mediator. It is up to the employer and the individual to determine how any fees will be paid; many times the parties split the fee, but sometimes an employer will agree to pay the entire fee. When the parties are serious about trying to work out their problems and are prepared for mediation, many disputes can be resolved in a single session.

ARBITRATION

In some circumstances, employees may be required to use a dispute resolution process that has been set up by the company. For example, when employees attempt to enforce their right to a benefit found in a personnel handbook or manual (i.e., a right allegedly granted to employees in an **implied contract**), courts may require them to use any grievance mechanism that is contained in that same handbook or manual. The rationale is that if the manual constitutes a contract, then all the provisions in the manual are part of that contract. If an employee wants the benefits of the manual, he or she is also bound by its other terms. The practical effect is that the employee may not be able to sue in court until all internal grievance procedures have been observed; even then, he or she may not be able to sue at all.

Similarly, employees who claim rights under collective-bargaining agreements are required to use the grievance mecha-

---

(i) TITLE VII RIGHTS AND COLLECTIVE-BARGAINING AGREEMENTS

At the time this book was written, the Supreme Court had taken the position that the arbitration provision in a collective-bargaining agreement cannot prevent an employee from suing his employer in court for violations of federal law. For example, suppose a union-represented employee files a grievance claiming he was fired because of his race and, therefore, that the employer did not have just cause for the discharge. An arbitrator finds that the employer did not breach the just-cause standard when it fired the employee. This decision does not prevent the employee from filing a lawsuit alleging the employer violated Title VII. While the court will take into account the arbitrator's decision, it will still arrive at its own independent conclusion regarding the case. In the coming years, however, it is possible that the Supreme Court will revisit this issue and change its position.

nisms specified in those agreements to enforce their rights. The overwhelming majority of collective-bargaining agreements contain grievance-and-arbitration provisions for enforcing contract rights. The grievance-and-arbitration procedure is described in the section on collective-bargaining agreements in chapter 13.

In **arbitration**, the parties submit their dispute to a neutral third party. Unlike a mediator, who helps the parties come up with their own solutions, the arbitrator, like a judge, issues a decision resolving the dispute. The arbitrator presides over a hearing, during which both parties have the opportunity to present evidence and testimony supporting their respective positions

(i) CAN EMPLOYEES BE FORCED TO ARBITRATE?

Courts will generally enforce a company-imposed requirement to arbitrate so long as the terms of the arbitration process are procedurally fair. The courts ask the following questions to decide whether the arbitration process is fair for employees:

- Is the arbitrator neutral?

- Can the employee receive the same remedy for a violation of the law as a court would order?

- Is there an adequate level of discovery allowing the employee to gather information about the claim?

- Does the process require a written decision explaining the reasoning on which the award is based?

- Is the cost of the process for the employee so expensive as to effectively preclude its use?

- Has the employer retained the right to change the procedures?

- Is the employer equally bound to submit to arbitration any dispute with the employee?

- Has the employee knowingly waived his or her right to have the claim heard by a judge or jury?

and make arguments to the arbitrator as to why their positions are correct.

After the hearing, the arbitrator issues a decision stating which party won the case and the prescribed remedy. For example, if the dispute involves the question whether an employer had the right to fire someone, the arbitrator could decide that the employer acted within its rights and that the employee is not entitled to a remedy. Or the arbitrator could decide that the employer was wrong, and direct the employer to reinstate the employee with back pay to make up for lost wages. Or the arbitrator could direct the employer to reinstate the employee without back pay.

The arbitration process is similar to a court hearing in that the parties have the opportunity to present their cases to a neutral third party with the authority to decide the dispute and issue a remedy. There are some differences, however. The process is less formal than going to court, and it is usually less expensive and quicker than court proceedings. There may, however, be less opportunity before the hearing to have access to all of the relevant documents and talk to all of the relevant witnesses.

⚠ WHAT IF I DON'T LIKE THE ARBITRATOR'S DECISION?

Generally speaking, the decision of an arbitrator is final and binding. If either party is dissatisfied with the decision, it can file an appeal with a court, but the scope of the court's review is very limited. Courts will not overturn an arbitrator's decision merely because they disagree with the arbitrator's findings of facts or legal conclusions. If, however, the arbitrator overstepped his or her bounds, there was evident partiality on the part of the arbitrator, the decision was procured by corruption, fraud, or undue means, or the arbitrator was guilty of misconduct that prejudiced the rights of a party, then a court may overturn an arbitration decision. Courts also will not enforce an arbitrator's award that would require a party to violate the law or a well-defined public policy.

ADMINISTRATIVE-AGENCY PROCEDURES

What if you can't resolve a workplace problem informally? What if you've tried to talk it out, maybe even tried mediation, but the two sides are still far apart?

The next step is usually to seek help from an administrative agency—such as the Equal Employment Opportunity Commission (EEOC) or the National Labor Relations Board (NLRB)—that enforces the law under which you think your rights are protected. (See Appendix II for a full listing of laws, enforcing agencies, and steps required for making a complaint.)

Seeking help from an administrative agency may be preferable to going to court in several ways. For one thing, the law often requires that an employee file a complaint with an administrative agency before filing a lawsuit. Sometimes employees can't sue at all, and the law is enforced solely through an administrative process. Even more important, going to an administrative agency costs no money, does not require a lawyer's help (though sometimes it is advisable), and keeps open the possibility of resolving the matter without a big fight. Almost all labor and employment laws provide for procedures (such as conciliation) aimed at helping disputing parties to reach an amicable settlement.

After an employee files a complaint with a government agency, an investigator is normally assigned to look into the case. Initially, the investigator will talk to the complaining party and seek to learn all the facts surrounding the claim. After obtaining information from the complaining party, the investigator will contact the employer to hear its side of the story. To complete its investigation, the investigator may also contact third-party witnesses to the relevant events.

When the investigation is completed, the agency will decide whether or not sufficient evidence exists to show that the law has been violated. If the agency decides that the claim has merit, it will contact the employer and the employee and attempt to settle the case. If settlement is unsuccessful, the next step will depend on which law is involved and what agency is handling

▶ **PREPARE YOURSELF**

After filing an administrative charge, you need to gather your evidence. Be sure to present to the investigator any written documentation affecting your case. For example, in a discharge case the following types of documents might be relevant:

- letter of termination;
- previous written warnings or other documentation of disciplinary action;
- personnel evaluations;
- company manual; and
- job description and pay stubs.

At this stage, you should also tell the investigator the names of other individuals who may have relevant information about your situation. If your state allows, you should attempt to obtain your personnel file from your employer (see the "Personnel Files" section of chapter 10 for a discussion of obtaining employee records).

the case. For example, the NLRB will issue a complaint and hold a hearing. If the EEOC is involved, the next step would be to file a lawsuit in court.

If the agency decides that the law has not been violated, in some cases that decision marks the end of the case. For example, under the National Labor Relations Act (NLRA) and Occupational Safety and Health Act (OSH Act) the agency (either the NLRB or OSHA) has sole authority to decide whether or not to pursue a case. Under Title VII, however, even if the EEOC decides that a case has no merit, an individual can still file a lawsuit in court.

How long does the administrative process take? The answer to this question depends on which agency is involved. For example, if the NLRB is involved, the investigation stage usually takes about forty-five days from the filing of a charge, though the time involved may vary based on the type of charge filed. The EEOC, however, generally takes several months and sometimes several years to complete an investigation.

COURT PROCEDURES

After going through the administrative process, what if you're still not satisfied? Many laws permit you to then file a lawsuit in court. Some laws allow you to proceed directly to court and file a lawsuit even if you haven't gone through the administrative process.

But should you sue? That's a decision that is highly individual; there are several factors to consider before making that decision. If you are suing your current employer, you should be aware that litigation causes hard feelings. Even though most employment laws have anti-retaliation provisions (see the "Anti-retaliation Laws" section of chapter 11), your relationship with your employer can easily be adversely affected by litigation.

Second, you need to consider the likelihood that you will win your lawsuit. While no lawyer can predict with 100 percent accuracy the outcome of any lawsuit, a lawyer can give you a good indication of how likely it is that you can win. Litigation entails a tremendous amount of time and money, and such expenditures may only make sense when the prospects of winning are high.

▶ **MAKE UP YOUR MIND**

If you intend to pursue a claim by filing a charge with a government agency or by filing a lawsuit in court, you need to make a decision in a timely manner. All laws have limitations periods. This means that if you don't file your charge or lawsuit within a specific period of time after the violation occurs (this period is different for each law), you lose your ability to "have your day in court." The time limits for the federal laws discussed in this book can be found in Appendix II.

Third, you should be aware that most lawsuits can take several years before they reach a courtroom. In the meantime, parties to a lawsuit will be required to give testimony in **depositions** (answering questions during the pretrial discovery process), and lawyers will file legal motions dealing with certain aspects of the case. All of these procedures involve paying for the attorney's time and efforts as well as expending your own time participating in the process.

Litigation is, of course, a very valuable mechanism for vindicating your rights and receiving compensation for wrongdoing. However, satisfaction with the process is much higher among those who know what to expect before they decide to sue.

WHEN DO YOU NEED A LAWYER?

Should you hire a lawyer in the event of a workplace dispute? As usual, it depends. One factor that will affect your decision is the process being used to deal with the dispute. Another is the stage of the process—in other words, you may not need a lawyer initially, but you may need one as the process gets more formal. A third factor is the size of the dispute: The more that is at stake, the more professional help makes sense.

Disputes that are still in the informal stages of resolution— that is, discussions between the employer and employee or mediation—may best be handled by the parties themselves. However, individuals who are uncomfortable with conflict, who feel at a disadvantage in expressing themselves, or who are unsure as to their rights and obligations may want to consult an attorney even at this early stage in the process.

If a dispute is relatively minor and is resolved amicably, neither side may need a lawyer to review the final settlement. But sometimes enough is at stake that it may be advisable to seek a lawyer's approval, even of a mediated settlement.

When government enforcement agencies become involved, it often is appropriate for an employer to retain an attorney. Enforcement agencies have the responsibility to ensure compliance with the law. When complaints are filed, they investigate and determine whether there is reason to believe the law has been violated. An attorney who understands the law and the investigation process can help to ensure that the government agency has access to the information necessary to understand the employer's conduct. A finding of no violation by the government may put the dispute to rest.

It may not be quite as important for an individual to have an attorney if government enforcement agencies are involved. The agency personnel know the law and have been trained to uncover the facts necessary to determine whether a violation has occurred. However, hiring an attorney at this stage often makes sense. An attorney can help the employee organize and present the information to the agency, highlight the probable legal issues involved, and suggest possible avenues of investigation. In effect, the attorney provides a safety net to ensure that the agency does not overlook critical information or issues.

ⓘ SPECIALIZED RULES REQUIRE SPECIALISTS

Arbitration, administrative hearings, and trials all have their own particular rules and procedures. Presenting a case successfully requires knowledge of the law and the rules of the process. Third-party decision makers—whether they are administrative law judges, arbitrators, or judges—rely on the parties to present all the evidence and arguments necessary for a decision. They don't independently investigate a case. A party can lose by failing to introduce an important piece of evidence, or by neglecting to inform the decision maker of the relevant case law affecting the issue. In some administrative hearings, such as before the NLRB or OSHA, a government attorney will present a case on behalf of the employee who filed the complaint. The attorney represents the public interest, and not the individual employee per se, but often the two interests are the same and the individual may not find it necessary to have separate representation.

Once a dispute reaches the **adjudication stage** (a hearing held before a neutral third party), it is usually a good idea for all parties to be represented by an attorney. This applies even to hearings outside the formal court system, such as in arbitration or before an administrative agency. In hearings before an administrative agency, an **administrative law judge (ALJ)** presides. An ALJ administers oaths, rules on evidence, takes testimony, makes findings of fact, and recommends conclusions of law.

FINDING THE RIGHT LAWYER

It's a good idea to choose a lawyer who regularly handles labor and employment law cases, since this is a complex and specialized area of law. How do you find one? It's helpful to get recommendations from other businesses, a union, or an acquaintance who has used a labor and employment lawyer. Your state or local bar association may have a lawyer referral service that can steer you towards lawyers specializing in this area. Or you may meet the income eligibility guidelines for representation by a Legal Services lawyer.

Many lawyers are willing to meet with you briefly without charge so that the two of you can get acquainted. At (or soon after) this first meeting, you can decide whether you want to hire that lawyer. Before you make that decision, you might want to ask:
- about the lawyer's experience and area of practice;
- who will be working on your case;
- about fees and costs (see below);
- about possible outcomes of the case; and
- how you can participate (and possibly lower the cost to yourself).

If you've made a complaint in a Title VII case, you can ask the court to appoint an attorney to represent you. Before the court will refer a case, it will consider your financial condition, the likelihood that you can win the case, and the efforts that you have made on your own to get an attorney. It may then make a

(i) LAWYER'S FEES

If you're considering a lawyer, you're naturally concerned with fees. In employment cases, attorneys representing employers generally charge an hourly rate for their services. Attorneys representing employees may charge an hourly rate or may represent employees in a **contingency fee arrangement.** In contingency fee cases, the fee is a percentage of the money awarded to you if you win. If you lose, you'll be liable for costs—filing fees, fees for serving summonses, costs of postage, costs of copying documents, costs of expert witnesses, and so on—but not the lawyer's time.

You'll want to discuss fees with each lawyer you interview. Try to get a feel for the likely range of fees you'll be charged; whether you will be billed at a lesser rate for associates and paralegals who work on the case; how long you have to pay fees; how you can help reduce them; and so on. Many labor statutes also provide for an award of attorney's fees to the plaintiff if he or she wins the case. This means that the defendant could be required to pay for the plaintiff's attorney.

referral of the case to an attorney, but it still cannot force an attorney to take the case.

THE WORLD AT YOUR FINGERTIPS

• *The American Bar Association Family Legal Guide* (2003) features a chapter on how to choose and use a lawyer (chapter 1) and a chapter on how the court system works (chapter 2). Some of this information is available online—visit *www.abanet. org/publiced/practical/home.html* and click on "Working with Lawyers."

• The website of the ABA Division for Public Education also provides easy-to-read information on how the court system works, and how arbitration works, at *www.abanet.org/publiced/courts/home.html*.

- *Alternative Dispute Resolution in a Nutshell* by Jacqueline Nolan-Haley (2001) features chapters describing the practical and legal aspects of mediation and arbitration.
- *Mediation in a Nutshell* by Kimberlee Kovach (2003) provides a good explanation of how mediation works.
- At *www.mediate.com*, you can find listings of mediators in every state.
- The website of the American Arbitration Association features information related to employment disputes and labor disputes. Visit *www.adr.org/Employment* and *www.adr.org/Labor* for rules, procedures, forms, and more.
- *How Arbitration Works: Elkouri & Elkouriorks* by Alan Miles Ruben et al. (2003) is a comprehensive guide to labor arbitration.

REMEMBER THIS

- If your company provides a mechanism for dealing with workplace problems, it may be a good idea to utilize that mechanism before seeking outside help.
- Mediation may help parties resolve a dispute to everyone's satisfaction.
- Mandatory arbitration provisions will be enforced by courts if the procedures outlined therein are fair.
- Many workplace laws create administrative agencies that investigate complaints involving violations of those laws.
- Some laws require employees to file a charge with an administrative agency, and some laws allow employees to file lawsuits.
- Whether an employee should contact a lawyer to handle a workplace dispute depends on the employee's own ability to deal with problems, the kind of dispute involved, and the process being used.

CHAPTER 16

Where Do You Go From Here?

How to Find More Information

Throughout this book, we've provided you with resources for finding more information on a variety of topics associated with workplace law. Not to belabor the issue, but we still have more to give you. Some of these resources may have been mentioned in previous chapters, but we think they're your best places to start. Also included are some reminders and tips you can use to go about getting more information. This chapter is broken up into the following subsections:

- We Can Work It Out: Seven Websites to Get You Started;
- This Book for Hire; and
- Don't Forget . . .

WE CAN WORK IT OUT: SEVEN WEBSITES TO GET YOU STARTED

The websites listed below feature substantial sections on topics associated with workplace law. Some of these sites are housed within larger sites; we've also included some specialty sites. You're bound to find what you're looking for at one of these sites, or from one of the links they provide. (Note: These are not arranged in any order of preference.)

The 'Lectric Law Library's Employment and Labor Topic Area—*www.lectlaw.com/temp.html*

The many topics featured here include: electronic privacy rights in the workplace, laws and regulations, sexual harassment, and how to file ERISA claims. This site also includes links to other pertinent information housed within the 'Lectric Law Library site.

Nolo—*www.nolo.com*

Go to "Rights & Disputes" and click on "Employee Rights" for information about your rights in the workplace. Topics include health and safety, fair pay, military leave, and more.

Employment Law Information Network—*www.elinfonet.com*

Designed for employment lawyers, in-house counsel, and human resources professionals, this site also features information that may be of interest to employees. It includes links to articles, a blog by employment lawyers, information on laws and regulations, and more.

U.S. Department of Labor—*www.dol.gov*

One-stop shopping for everything you need to know regarding wages, benefits, laws, links to state labor offices, disability, equal opportunity, forms, and more. Among other categories, the site is organized by topic, by intended audience, and by its top-twenty requested items.

National Labor Relations Board—*www.nlrb.gov*

This site features manuals, forms, news, and other information pertaining to the National Labor Relations Act.

Cornell's Legal Information Institute—*straylight.law.cornell.edu/topics/index.html*

The LII website offers a variety of topical legal information; scroll down to "Employment Law" for information about workplace safety, pension, workers' compensation, and more.

DisabilityInfo.gov—*www.disabilityinfo.gov*

This site features a section on employment geared toward employees, employers, and those seeking jobs.

THIS BOOK FOR HIRE

Listed below are some books you might wish to explore if you want to learn more about the law of the workplace. But don't stop with these; you can find many more at your local library, as well as at Amazon.com and other online bookstores.

For Employees

Employees' Rights: Your Practical Handbook to Workplace Law by Richard C. Busse (Sourcebooks, January 2004).

Fired, Laid Off Or Forced Out: A Complete Guide To Severance, Benefits And Your Rights When You're Starting Over by Richard C. Busse (Sphinx Publishing, February 2005).

Every Employee's Guide to the Law by Lewin G. Joel III (Pantheon, September 2001).

Your Rights in the Workplace by Barbara Kate Repa (Nolo, November 2002).

For Employers

Employer's Rights: Your Legal Handbook from Hiring to Termination and Everything in Between by Charles H. Fleischer (Sphinx Publishing, January 2004).

The Employer's Legal Handbook by Fred S. Steingold (Nolo, June 2005).

Working with Independent Contractors: The Employer's Legal Guide by Stephen Fishman (Nolo, July 2005).

DON'T FORGET . . .

Check local venues for courses, lectures and seminars, and expert panels related to workplace and labor law, including various panels associated with specialized topics (such as pensions, health care, and unemployment). Start with your local library, bar association, area colleges, and senior citizens' centers to see what's in the works, or to suggest a topic for upcoming events. Local radio and TV stations also feature experts on employment matters, so get with the programs. You might also want to check national programs on radio stations and TV channels such as CNN and CNBC for salient information. If you don't have cable TV, don't forget that most channels also have websites.

The Internet is also a great resource. Countless posting boards, user groups, mailing lists, and chat rooms exist in cyberspace; many of these could help you in your quest for knowledge and provide a "been there, done that" perspective on issues you're facing. Communicating with others who have been in your position is a great way to learn about other avenues to explore and pitfalls to avoid. Some websites may also provide an area where you can send in your questions and get answers. And many of the sites associated with employment law include online tools (such as forms) you can use for free.

That's about all for now. Your next job is to begin checking out the resources we've provided. We welcome your comments and suggestions for future editions of this book. Please visit us on the Web at *www.abanet.org/publiced/*, or drop us a line via e-mail at *abapubed@abanet.org*.

APPENDIX I

Defining the Terms Found in Federal Law

Most of the terms used in federal employment laws have an obvious meaning and do not need definition here. A few terms, however, bear special scrutiny:

CITIZENSHIP

The **Immigration Reform and Control Act (IRCA)** prohibits discrimination based on citizenship status. As it is defined in the statute, "citizenship status" includes only those individuals who are actually U.S. citizens or lawfully admitted aliens who have applied for naturalization. Thus, a lawfully admitted alien who has resided in the United States for ten years and has taken no steps to apply for citizenship would not be protected from citizenship discrimination under IRCA. However, a lawfully admitted alien who has taken steps to become naturalized could not be denied a job just because he was not currently a citizen.

DISABILITY

Both the **Americans with Disabilities Act (ADA)** and the **Rehabilitation Act** prohibit discrimination against any qualified individual with a disability. An individual with a disability is one who:

1. has a physical or mental impairment that substantially limits a major life activity;

2. has a record of having such a physical or mental impairment; or

3. is regarded as having such an impairment.

ⓘ MISPERCEPTIONS OF DISABILITY

The EEOC provides the following example of a case in which an individual is regarded as having a disability: An employee has a mild form of strabismus (crossed eyes). The impairment only slightly affects her ability to see, but the employer mistakenly believes that the impairment prevents the employee from seeing all printed material. As a result, the employer refuses to promote the employee to a supervisory position that would require her to review the written work of others. Although the employee does not actually have a disability, she is *regarded* as having an impairment that substantially limits her ability to see.

The term is defined broadly to include any physiologically based impairment or any mental or psychological impairment. It does not, however, include mere physical characteristics or cultural, economic, or environmental impairments. For example, an individual with dyslexia has a disability, but an individual who is illiterate does not. A person who is a dwarf has a disability, but a person who is short does not.

To fall within the auspices of the statute, the impairment must cause a substantial limitation to a major life activity. Temporary conditions, such as a broken leg or a cold, are not considered substantial limitations. For statutory purposes, major life activities include walking, eating, seeing, speaking, caring for oneself, or working.

To determine whether a disability constitutes a substantial limitation, courts take into account the following factors:
- the nature and severity of the impairment;
- how long the impairment will last—i.e., whether it is temporary, permanent or long-term;

- how the impairment affects the individual's major life activities as compared to those of the average person; and
- how medicines or devices may alleviate the impact of the impairment.

Whether an impairment constitutes a substantial limitation is an individualized assessment. Two persons may have the same medical impairment but be affected by it differently; one may be substantially limited while the other person is not.

A second meaning of the term "disability" encompasses any person who no longer has a disability but has a record of a disability, such as a person who has successfully recovered from tuberculosis, or a person who was diagnosed with cancer but did not in fact have (or no longer has) cancer.

A third meaning of the term takes into account misperceptions that other people may have about an individual. For example, an employer may mistakenly believe that a person has an impairment that substantially limits a major life activity, when in fact the impairment is non-limiting.

In order to be protected under the ADA or the Rehabilitation Act, an individual not only must have a disability, but also must be **qualified**. People with disabilities are "qualified" under these statutes if they "satisfy the requisite skill, experience, education and other job-related requirements." For example, if a person with epilepsy applies for a job as a teacher but does not possess a teaching certificate, then he or she is not a "qualified" individual, and therefore is not protected under the law despite his or her disability.

Certain types of conditions are not considered disabilities under the ADA, including homosexuality, transvestism, transsexualism, bisexuality, sexual-behavior disorders, compulsive gambling, kleptomania, pyromania, or current illegal drug use.

(Note that the above discussion defines "impairment" for purposes of the ADA and Rehabilitation Act only; some state laws may have different standards for defining the term, which may offer protection for a wider array of medical conditions.)

EMPLOYEES ENGAGED IN
INTERSTATE COMMERCE

The **Fair Labor Standards Act (FLSA)** applies to employees engaged in interstate commerce. The Wage and Hour Division of the Department of Labor has identified five general categories of employees who are considered to be engaged in interstate commerce:

1. employees participating in the actual movement of commerce—for example, employees in the telephone, transportation, or insurance industries;

2. employees performing work related to the **instrumentalities of commerce**—for example, employees who maintain and repair roads and bridges, or employees who work at airports and bus stations;

3. employees who regularly cross state lines in performing their duties, such as traveling salespersons;

4. employees who produce or work on goods for commerce—for example, assembly workers in auto plants, coal miners, and shipping department employees; and

5. employees who work in a closely related process or occupation essential to producing goods for commerce—for example, employees who build machines used in auto plants.

NATIONAL ORIGIN

Title VII prohibits discrimination based on national origin. The term "national origin" encompasses not only the place of origin of an individual and his or her ancestors, but also the possession by that individual of physical, cultural, or linguistic characteristics of a national-origin group. For example, if an employer hires individuals who are born in Mexico, but refuses to hire anyone who speaks with a Mexican accent, then the employer has discriminated based on national origin. National origin does not include citizenship status. Thus, an employer may have a policy requiring all employees to be U.S. citizens without discriminating based on national origin under Title VII. (Such a policy, however, would run afoul of the requirements of the IRCA, which prohibits discrimination based on citizenship status.)

PRIVATE-SECTOR EMPLOYER

This term refers to nongovernmental employers. Any employer that is not a public-sector employer is a private-sector employer. Individuals who work for nongovernmental employers are called **private-sector employees.**

PROTECTED CLASS

The various antidiscrimination laws were passed to prohibit employers from taking adverse employment actions against individuals because of their membership in protected classes. Different laws define the term "protected class" differently. For example, protected classes under Title VII are race, sex, religion, national origin, and color; under the ADA, the protected class is disability. Under some state laws, marital status and/or sexual orientation are protected classes. Antidiscrimination laws are based on the premise that just because a person is in a protected class, he or she should not be treated any differently than someone who is not a member of that class. Such laws are aimed at ensuring equality of treatment, not preferential treatment.

PUBLIC-SECTOR EMPLOYER

This term refers to employers that are governments, governmental agencies, or political subdivisions of a government. For example, a state department of motor vehicles, a city school district, and the United States Department of Agriculture are all public-sector employers. The term for people who work for government employers is **public-sector employees,** though in this book we refer to them simply as "government employees."

RACE

Title VII's prohibition against race discrimination protects not only members of minority racial groups, but also individuals of all races—including Caucasians.

RELIGION

Title VII prohibits discrimination because of religion. For purposes of Title VII, the term "religion" encompasses not only membership in an established religious group, but also an individual's sincerely held religious beliefs, whether or not that individual is connected with any institutional religious group. The term also encompasses all aspects of religious observance, practice, and belief. For example, an individual who does not belong to any church, but who sincerely believes that she should read the Bible for two hours every day, may be protected under Title VII. If her employer fires her for reading the Bible during her lunch break, the employer may have violated Title VII's prohibition against religious discrimination.

Title VII grants an exemption from the prohibition against religious discrimination to religious corporations and educational institutions so that such employers may lawfully express a preference for employees of a particular religion. For example, a Catholic school may prefer to hire a teacher who is Catholic over one who is Protestant. This exemption applies only to religious preferences; however, it does not allow religious institutions to discriminate based on race, sex, national origin, age, or disability.

ⓘ YOU DON'T ACT LIKE A WOMAN!

Courts are increasingly recognizing that sex discrimination also includes **sex stereotyping**. Sex stereotyping involves discrimination based on an individual's failure to conform to certain socially expected behaviors associated with his or her gender. For example, taking adverse employment action against a woman for her failure to act feminine can constitute sex stereotyping in violation of Title VII. This was what happened in a notable case brought before the Supreme Court, in which a woman was accused of being "macho," in need of "a course in charm school," "a lady using foul language," or "a tough-talking somewhat masculine hard-nosed manager."

SEX

Title VII prohibits discrimination based on sex. "Sex" means a person's gender—not his or her sexual orientation. "Sex" has also been defined to include pregnancy, childbirth, and related medical conditions. Thus, an employer that fires a woman because she becomes pregnant discriminates against her based on her sex; but an employer that refuses to promote a woman because she is a lesbian has not violated Title VII. (In the second instance, however, the employer may be in violation of state, city, or municipal law in those jurisdictions that prohibit sexual-orientation discrimination.)

APPENDIX II
Labor and Employment Laws

This appendix provides a handy summary of the federal laws discussed in this book. It contains a general description of which types of employers are regulated by each law, what each law requires, and how each law is enforced. For more information on these laws, see the appropriate sections of the main text.

EMPLOYMENT DISCRIMINATION LAWS

These federal laws generally prohibit employers from discriminating against employees and applicants. They cover hiring, firing, and terms and conditions of employment. They protect employees and applicants who are members of an identified class of protected individuals.

Title VII of the Civil Rights Act of 1964 (Title VII)

This is perhaps the most important federal antidiscrimination law.

What It Does: Prohibits employment discrimination based on race, color, religion, sex, or national origin.

Who Is Covered: All government and private-sector employers employing at least fifteen employees. Unions having at least fifteen members and employment agencies also are covered.

Where to Find It in the Law Books: 42 U.S.C. secs. 2000e–2000e-17

Where to Find More Information: The primary source of information about Title VII is the **Equal Employment Opportunity Commission (EEOC)**, 1801 L Street, N.W., Washington, D.C. 20507. The EEOC has regional offices in most major cities throughout the U.S. The EEOC publishes brochures that explain the law and describe the charge-filing process. You can

▶ FINDING FEDERAL LAWS

Federal laws are collected in a series of books called the U.S. Code. Every federal law is assigned a title number and a section number. The title number indicates the law's general category; laws with the same title numbers deal with related matters. For example, many labor laws are found in Title 29. The section number refers to the specific place within the title where a law can be found. Thus, you can find the Age Discrimination in Employment Act (ADEA) at Title 29 of the U.S. Code beginning at section 621. This is written as "29 U.S.C. sec. 621."

obtain these brochures by calling (800) 669–4000, or by accessing the EEOC's website at *www.eeoc.gov.*

There also are several private organizations that deal with problems related to employment discrimination. You can contact the NAACP Legal Defense and Education Fund at 99 Hudson Street, 16th Floor, New York, NY 10013, or online at *www. naacpldf.org;* the National Women's Law Center at 11 Dupont Circle, N.W., Suite 800, Washington, D.C. 20036, or online at *www.nwlc.org;* the Mexican American Legal Defense and Education Fund at 634 South Spring Street, 11th Floor, Los Angeles, CA 90014, or online at *www.maldef.org;* the Asian-American Legal Defense and Education Fund at 99 Hudson Street, 12th Floor, New York, NY 10013, or online at *www.aaldef.org;* or the American-Arab Anti-Discrimination Committee at 4201 Connecticut Avenue, N.W., Suite 300, Washington, D.C. 20008, or online at *www.adc.org.*

Who Enforces It: The Equal Employment Opportunity Commission (EEOC) investigates complaints of Title VII violations. It also has the authority to file lawsuits in federal court to enforce the statute. Individuals may also file lawsuits in either state or federal court alleging that their rights under the law have been violated.

Going to the EEOC: First, the statute requires you to file a charge with the EEOC. You must file the charge in writing and describe the conduct that you claim violates the law. You can file your charge in one of the EEOC's regional offices, which exist in most major cities. The courts will dismiss any lawsuit that is filed without first filing a charge with the EEOC and giving the EEOC an opportunity to investigate the claim.

Second, there are time limits for filing a charge with the EEOC. If you miss the deadline for filing a charge, you lose your opportunity to have your case heard either before the EEOC or in court. The time limit for filing depends on whether the issue you are complaining about violates the antidiscrimination law in your state.

In states that have an antidiscrimination law covering the matter in question, you often must file a charge with the state agency responsible for enforcing the state law before you can file with the EEOC. However, many states have "work-sharing" agreements with the EEOC, which eliminate the need for you to file claims with both the state agency and the EEOC.

In states where a charge must first be filed with a state agency, the agency must have at least sixty days to investigate the complaint. After sixty days, you then can file the charge with the EEOC. The deadline for filing the charge with the EEOC is three hundred days from the date the unlawful discrimination occurred, or within thirty days after the state agency completes its investigation, whichever occurs first.

In states where there are no antidiscrimination laws covering the matter in question, you must file your charge with the EEOC within 180 days from the date of the discriminatory act.

After your charge is filed with the EEOC, the agency investigates the complaint to determine whether there is reasonable cause to believe the law was violated. If the EEOC finds reasonable cause, it enters into **conciliation** with your employer and tries to settle the case. If settlement is unsuccessful, the EEOC will send you a letter informing you that you have ninety days to file a lawsuit in court. This is called a **right-to-sue letter.**

Although the EEOC has the authority to file lawsuits in court, it does so only in a small percentage of cases. Most of the time, you must pursue a lawsuit on your own.

After its investigation, if the EEOC decides there is no reasonable cause to believe the law was violated, it will still send you
a right-to-sue letter. The law gives you the right to have a court
determine the merits of your complaint, even when the EEOC
decides it has no merit. The statute of limitations for filing the
lawsuit expires ninety days from the date you receive the right-
to-sue letter. (**Statutes of limitation** are time deadlines set by
law for filing lawsuits. If a suit is filed after the time limit set by
the statute has expired, the suit will almost always be dismissed
by the court.)

▶ **DIFFERENT PROCESS FOR EMPLOYEES
OF THE FEDERAL GOVERNMENT**

If you're an employee of the federal government, you must follow a different procedure than private-sector employees in order to make a Title VII
claim. All agencies of the federal government employ equal-employment-
opportunity (EEO) counselors whose job is to try to resolve discrimination
complaints. A federal employee must first file any charge with the EEO
counselor within forty-five days of the date of the discriminatory act. The
counselor investigates the matter and attempts to resolve the complaint. If
you're not satisfied with the counselor's proposed settlement, then within
fifteen days you must either request a hearing on the complaint or request
a decision by the head of the agency without a hearing. If you request a
hearing, the hearing will be conducted by an independent administrative-
law judge, who will then issue a decision. The judge's decision will then be
sent to the agency head, who may reject, accept, or modify it.

After the agency head issues a decision, you have three options: accept
the decision of the agency head, file an appeal with the EEOC within
thirty days, or file a lawsuit in court within ninety days.

If you decide to appeal to the EEOC, the EEOC has 180 days to review
your file and make a final decision. If you are not satisfied with the
EEOC's final decision, you can file a lawsuit in court within ninety days of
receiving the decision.

(i) REMEDYING YOUR LOSS

Compensatory Damages. These are damages for the *indirect* injuries you suffer as a natural consequence of the wrongdoer's act. An example of compensatory damages would be payment for pain and suffering you incur as a result of the law's violation.

Injunctive Relief. This is a court order directed at wrongdoers, requiring them to engage (or not engage) in certain types of action. For example, an order might tell a wrongdoer to stop violating the law and to refrain from doing so in the future. Or an order might require the wrongdoer to take certain affirmative steps to restore a situation to the way it would have been had the law not been violated.

Make-Whole Remedy. This type of remedy puts you in the position you would have been in had there been no violation of the law. For example, let's say you're illegally terminated from your job. Your make-whole remedy would include:

- reinstatement to the job;
- payment of the wages you would have earned (with interest) had you remained employed;
- payment of any bonuses, vacation pay, or other types of payments you would have earned had you remained employed;
- accrual of seniority and pension benefits with which you would have been credited had you remained employed; and
- payment for any medical expenses you incurred that would have been covered under the employer's health insurance plan.

The elements of the make-whole remedy will vary depending on the type of injury suffered.

Punitive Damages. These damages are intended to punish the wrongdoer *and* deter others from engaging in similar conduct. The money goes to you, not the government. Courts award these damages when a wrongdoer acts with malice or reckless indifference to your rights. Punitive damages are not available in all labor and employment law cases.

If You Win: What will you get if you win? The remedies available include **compensatory damages, injunctive relief, make-whole remedies,** and, where appropriate, punitive damages. In cases involving intentional discrimination (but not adverse impact), a court will also award **compensatory damages** and, where appropriate, **punitive damages.** (See the sidebar entitled "Remedying Your Loss" on page 264.)

Compensatory and punitive damage amounts are capped based on the size of the employer. For example, small employers with fewer than 101 employees are liable for no more than $50,000 total in compensatory and punitive damages; employers with more than five hundred employees are liable for no more than $300,000 total. In adverse-impact cases, only make-whole and injunctive relief is available. The court in its discretion may (in either type of case) award attorney's fees to the prevailing party.

Section 1981

This is a very old law, dating from the years just after the Civil War.

What It Does: Prohibits employment discrimination based on race or ethnicity.

Who Is Covered: All government and private-sector employers, regardless of size.

Where to Find It in the Law Books: 42 U.S.C. sec. 1981

Who Enforces It: Private individuals, through lawsuits. There is no federal agency with authority to enforce this law. Individuals may file lawsuits in either state or federal court alleging violations of their rights under this statute.

Going to Court: You can file suit directly in federal or state court; you don't first have to take any administrative steps. The time limit for filing some types of employment discrimination claims under Section 1981 is four years; the limit for other types of claims is based on the state statute of limitations for personal-injury suits—usually two or three years from the date of the event giving rise to the suit.

If You Win: You might get injunctive relief, make-whole remedies, compensatory and punitive damages, and reasonable attorney's fees.

Section 1983

This law is a companion to Section 1981, and also dates from the years after the Civil War.

What It Does: Prohibits discrimination in employment because of membership in a protected class, and limits the ability of an employer to interfere with the constitutional rights of its employees.

Who Is Covered: All state- and local-government employers, regardless of size.

Where to Find It in the Law Books: 42 U.S.C. sec. 1983

Who Enforces It: Private individuals, through lawsuits. There is no government agency with authority to enforce this law. Individuals may file lawsuits in either state or federal court alleging violations of their rights under this statute.

Going to Court: You can file suit directly in court for violations; you don't first have to take any administrative steps. The time limit for filing the lawsuit is based on the state statute of limitations for personal-injury suits—usually two or three years from the date of the event giving rise to the suit.

If You Win: You might get injunctive relief, make-whole remedies, compensatory damages, and reasonable attorney's fees. Punitive damages may be awarded against individuals (not against government entities) when they act with reckless disregard of a plaintiff's rights.

The Age Discrimination in Employment Act (ADEA)

What It Does: Prohibits employment discrimination based on the fact that an employee or job applicant is forty years of age or older.

Who Is Covered: Public- and private-sector employers

employing at least twenty people, along with unions and employment agencies.

Where to Find It in the Law Books: 29 U.S.C. secs. 621–34

Where to Find More Information: Contact the EEOC at *www.eeoc.org* or the American Association of Retired Persons at 601 E Street, N.W., Washington, D.C. 20049, or online at *www.aarp.org*.

Who Enforces It: The EEOC has enforcement authority under the ADEA both to investigate complaints and file lawsuits. Individuals may also file lawsuits in either state or federal court alleging violations of the ADEA.

Going to the EEOC: Procedures are slightly different than those for enforcing Title VII. As with Title VII, you must file a written charge with the EEOC. The time limits for filing this charge depend on whether there is a state law that prohibits age discrimination. The same 180-day/300-day time limits apply as under Title VII (see above). In those states with age discrimination laws, you are not required to file with the applicable state agency before filing with the EEOC; as long as you ultimately file with both, the order of the filings doesn't matter. The remainder of the enforcement procedure is the same: an investigation, an attempt to conciliate, and the issuance of a right-to-sue letter.

The procedures in place for federal employees are the same as those that apply under Title VII.

Going to Court: You can't file suit without going first to the EEOC and getting a right-to-sue letter. You have ninety days from the date you receive the right-to-sue letter to file a lawsuit in court. Employees who work for a state government, however, cannot sue their employers; state governments enjoy sovereign immunity. The EEOC may file a lawsuit against the state.

If You Win: The remedies available under the ADEA include injunctive relief and make-whole remedies. In those cases where an employer acted with reckless disregard for the rights of the employee, the employer must pay the employee **liquidated damages**. For example, if the employer owes the employee $25,000 in back pay, liquidated damages would equal an addi-

tional $25,000. The courts also award attorney's fees to success-
ful plaintiffs.

Title I of the Americans with Disabilities Act (ADA)

What It Does: Prohibits employment discrimination against qualified individuals with a disability.

Who Is Covered: All state- and local- government employers
and private-sector employers employing at least fifteen employees. Unions having at least fifteen members and employment
agencies are also covered.

Where to Find It in the Law Books: 42 U.S.C. sec.
12101–11

Where to Find More Information: Contact the EEOC (see
the Title VII entry above for full contact information). Several
private organizations also focus on disability rights issues: Contact the Disability Rights Education and Defense Fund, Inc., at
2212 6th St., Berkeley, CA 94710, or access its website at
www.dredf.org; the Judge David L. Bazelon Center for Mental
Health Law at 1101 15th St., N.W., Suite 1212, Washington,
D.C. 20005, or access its website at *www.bazelon.org*; or the
Disability Rights Center at P.O. Box 2007, Augusta, ME 04338,
or access their website at *www.drcme.org*.

Who Enforces It: The EEOC has the authority to investigate complaints and file lawsuits under the ADA. After exhaust-
ing administrative procedures, individuals may also file lawsuits
in either state or federal court alleging violations of the ADA.
Employees who work for a state government, however, cannot
sue their employer; state governments enjoy sovereign immunity.
The EEOC may file a lawsuit against the state.

Going to the EEOC: The administrative procedures required under the ADA are exactly the same as those required
under Title VII.

If You Win: The same remedies available under Title VII are
also available under the ADA.

The Rehabilitation Act

What It Does: Prohibits employment discrimination against qualified individuals with disabilities.

Who Is Covered: Executive-branch agencies of the federal government, the U.S. Postal Service, federal-government contractors and subcontractors whose contracts are in excess of $10,000, and programs that receive federal funds, including state and local governments.

Where to Find It in the Law Books: 29 U.S.C. secs. 706(8), 791, 793–94(a)

Where to Find More Information: The same private organizations that are concerned with legal issues under the ADA are also familiar with issues arising under the Rehabilitation Act. You can also access more information at *www.dol.gov/esa/ofccp.*

Who Enforces It: The enforcement mechanisms for this statute vary depending on the employer. If the employer is the federal government or the United States Postal Service, then the EEOC has the authority to investigate complaints and file lawsuits. If the employer is a federal contractor or subcontractor, the responsibility for enforcement lies with the Office of Federal Contract Compliance Programs (OFCCP) of the Department of Labor. The OFCCP has offices located in six cities across the U.S.: New York, Philadelphia, Atlanta, Chicago, Dallas, and San Francisco. If the employer is a program that receives federal funding, a private individual can file a lawsuit directly; there is no government agency responsible for enforcement under these circumstances.

How to Enforce the Rehabilitation Act Against the Federal Government: The enforcement process is exactly the same as the process used by federal-government employees under Title VII. The remedies available are also the same as those available under Title VII.

How to Enforce the Rehabilitation Act Against Federal Contractors: An individual must file a written complaint with the OFCCP within 180 days of the date of the unlawful discrimination. The OFCCP investigates and determines what type of action to take.

If the OFCCP decides that the law has been violated, it enters into conciliation with the employer and tries to settle the case. If settlement is unsuccessful, a hearing is held before an administrative law judge (ALJ). The decision of the ALJ is appealable to the Department of Labor. The final decision of the Department of Labor can be appealed to a federal district court.

If a violation is found, the government may terminate the contract, bar the contractor from further government business, or order the contractor to make whole the employee against whom it discriminated.

Individuals cannot file their own lawsuits alleging violations of the Rehabilitation Act by federal contractors. The OFCCP has the exclusive authority to enforce the law.

How to Enforce the Rehabilitation Act Against Programs that Receive Federal Funds: There is no government agency that enforces the Rehabilitation Act against recipients of federal funds. Individuals may file a lawsuit directly in federal court. There is no uniform statute of limitations for filing a lawsuit. The deadline is based on the most closely analogous state statute of limitations, which can vary from one year in some states to six years in others. Successful plaintiffs are entitled to injunctive relief, make-whole remedies, compensatory and punitive damages, and reasonable attorney's fees.

Uniformed Services Employment and Reemployment Rights Act of 1994 (USERRA)

What It Does: Prohibits employment discrimination because of an employee's or applicant's past, current, or future military obligations. It also requires employers to reinstate to their former jobs, upon honorable completion of their military duty, employees who have served in the uniformed services.

Who Is Covered: All public- and private-sector employers, regardless of size.

Where to Find It in the Law Books: 38 U.S.C. secs. 4301–33

Where to Find More Information: Contact the Department of Labor, Veterans' Employment and Training Service, 200 Constitution Avenue, N.W., Washington, D.C. 20210, or access its website at *www. dol.gov/vets/*; the National Veterans Legal Services Project, 2001 S Street, N.W., Suite 610, Washington, D.C. 20009, or access its website at *www.nvlsp.org*.

Who Enforces It: The Office of Veterans' Employment and Training Service (VETS) of the Department of Labor has the responsibility for investigating complaints under USERRA. Individuals may also file lawsuits in federal court to enforce their rights.

Going to VETS: An individual who is employed by a state or local government or a private-sector employer is not required to first file a complaint with VETS. He or she may file a lawsuit directly in court, without following any administrative procedure. There is no statute of limitations for filing a lawsuit. The only rule is that a plaintiff may not unreasonably delay filing a suit so as to cause prejudice to the defendant's ability to present its case.

An individual may, however, file a charge with the VETS

(i) SPECIAL RULES FOR EMPLOYEES OF THE FEDERAL GOVERNMENT

An individual who is employed by the federal government cannot file a lawsuit under USERRA directly in court. Federal employees must first file a charge with the VETS office. If, after finding merit to the charge, VETS is unsuccessful in its attempt to settle the case, the employee may request that the charge be referred to the Office of Special Counsel for the Merit Systems Protection Board (MSPB). It is within the discretion of the special counsel to decide whether to prosecute the case before the MSPB. If the special counsel decides not to prosecute, the individual may then file a complaint directly with the MSPB.

office. Filing an administrative charge may help to resolve the problem without the necessity of a lawsuit.

Once a charge is filed, VETS is required to investigate and, if it finds merit to the charge, attempt to resolve the problem. VETS notifies the charging party of the outcome of the investigation and provides information about further enforcement options.

If VETS is unsuccessful in resolving the charge, the individual can ask the Department of Labor to refer the case to the U.S. attorney general for prosecution. It is within the discretion of the attorney general to decide if it will prosecute the case. The individual always has the option of bringing his or her own private lawsuit in court.

If You Win: The remedies available include injunctive relief, make-whole remedies, and liquidated damages. The court may, in its discretion, award reasonable attorney's fees.

Immigration Reform and Control Act (IRCA)

What It Does: Prohibits discrimination with regard to hiring, recruiting, or discharging employees based on national origin or citizenship status. It also prohibits employers from hiring illegal aliens and requires employers to verify the work eligibility status of all applicants for employment.

Who Is Covered: All private-sector employers that employ three or more employees.

Where to Find It in the Law Books: 8 U.S.C. secs. 1324a–c

Where to Find More Information: Contact the Department of Justice, Office of the Special Counsel for Immigration-Related Unfair Employment Practices, P.O. Box 27728, Washington, D.C. 20038, (800) 255–7688, or access its website at *www.justice. gov/crt/osc/*; the League of United Latin American Citizens at 2000 L Street, N.W., Suite 610, Washington, D.C. 20036, or access its website at *www.lulac.org*; the Mexican American Legal Defense and Educational Fund at 634 South Spring Street, 11th Floor, Los Angeles, CA 90014.

Who Enforces It: The Office of the Special Counsel for Immigration-Related Unfair Employment Practices, Department of Justice, has the authority to investigate and prosecute charges. Individuals cannot file private lawsuits; they must use the administrative process.

Going to the Special Counsel: An individual who believes his or her rights under IRCA were violated must file a written complaint with the special counsel within 180 days from the date of the alleged violation. The special counsel investigates the case and within 120 days decides whether or not to prosecute the case. If the special counsel decides to prosecute the case, he or she files a complaint before a Department of Justice ALJ. If the special counsel decides not to prosecute the case, the counsel must notify the charging party, who then has ninety days to file his or her own complaint with the Department of Justice.

The ALJ holds a hearing and issues a decision. The decision of the ALJ can be appealed to the federal court of appeals within sixty days after the decision is issued.

If You Win: The remedy for a violation is a make-whole order. An employer may also be subject to civil fines of between $250 and $3,000. (**Civil fines** are paid to the government, not to the plaintiff.)

EXECUTIVE ORDERS

Executive Orders are issued by the President to regulate the conduct of employers who do business with agencies of the federal government.

Executive Order 11246

What It Does: Prohibits employment discrimination based on race, color, religion, sex, or national origin.

Executive Order 11141

What It Does: Prohibits employment discrimination based on age.

Executive Order 12989

What It Does: Prohibits executive-branch agencies from entering into contracts with any employer that knowingly hires illegal aliens.

Who Is Covered by Executive Orders: All private-sector employers who have contracts with the federal government.

Where to Find Executive Orders in the Law Books: Executive Orders are reprinted in Title 3 of the Code of Federal Regulations.

Who Enforces Executive Orders: The Office of Federal Contract Compliance Programs (OFCCP) of the Department of Labor is responsible for ensuring compliance with the antidiscrimination mandates of Executives Orders 12086 and 11141. Each federal agency is responsible for ensuring contractor compliance under Executive Order 12989. Individuals cannot file lawsuits in court to enforce executive orders; they may, however, file complaints with an appropriate agency notifying it of possible noncompliance with an executive order.

Enforcement Procedures for Executive Orders: If the agency responsible for ensuring compliance with an executive order determines, after an investigation, that a contractor is not in compliance, it will notify the contractor of its decision. The contractor has the opportunity to contest the decision, in which case a hearing is held before an ALJ. The decision of the ALJ is appealable to the Department of Labor. The final decision of the Department of Labor can be appealed to a federal district court.

Consequences of Noncompliance with an Executive Order: A contractor found to be in noncompliance can have its current contract terminated, may be barred from entering into future government contracts, or may be required to take appropriate action to bring it into compliance with the mandates of the executive order.

UNION MANAGEMENT LAWS

These laws prohibit discrimination in employment because an employee has joined (or refused to join) a labor organization, or because an employee has engaged (or refused to engage) in union or other protected, concerted activity. The laws also impose restrictions on labor organizations and establish election procedures for determining whether employees want to be represented by a union.

National Labor Relations Act (NLRA)

What It Does: Regulates the labor-management relationship, prohibits discrimination based on union and concerted activity, and establishes election procedures for certification of unions as bargaining representatives.

Who Is Covered: All private-sector employers that have an impact on interstate commerce. The dollar volume of business generated by a company determines whether its operations impact interstate commerce. For example, the NLRA covers retail and service establishments with annual gross receipts of at least $500,000. It also covers labor unions. Specifically excluded from coverage are public-sector employers, railway and airline employers, supervisory and managerial employees, domestic employees, independent contractors, and individuals who are employed as agricultural laborers.

Where to Find It in the Law Books: 29 U.S.C. secs. 141–97

Where to Find More Information: Contact the National Labor Relations Board at 1099 14th Street, N.W., Washington, D.C. 20570. The NLRB offers free pamphlets that explain the rights and procedures associated with the law; to request them, call (866) 667–6572, or access the NLRB website at

ⓘ THERE'S ALWAYS AN EXCEPTION

There is one exception to the general rule that an individual cannot file a private lawsuit under the NLRA. The exception arises when a union violates its duty of fair representation. In that case, an employee may file his or her own lawsuit in either federal or state court within six months. Employers also have the right to file a lawsuit in federal court to recover damages for losses sustained as a result of a union engaging in a secondary boycott. There is no uniform time limit for filing such a lawsuit; the limit will vary based on the jurisdiction in which the suit is filed. Deadlines may be as soon as one year or as long as three years from the date of violation.

www.nlrb.gov. Local labor unions in your community may also have information concerning employee rights under this law.

Who Enforces It: The National Labor Relations Board (NLRB) has the exclusive authority to investigate charges, prosecute complaints, and conduct elections. With few exceptions, individuals cannot file their own lawsuits in court.

Going to the NLRB: Individuals who believe their rights have been violated must file a written charge with the NLRB within six months of the date of the alleged violation. There are regional offices located in most major cities. The NLRB investigates the case and decides if there is reasonable cause to believe the law was violated. If it finds no reasonable cause, it will dismiss the charge and inform the charging party by letter. The charging party has the right to appeal the dismissal to the Office of the General Counsel of the NLRB in Washington, D.C. The decision of the general counsel is final and nonappealable.

If the NLRB finds reasonable cause to believe the law was violated, it will first attempt to settle the case. If settlement is unsuccessful, it will issue a complaint. If further settlement attempts are unsuccessful, a hearing will be held before an administrative law judge (ALJ). The decision of the ALJ is appealed to the NLRB in Washington. The NLRB's decision is subject to review by the federal courts of appeals.

If You Win: The remedies for violations are injunctive relief, make-whole remedies, and a requirement that the offending party post a notice in the workplace (or at the union's place of business) informing the employees of the outcome of the case. The remedies in cases alleging a violation of the union's duty of fair representation are make-whole orders, compensatory damages, and, in appropriate cases, reasonable attorney's fees.

Railway Labor Act (RLA)

What It Does: Regulates the labor-management relationship, prohibits discrimination based on union activity, and establishes election procedures for certification of unions as bargaining representatives.

Who Is Covered: All railroads and airlines.

Where to Find It in the Law Books: 45 U.S.C. secs. 151–88

Where to Find More Information: Contact the Chief of Staff of the National Mediation Board at Suite 250 East, 1301 K Street, N.W., Washington, D.C. 20572, or online at *www.nmb.gov.*

Who Enforces It: There are two federal administrative agencies responsible for enforcing the RLA. The National Mediation Board (NMB) regulates the union election process and acts as mediator in helping employers and unions negotiate contracts. The National Railroad Adjustment Board (NRAB) acts as an arbitration agency to resolve disputes concerning the application and interpretation of contracts between unions and employers. The offices of the NRAB are in Chicago, Illinois. Only if a dispute does not fall within the jurisdiction of either the NMB or the NRAB may an individual file his or her own lawsuit in federal court.

Going to Court: In those cases dealing with employer discrimination where there is no union representation, or cases alleging a violation of the duty of fair representation, individuals covered by the RLA can file private lawsuits in federal court. The time limit for filing a lawsuit is six months from the date of the alleged violation. Once a union represents the employees, however, almost all disputes must be submitted to an adjustment board.

If You Win: Successful plaintiffs are entitled to injunctive relief and make-whole remedies. The courts are divided on whether punitive damages are available. In some cases, criminal penalties can be imposed on employers, but this sanction is rarely used.

Federal Labor Relations Act (FLRA)

What It Does: Regulates the labor-management relationship, prohibits discrimination based on union and concerted activity, and establishes election procedures for certification of unions as bargaining representatives.

Who Is Covered: Employers that are executive agencies of the federal government. Supervisory and managerial personnel are excluded from the protections of the law.

Where to Find It in the Law Books: 5 U.S.C. secs. 7101–35

Where to Find More Information: Contact the Federal Labor Relations Authority at 607 14th Street, N.W., Washington, D.C. 20424, or access its website at *www.flra.gov*.

Who Enforces It: There are two federal agencies with authority under the FLRA. The Federal Labor Relations Authority (FLR Authority) has the exclusive responsibility to investigate and adjudicate complaints alleging violations of rights under the FLRA and to regulate the election process. The Federal Service Impasses Panel provides assistance to unions and employers in resolving impasses that occur during contract negotiations. This agency does not handle problems or complaints filed by individual employees. Individuals may not file private lawsuits under this statute; they must file their complaints with the FLR Authority.

Going to the FLR Authority: The procedures for enforcing the law are modeled after those found in the NLRA. An aggrieved employee must file a charge with the regional office of the authority within six months of the discriminatory act. The authority investigates the charge, and if reasonable cause exists to believe the FLRA was violated, and if attempts to settle are unsuccessful, a hearing will be held before an administrative law judge. The ALJ's decision is appealable to the three members who comprise the adjudicatory board of the FLR authority. The decisions of this panel are appealable to the federal courts of appeals.

If You Win: Remedies for violations of the FLRA are injunctive relief, make-whole remedies, and a notice posted at the workplace informing employees of the outcome of the case.

Labor Management Reporting and Disclosure Act (LMRDA)

What It Does: Regulates the operation of labor organizations, their relationship to their members, and the conduct of internal union elections.

(i) THERE'S ALWAYS AN EXCEPTION

Each individual union member has the private right to bring a lawsuit in federal court to enforce the LMRDA. There is an exception, however, regarding challenges to internal union elections. In such cases, a union member must first invoke and attempt to exhaust any internal union procedures available under the union constitution and bylaws for challenging elections. If the union member is dissatisfied with the outcome of the internal union process, he or she may then file a complaint with the Office of Labor-Management Standards (LMS) of the Department of Labor within one month after the internal union procedures have been completed or within three months after the member first invoked such procedures. LMS has district offices located in major cities throughout the U.S.

The Office of LMS investigates each complaint and, if it finds reasonable cause to believe the law was violated and that the violation may have affected the outcome of the election, it will attempt to settle the case. If settlement is unsuccessful, the secretary of labor will file suit in court. The remedy for a successful challenge to a union election is to void the results of the election and direct the holding of a new election.

Who Is Covered: All private-sector labor unions.

Where to Find It in the Law Books: 29 U.S.C. secs. 401–531

Where to Find More Information: Contact the Office of Labor-Management Standards, Department of Labor, at 200 Constitution Avenue, N.W., Washington, D.C. 20210. This office offers free publications describing rights and responsibilities under the LMRDA; request them by calling (866) 4-USA-DOL or by visiting *www.dol.gov/esa/olms_org.htm.*

Who Enforces It: Each individual union member possesses a private right to bring a lawsuit in federal court to enforce most of the provisions of the LMRDA. The time limit for filing most individual lawsuits under the LMRDA is based on the most closely analogous state statute of limitations; there is no uniform time limit.

If You Win: An individual who brings a private cause of action under the LMRDA is entitled to injunctive relief, compensatory damages, make-whole relief where appropriate, and, in limited circumstances, reasonable attorney's fees.

WAGE AND HOUR LAWS

These laws set minimum wage amounts that employers must pay to certain classes of employees, and limit the hours of work for employees under the age of eighteen.

Fair Labor Standards Act (FLSA)

What It Does: Sets minimum wage and overtime requirements and regulates the employment of child labor.

Who Is Covered: Private-sector employers who have at least two employees engaged in interstate commerce activities and whose annual volume of business is at least $500,000. Hospitals and educational institutions are also covered. Employees who work for state government, however, cannot sue their employers; state governments enjoy sovereign immunity.

The statute also covers individual employees who are engaged in interstate commerce, even if their employers do not gross $500,000 a year.

Where to Find It in the Law Books: 29 U.S.C. secs. 201–19

Where to Find More Information: Contact the Department of Labor, Wage and Hour Division, at 200 Constitution Avenue, N.W., Washington, D.C. 20210. Free pamphlets explaining the law are available by calling (866) 4-USA-DOL or by visiting *www.dol.gov/esa/whd/*.

Who Enforces It: The Wage and Hour Division of the Department of Labor has the authority to investigate complaints and file lawsuits in court. Any individual may also institute legal action in state or federal court. There is no requirement that an individual file an administrative charge before going to court. An individual may, however, file a charge with the Wage and Hour Division.

Going to the Wage and Hour Division: Once an individual files a charge, the division will investigate and, if it finds a violation, attempt to get the employer to voluntarily agree to a settlement. If settlement is not possible, the Department of Labor may file a lawsuit; it is not, however, required to file suit.

Going to Court: The statute of limitations for filing a lawsuit is two years. If the employer acted with reckless disregard as to whether its conduct violated the law, the deadline is extended to three years. An individual can file a lawsuit in either state or federal court.

If You Win: Successful plaintiffs are entitled to injunctive relief, payment of the wages owed, liquidated damages in an amount equal to the wages owed, and reasonable attorney's fees. An employer can avoid having to pay liquidated damages if it can prove that it acted in good faith and with reasonable grounds for believing its actions were legal.

Equal Pay Act (EPA)

What It Does: Requires employers to pay equal wages to male and female employees who are performing substantially equivalent work.

Who Is Covered: The same employers that are covered under the FLSA.

Where to Find It in the Law Books: 29 U.S.C. sec. 206(d)

Where to Find More Information: Contact the EEOC (see the Title VII entry at the beginning of this appendix for full contact information); or 9to5, the National Association of Working Women, at 152 W. Wisconsin Avenue, Suite 408, Milwaukee, WI 53203, or online at *www.9to5.org.*

Who Enforces It: The EEOC has the authority to investigate complaints and file lawsuits. Individual workers may also file lawsuits.

Going to the EEOC: Individuals are not required to file a charge with the EEOC before filing a lawsuit. If a charge is filed, however, the EEOC will investigate and determine whether there is reasonable cause to believe a violation has occurred. If the EEOC finds a violation, it will attempt conciliation. If settlement is unsuccessful, the EEOC may file a lawsuit, but is not required to do so.

Going to Court: Individuals may file private lawsuits in either state or federal court. The time limit is two years; if the employer acted with reckless disregard as to whether its conduct violated the law, the deadline is extended to three years.

If You Win: The remedies are the same as those available under the FLSA.

Walsh-Healey Public Contracts Act

What It Does: Regulates wage payments.

Who Is Covered: Federal government contractors with a contract for the purchase of supplies in excess of $10,000.

Where to Find It in the Law Books: 41 U.S.C. secs. 35–45

Who Enforces It: The Wage and Hour Division, Department of Labor. Only in very limited circumstances can an employee file a lawsuit in court.

Going to the Department of Labor: Employees can notify the agency with which their employer has its contract of the employer's noncompliance. That agency will then notify the Department of Labor. If the secretary of labor determines that the contractor has violated wage requirements, it can withhold payment under the contract and use the money to pay the required wage amounts to the employees. It can also bar the contractor from further government work.

Davis-Bacon Act

What It Does: Requires employers to pay construction workers the prevailing-area wage and fringe-benefit rates.

Who Is Covered: Employers with federal construction project contracts with a value exceeding $2,000.

Where to Find It in the Law Books: 40 U.S.C. secs. 3141–44, 3146, 3147

Who Enforces It: This law is enforced by the Wage and Hour Division of the Department of Labor. The same process used for enforcing the Walsh-Healey Act applies to the Davis-Bacon Act.

Service Contract Act

What It Does: Regulates wage payments to employees working under federal service contracts.

Who Is Covered: Federal contractors and subcontractors who provide services to the federal government.

Where to Find It in the Law Books: 41 U.S.C. secs. 351–58

Who Enforces It: The Wage and Hour Division of the Department of Labor. The enforcement process is the same as that for the Walsh-Healey and Davis-Bacon Acts.

WORKPLACE SAFETY LAWS

These laws are administered by federal agencies with the authority to promulgate health and safety rules for the workplace, and to require employers to comply with such standards.

Occupational Safety and Health Act (OSH Act)

What It Does: Regulates workplace safety and health.

Who Is Covered: Private-sector employers affecting interstate commerce, but excluding the mining industry.

Where to Find It in the Law Books: 29 U.S.C. secs. 651–78

Where to Find More Information: Contact the Occupational Safety and Health Administration at 200 Constitution Avenue, N.W., Washington, D.C. 20210. A catalogue of publications dealing with health and safety issues is available by calling (866) 4-USA-DOL or by visiting *www.osha.gov.*

Who Enforces It: The Occupational Safety and Health Administration (OSHA) has the exclusive authority to enforce the OSH Act. In some states, such as California, the Occupational Safety and Health Administration has ceded jurisdiction to a state agency that performs the same function. Individual workers cannot file their own lawsuits.

Going to OSHA: Employees can file either oral or written complaints with OSHA alleging that a workplace condition constitutes a safety or health hazard. There are regional and area of-

(i) WHEN THE OSHA INSPECTOR CALLS

During an inspection, the OSHA investigator will meet with the employer, explain the nature of the inspection, and may review employer documents pertaining to workplace injuries and hazards. The inspector will then perform a "walk-around" of the plant to physically inspect the workplace. The employer and a representative of the employees are allowed to accompany the inspector on the walk-around. The inspector may also talk with employees and ask them questions. At the end of the inspection, the inspector will informally tell the employer of any possible violations that may have been uncovered during the investigation.

fices located in cities throughout the U.S. Upon receiving a complaint, OSHA will decide if there are reasonable grounds for believing a violation of the law exists. If it has reason to believe there is a violation, it will either send a letter to the employer regarding the alleged violation and suggesting how to correct the problem, or it will send an inspector to the workplace to conduct an on-site safety inspection. OSHA also has the authority to conduct workplace inspections at its own discretion.

If violations are uncovered during an inspection, OSHA will send the employer a citation that lists each violation and describes what the employer must do to fix the problem or problems. The employer may also be fined, in an amount based on the seriousness of the violation. An employer can also be subject to criminal liability and imprisonment for willful violation of an OSH Act standard that results in an employee's death. The citation is required to be posted at the workplace in the areas where violations have taken place. If an employer contests a citation or the penalty, it must file a notice within fifteen days. A hearing will be held before an ALJ of the Occupational Safety and Health Review Commission, who will then issue a decision. The ALJ's decision is appealable to the Review Commission; the decision of the Review Commission is appealable to the federal courts of appeals.

Mine Safety and Health Act

What It Does: Regulates workplace safety and health.

Who Is Covered: Employers engaged in the mining industry.

Where to Find It in the Law Books: 30 U.S.C. secs. 801–962

Who Enforces It: The Mine Safety Health Administration (MSHA) has exclusive authority for enforcing the law. Individuals cannot file private lawsuits.

Where to Find More Information: Contact the Mine Safety and Health Administration at 1100 Wilson Blvd., 21st Floor, Arlington, VA 22209, by phone at (202) 693–9400, or online at *www.msha.gov*.

Going to the MSHA: The enforcement process is substantially the same as that under OSHA.

PENSION AND WELFARE BENEFITS

Employee Retirement Income Security Act (ERISA)

What It Does: Regulates employee pension and welfare benefit plans.

Who Is Covered: Private-sector employers whose business affects interstate commerce or whose pension and welfare plans are "qualified" under the federal tax laws.

Where to Find It in the Law Books: 29 U.S.C. secs. 1001–1461

Where to Find More Information: Contact the Department of Labor, Employee Benefits Security Administration, at 200 Constitution Avenue, N.W., Washington, D.C. 20210. Publications providing information about rights and duties under ERISA can be obtained by calling (866) 444–3272, or by visiting *www.dol.gov/ebsa/*. You can also contact the Pension Rights Center at 1350 Connecticut Avenue, Suite 206, Washington, D.C. 20036, or online at *www.pensionrights.org*; or the American Association of Retired Persons at 601 E Street, N.W., Washington, D.C. 20049, or online at *www.aarp.org*. Both of these organizations can provide you with information concerning pension rights under ERISA.

Who Enforces It: The Secretary of Labor is responsible for investigating violations of ERISA, and can file a lawsuit to enforce the statute. Individual employees can also file lawsuits to enforce their rights under ERISA.

Going to Court: Employees alleging violations of ERISA with respect to the payment of benefits are required to use any dispute resolution procedures contained in the pension plan before filing a lawsuit. Claims for any other violations of ERISA may be brought directly in federal court. Individuals are not required to file administrative charges before filing a lawsuit. The statute of limitations for filing a suit with respect to the denial of benefits expires six years from the date of the unlawful act, or three years from the date the plaintiff had actual knowledge of the violations, whichever is earlier. The time limit for filing suit for unlawful interference with an employee's rights under ERISA is based on the most closely analogous state statute of limitations.

If You Win: Available remedies are injunctive relief and make-whole remedies.

OTHER TERMS OF EMPLOYMENT

Worker Adjustment and Retraining Notification Act (WARN Act)

What It Does: Requires employers to give advance notice of plant closings or mass layoffs.

Who Is Covered: Private-sector employers with one hundred or more employees.

Where to Find It in the Law Books: 29 U.S.C. secs. 2102–09

Where to Find More Information: Information on the WARN Act is available at the Department of Labor website at *www.dol.gov/dol/compliance/comp-warn.htm.*

Who Enforces It: Individual workers, unions, or a unit of local government may file a suit in federal district court to enforce the law.

Going to Court: There are no administrative prerequisites to filing a lawsuit. The deadline for filing a lawsuit is based on the most closely analogous state statute of limitations; this can be anywhere from two to six years.

If You Win: Successful plaintiffs are entitled to back pay for each day the law was violated, up to a maximum of sixty days. The court may also award reasonable attorney's fees.

Family and Medical Leave Act (FMLA)

What It Does: Requires covered employers to grant an eligible employee up to twelve weeks of unpaid leave during a twelve-month period for the birth and care of a newborn child; for the placement with the employee of a child for adoption or foster care; to care for an immediate family member with a serious health condition; or because of the employee's own serious health condition. Upon return from FMLA leave, an employee typically must be returned to his or her original job, or to an equivalent job with equivalent pay, benefits, and other terms and conditions of employment.

Who Is Covered: Private-sector employers that employ fifty or more employees, and all public-sector employers regardless of the number of employees.

Where to Find It in the Law Books: 29 U.S.C. secs. 2601, 2611–19

Where to Find More Information: Contact the Office of the Administrator, Wage and Hour Division, Department of Labor, 200 Constitution Avenue, N.W., Washington, D.C. 20210. Information on the FMLA can be accessed at the Department of Labor website at *www.dol.gov/esa/whd/fmla/*.

Who Enforces It: The secretary of labor has the authority to investigate complaints of violations and can institute a lawsuit to enforce the statute. Individuals can file a complaint alleging a violation of the FMLA with the local office of the Wage and Hour Division of the Department of Labor. Individual employees also have the right to sue their employers for violations of the law.

Going to Court: Individual employees may file suit directly in federal or state court. Employees can file charges with the Department of Labor, but are not required to do so. The statute of limitations for filing a lawsuit is two years.

If You Win: Successful plaintiffs are entitled to make-whole relief. If an employee did not lose any employment benefits, he or she is entitled to reimbursement of the costs incurred as a direct result of being denied leave, up to a maximum of twelve weeks' wages. The court will also award liquidated damages unless the employer proves it acted in good faith with reasonable grounds for believing it did not violate the law. Plaintiffs are also entitled to reasonable attorney's fees.

Employee Polygraph Protection Act (EPPA)

What It Does: Prohibits employers from requiring employees to submit to lie detector tests, except under strictly limited circumstances.

Who Is Covered: All private-sector employers whose business affects interstate commerce.

Where to Find It in the Law Books: 29 U.S.C. secs. 2001–09

Where to Find More Information: Access the Department of Labor website at *www.dol.gov/esa/whd/polygraph*.

Who Enforces It: The secretary of labor has authority to investigate complaints of violations and can file suit to enforce the law. Individual employees also have the right to sue their employers in state or federal court for violations of the law.

Going to Court: There are no administrative prerequisites to filing a lawsuit under this statute. The time limit for filing suit is three years.

If You Win: Available remedies are make-whole relief, injunctive relief, and reasonable attorney's fees. If the lawsuit is brought by the secretary of labor, the employer can also be liable for a civil penalty of no more than $10,000.

Jury System Improvements Act

What It Does: Prohibits discipline or discharge of employees for serving jury duty in federal court.

Who Is Covered: All public- and private-sector employers.

Where to Find It in the Law Books: 28 U.S.C. sec. 1875

Who Enforces It: Individual employees can sue their employers in federal court.

Going to Court: There are no administrative prerequisites for enforcing this statute. The time limit for filing suit is based on the most closely analogous state statute of limitations, which will vary by jurisdiction.

If You Win: Available remedies include make-whole relief and reasonable attorney's fees. A court may also impose a civil fine of not more than $1,000.

INDEX

401(k) plans, 103, 177

accommodation, reasonable.
    See reasonable accommo-
    dation
actors, child, 28
ADA. *See* Americans with
    Disabilities Act
ADEA. *See* Age Discrimina-
    tion in Employment Act
adjudication stage, 246
adjustment board, 218
administrative-agency proce-
    dures, 241–43, 245
administrative employees,
    78
administrative law judge
    (ALJ), 245, 246, 270,
    273, 274, 276–77, 285
adoption. *See* family leave
advanced knowledge
    (defined), 77–78
adverse employment actions,
    201–2
adverse-impact discrimina-
    tion, 18, 19–20, 35–37,
    55, 59, 130–31
affirmative-action plan
    (AAP), 60–63
Age Discrimination in Em-
    ployment Act (ADEA),
    266–68
    adverse-impact discrimina-
    tion under, 20
    affirmative action plans
    and, 60
    anti-retaliation clauses in,
    161–62
    bona fide occupational
    qualification under, 35
    coverage, 17
    described, 6, 15–16
    employee termination
    under, 160
    harassment claims under,
    124
    health insurance and, 98
    hiring questions viewed by,
    42
    layoffs under, 174
    legislators covered under,
    222
    overseas employees cov-
    ered, 22

retirement under, 176–77
    sovereign immunity princi-
    ple, 23
    state laws supplementing, 9
    tests under, 55
    U.S. Code section for, 261
agricultural workers, 9, 86,
    186, 195
AIDS/HIV testing, 58
airline flight personnel
    drug testing of, 33, 229
    hours of work regulations,
    84
    unions and, 194, 218, 277
Alabama
    at-will employee termina-
    tion in, 166
    workers' compensation
    laws, 86
Alaska
    garnishment restrictions,
    82
    polygraph test prohibitions,
    56, 151
alcohol, off-duty use of, 52,
    131
aliens. *See* resident aliens,
    permanent; unauthorized
    aliens
American Arbitration Associ-
    ation, 237, 248
American Civil Liberties
    Union (ACLU), 226, 227
American Polygraph Associa-
    tion, 155
Americans with Disabilities
    Act (ADA), 268
    affirmative action plans
    and, 60
    anti-retaliation clauses in,
    161–62
    coverage, 17
    described, 7, 16
    disability defined in,
    253–55
    employee leave and, 115
    employee termination
    under, 160
    government employees and,
    221–22
    harassment claims under,
    124
    health insurance and,
    98–101

hiring questions viewed by,
    42–43
    job requirements and,
    38–40
    legislators covered under,
    222
    medical files under,
    148–49
    overseas employees cov-
    ered, 22
    protected class defined by,
    257
    refusal to accommodate
    discrimination under,
    20–21, 48–51, 96–97
    sovereign immunity princi-
    ple, 23
    state laws supplementing, 9
    tests under, 55–59
    "undue hardship" defined
    under, 50–51
anti-retaliation laws, 139,
    161–62, 182, 243
antidiscrimination legislation,
    15–26
    employee benefits and, 67,
    97–102
    employee discipline and,
    145–48
    employee layoffs and, 172
    employee leave and,
    114–15, 117
    employee termination and,
    160–61
    employment agencies and,
    62
    executive orders, 273–75
    federal laws, 15–21
    government employees and,
    221, 224
    hiring decisions under,
    33–43, 63–64
    hiring halls and, 217
    job advertisements and de-
    scriptions under, 40–41
    lists of, 6–7, 260–73
    medical tests and, 58
    polygraph tests and, 152
    protected classes defined
    by, 257
    state and local laws, 9,
    22–23, 52
    unauthorized aliens and,
    31, 32

ABOUT THE AUTHOR

Barbara J. Fick is an associate professor of law at Notre Dame Law School, specializing in labor and employment law, international and comparative labor law, and dispute resolution. She is a member of the George Higgins Labor Research Center and a faculty fellow of the Joan B. Kroc Institute for International Peace Studies at Notre Dame. She has written numerous scholarly articles on labor and employment law, and has delivered papers and lectures in Central and Eastern Europe, Central Asia, the Middle East, and the United States. She has also served as a mediator and arbitrator and expert witness in labor relations cases. Before joining the faculty at Notre Dame, she was a field attorney with the National Labor Relations Board.